SAM WALTON

MADE IN AMERICA

MY STORY

SAM WALTON

MADE IN AMERICA

MY STORY

BY

SAM WALTON

WITH JOHN HUEY

DOUBLEDAY

New York   Toronto   London   Sydney   Auckland

PUBLISHED BY DOUBLEDAY
a division of Random House, Inc.

DOUBLEDAY and the portrayal of an anchor with a dolphin
are trademarks of Doubleday,
a division of Random House, Inc.

*Photographs without credits appear
courtesy of the Walton family.*

Book design by Marysarah Quinn

Library of Congress Cataloging-in-Publication Data
Walton, Sam, 1918–1992
    Sam Walton, made in America : my story / Sam Walton with John Huey.
    p.   cm.
    Includes bibliographical references and index.
    1. Walton, Sam, 1918–1992. 2. Wal-Mart (firm)—History. 3. Businessmen—
United   States—Biography.   4.   Millionaires—United   States—Biography.   5.
Discount stores (Retail trade)—United States—History. I. Huey, John. II. Title.
HC102.5W35A3   1992
381'.148'092—dc20
[B]
          92-18874
          CIP

ISBN 0-385-51120-5

CONTENTS

ACKNOWLEDGMENTS

Life has been great to me, probably better than any man has a right to expect. At home, I've been blessed with a wife and family who've stuck together and loved each other and indulged my lifelong obsession with minding the store. At work, my business life has been spent in lockstep with an incredible group of Wal-Mart associates who have put up with all my aggravation and bullheadedness and pulled together to make what once appeared truly impossible now seem expected and routine.

So first, I want to dedicate this book to Helen Robson Walton and the four fine kids she raised—with some help along the way from the old man—our sons Rob, John, and Jim, and our daughter Alice.

Then I want to dedicate it to all my partners—and I wish I could recognize every one of you individually, but we've talked over the years and you know how I feel about you—and to all 400,000 of my associate-partners who've made this wild, wild

Wal-Mart ride so much fun and so special. Much of this book is really your story.

Earlier on, there were fewer of us. Jackie Lancaster, our first floor manager in Newport, Arkansas. Inez Threet, Ruby Turner, Wanda Wiseman, Ruth Keller—my first four associates when we opened Walton's Five and Dime in Bentonville on August 1, 1951. What would we have done without those early managers? Most of them risked so much by leaving good jobs with much larger variety chains to join up with a one-horse outfit run by an overactive dreamer down in Bentonville—people like Clarence Leis, Willard Walker, Charlie Baum, Ron Loveless, Bob Bogle, Claude Harris, Ferold Arend, Charlie Cate, Al Miles, Thomas Jefferson, Gary Reinboth. There was Bob Thornton, Darwin Smith, Jim Henry, Phil Green, and Don Whitaker. And I can't forget Ray Thomas, Jim Dismore, Jim Elliott, or John Hawks. Ron Mayer made special contributions, and Jack Shewmaker had as much to do with making Wal-Mart a great company as anybody. John Tate has provided valuable counsel all along the way.

Of course, Wal-Mart wouldn't be what it is today without a host of fine competitors, most especially Harry Cunningham of Kmart, who really designed and built the first discount store as we know it today, and who, in my opinion, should be remembered as one of the leading retailers of all time.

Still, I think I'll hold on to my Wal-Mart stock, knowing that David Glass is at the wheel, steering a great team: Don Soderquist, Paul Carter, and A. L. Johnson. And when I think about young guys like Bill Fields and Dean Sanders and Joe Hardin running huge parts of the company, I know that one day they'll put us all to shame.

Of course, my number-one retail partner from our third store on has been my brother, James L. "Bud" Walton, who has a few things of his own to say about me in this book—not all of them flattering. Bud's wise counsel and guidance kept us from many a mistake. My nature has always been to charge, to say let's do it now. Often, Bud would advise taking a different direction, or maybe changing the timing. I soon learned to listen to him because he has exceptional judgment and a great deal of common sense.

Finally, I hope there's a special place in heaven reserved for my two secretaries, Loretta Boss, who was with me for twenty-five years, and Becky Elliott, who's been with me now for three years. They deserve it after what they've put up with here on earth.

—SAMUEL MOORE WALTON
Bentonville, Arkansas

FOREWORD

Hello, friends, I'm Sam Walton, founder and chairman of Wal-Mart Stores. By now I hope you've shopped in one of our stores, or maybe bought some stock in our company. If you have, you probably already know how proud I am of what is simply the miracle that all these Wal-Mart associates of mine have accomplished in the thirty years since we opened our first Wal-Mart here in northwest Arkansas, which Wal-Mart and I still call home. As hard as it is to believe sometimes, we've grown from that one little store into what is now the largest retailing outfit in the world. And we've really had a heck of a time along the way.

I realize we have been through something amazing here at Wal-Mart, something special that we ought to share more of with all the folks who've been so loyal to our stores and to our company. That's one thing we never did much of while we were building Wal-Mart, talk about ourselves or do a whole lot of bragging outside the Wal-Mart family—except when we had to convince some banker or some Wall Street financier that we intended to amount to something someday, that we were worth taking a chance on. When folks have asked me, "How did Wal-Mart do it?" I've usually been flip about answering them. "Friend, we just got after it and stayed after it," I'd say. We have always pretty much kept to ourselves, and we've had good reasons for it; we've been very protective of our business dealings and our home lives, and we still like it that way.

But as a result, a whole lot of misinformation and myth and half-truths have gotten around over the years about me and about Wal-Mart. And I think there's been way too much attention paid to my personal finances, attention that has caused me and my family a lot of extra trouble in our lives—though I've just ignored it and pretty much gone about my life and the business of Wal-Mart as best I could.

None of this has really changed. But I've been fighting cancer for a while now, and I'm not getting any younger anyway. And lately a lot of folks—including Helen and the kids, some of our executives here at the company, and even some of the associates in our stores—have been fussing at me that I'm really the best person to tell the Wal-Mart tale, and that—like it or not—my life is all wrapped up in Wal-Mart, and I should get it down right while I still can. So I'm going to try to tell this story the best I'm able to, as close to the way it all came about as I can, and I hope it will be almost as interesting and fun and exciting as it's been for all of us, and that it can capture for you at least something of the spirit we've all felt in building this company. More than anything, though, I want to get across once and for all just how important Wal-Mart's associates have been to its success.

This is a funny thing to do, this looking back on your life trying to figure out how all the pieces came together. I guess anybody would find it a little strange, but it's really odd for somebody like me because I've never been a very reflective fellow, never been one to dwell in the past. If I had to single out one element in my life that has made a difference for me, it would be a passion to compete. That passion has pretty much kept me on the go, looking *ahead* to the next store visit, or the next store opening, or the next merchandising item I personally wanted to promote out in those stores—like a minnow bucket or a Thermos bottle or a mattress pad or a big bag of candy.

As I do look back though, I realize that ours is a story about the kinds of traditional principles that made America great in the first place. It is a story about entrepreneurship, and risk, and hard work, and knowing where you want to go and being willing to do what it takes to get there. It's a story about believing in your idea even when maybe some other folks don't, and about sticking to your guns. But I think more than anything it proves there's absolutely no limit to what plain, ordinary working people can accomplish if they're given the opportunity and the encouragement and the incentive to do their best. Because that's how Wal-Mart became Wal-Mart: ordinary people joined together to accomplish extraordinary things. At first, we amazed ourselves. And before too long, we amazed everybody else, especially folks who thought America was just too complicated and sophisticated a place for this sort of thing to work anymore.

The Wal-Mart story is unique: nothing quite like it has been done before. So maybe by telling it the way it really happened, we can help some other folks down the line take these same principles and apply them to their dreams and make them come true.

SAM WALTON

MADE IN AMERICA

MY STORY

CHAPTER 1

LEARNING TO VALUE A DOLLAR

"I was awake one night and turned on my radio, and I heard them announce that Sam Walton was the richest man in America. And I thought, 'Sam Walton. Why, he was in my class.' And I got so excited."

—HELEN WILLIAMS,
*former history and speech teacher
at Hickman High School in
Columbia, Missouri*

Success has always had its price, I guess, and I learned that lesson the hard way in October of 1985 when *Forbes* magazine named me the so-called "richest man in America." Well, it wasn't too hard to imagine all those newspaper and TV folks up in New York saying "Who?" and "He lives where?" The next thing we knew, reporters and photographers started flocking down here to Bentonville, I guess to take pictures of me diving into some swimming pool full of money they imagined I had, or to watch me light big fat cigars with $100 bills while the hootchy-kootchy girls danced by the lake.

I really don't know what they thought, but I wasn't about to cooperate with them. So they found out all these exciting things about me, like: I drove an old pickup truck with cages in the back for my bird dogs, or I wore a Wal-Mart ball cap, or I got my hair cut at the barbershop just off the town square—somebody with a telephoto lens even snuck up and took a picture of me in the barber chair, and it was in newspapers all over the country. Then folks we'd never heard of started calling us and writing us from all over the world and coming here to ask us for money. Many of them represented worthy causes, I'm sure, but we also heard from just about every harebrained, cockamamy schemer in the world. I remember one letter from a woman who just came right out and said, "I've never been able to afford the $100,000 house I've always wanted. Will you give me the money?" They still do it to this day, write or call asking for a new car, or money to go on a vacation, or to get some dental work—whatever comes into their minds.

Now, I'm a friendly fellow by nature—I always speak to folks in the street and such—and my wife Helen is as genial and outgoing as she can be, involved in all sorts of community activities, and we've always lived very much out in the open. But we really thought there for a while that this "richest" thing was going to ruin our whole lifestyle. We've always tried to do our share, but all of a sudden everybody expected us to pay their way too. And nosy people from the media would call our house at all hours and get downright rude when we'd tell them no, you can't bring a TV crew out to the house, or no, we don't want your magazine to spend a week photographing the lives of the Waltons, or no, I don't have time to share my life story with you. It made me mad, anyway, that all they wanted to talk about was my family's personal finances. They weren't even interested in Wal-Mart, which was probably one of the best business stories going on anywhere in the world at the time, but it never even occurred to them to ask about the company. The impression I got is that most media folks—and some Wall Street types too—either thought we were just a bunch of bumpkins selling socks off the back of a truck, or that we were some kind of fast buck artists or stock scammers. And when they did write about the company they either got it wrong or just made fun of us.

So the Walton family almost instinctively put a pretty tight lid on personal publicity for any of us, although we kept living out in the open and going around visiting folks in the stores all the time. Fortunately, here in Bentonville, our friends and neighbors protected us from a lot of these scavengers. But I did get ambushed by the "Lifestyles of the Rich and Famous" guy at a tennis tournament I was playing in, and Helen talked to one of the women's magazines for an article. The media usually portrayed me as a really cheap, eccentric recluse, sort of a hillbilly who more or less slept with his dogs in spite of having billions of dollars stashed away in a cave. Then when the stock market crashed in 1987, and Wal-Mart stock dropped along with everything else in the market, everybody wrote that I'd lost a half billion dollars. When they asked me about it I said, "It's only paper," and they had a good time with that.

But now I'd like to explain some of my attitudes about money —up to a point. After that, our finances—like those of any other normal-thinking American family—are nobody's business but our own. No question about it, a lot of my attitude toward money stems from growing up during a pretty hardscrabble time in our country's history: the Great Depression. And this heartland area we come from out here—Missouri, Oklahoma, Kansas, Arkansas —was hard hit during that Dust Bowl era. I was born in Kingfisher, Oklahoma, in 1918 and lived there until I was about five, but my earliest memories are of Springfield, Missouri, where I started school, and later of the little Missouri town of Marshall. After that, we lived in Shelbina, Missouri, where I started high school, and still later Columbia, where I finished high school and went on to college.

My dad, Thomas Gibson Walton, was an awfully hard worker who got up early, put in long hours, and was honest. Completely, totally honest, remembered by most people for his integrity. He was also a bit of a character, who loved to trade, loved to make a deal for just about anything: horses, mules, cattle, houses, farms, cars. Anything. Once he traded our farm in Kingfisher for another one, near Omega, Oklahoma. Another time, he traded his wristwatch for a hog, so we'd have meat on the table. And he was the best negotiator I ever ran into. My dad had that unusual instinct to know how far he could go with someone—and did it in a way that he and the guy always parted friends—but he would embarrass me with some of the offers he would make, they were so low. That's one reason I'm probably not the best negotiator in the world; I lack the ability to squeeze that last dollar. Fortunately, my brother Bud, who has been my partner from early on, inherited my dad's ability to negotiate.

Dad never had the kind of ambition or confidence to build much of a business on his own, and he didn't believe in taking on debt. When I was growing up, he had all sorts of jobs. He was a banker and a farmer and a farm-loan appraiser, and an agent for both insurance and real estate. For a few months, early in the Depression, he was out of work altogether, and eventually he went to work for his brother's Walton Mortgage Co., which was an agent for Metropolitan Life Insurance. Dad became the guy who had to service Metropolitan's old farm loans, most of which were in default. In twenty-nine and thirty and thirty-one, he had to repossess hundreds of farms from wonderful people whose families had owned the land forever. I traveled with him some, and it was tragic, and really hard on Dad too—but he tried to do it in a way that left those farmers with as much of their self-respect as he could. All of this must have made an impression on me as a kid, although I don't ever remember saying anything to myself like "I'll never be poor."

We never thought of ourselves as poor, although we certainly didn't have much of what you'd call disposable income lying around, and we did what we could to raise a dollar here and there. For example, my mother, Nan Walton, got the idea during the Depression to start a little milk business. I'd get up early in the morning and milk the cows, Mother would prepare and bottle the milk, and I'd deliver it after football practice in the afternoons. We had ten or twelve customers, who paid ten cents a gallon. Best of all, Mother would skim the cream and make ice cream, and it's a wonder I wasn't known as Fat Sam Walton in those days from all the ice cream I ate.

I also started selling magazine subscriptions, probably as young as seven or eight years old, and I had paper routes from the seventh grade all the way through college. I raised and sold rabbits and pigeons too, nothing really unusual for country boys of that era.

I learned from a very early age that it was important for us kids to help provide for the home, to be contributors rather than just takers. In the process, of course, we learned how much hard work it took to get your hands on a dollar, and that when you did it was worth something. One thing my mother and dad shared completely was their approach to money: they just didn't spend it.

BUD WALTON:

"People can't understand why we're still so conservative. They make a big deal about Sam being a billionaire and driving an old pickup truck or buying his clothes at Wal-Mart or refusing to fly first class.

"It's just the way we were brought up.

"When a penny is lying out there on the street, how many people would go out there and pick it up? I'll bet I would. And I know Sam would."

STEPHEN PUMPHREY, PHOTOGRAPHER:

"Once I was setting up to photograph Sam out on the tarmac of some little airport in Missouri. He was over filing a flight plan, and I threw a nickel down on the pavement—trying to be cute—and said to my assistant: 'Let's see if he picks it up.' Planes are landing and taking off, and Sam comes walking over in a big hurry, a little put out that he has to pose for another picture. 'Okay,' he says, 'where do you want me to stand—on that nickel?' "

By the time I got out in the world ready to make something of myself, I already had a strongly ingrained respect for the value of a dollar. But my knowledge about money and finances probably wasn't all that sophisticated in spite of the business degree I had. Then I got to know Helen's family, and listening to her father, L. S. Robson, was an education in itself. He influenced me a great deal. He was a great salesman, one of the most persuasive individuals I have ever met. And I am sure his success as a trader and a businessman, his knowledge of finance and the law, and his philosophy had a big effect on me. My competitive nature was such that I saw his success and admired it. I didn't envy it. I admired it. I said to myself: maybe I will be as successful as he is someday.

The Robsons were very smart about the way they handled their finances: Helen's father organized his ranch and family businesses as a partnership, and Helen and her brothers were all partners. They all took turns doing the ranch books and things like that. Helen has a B.S. degree in finance, which back then was really unusual for a woman. Anyway, Mr. Robson advised us to do the same thing with our family, and we did, way back in 1953. What little we had at the time, we put into a partnership with our kids, which was later incorporated into Walton Enterprises.

Over the years, our Wal-Mart stock has gone into that partnership. Then the board of Walton Enterprises, which is us, the family, makes decisions on a consensus basis. Sometimes we argue, and sometimes we don't. But we control the amount we pay out to each of us, and everybody gets the same. The kids got as much over the years as Helen and I did, except I got a salary, which my son, Jim, now draws as head of Walton Enterprises. That way, we accumulated funds in Enterprises rather than throwing it all over the place to live high. And we certainly drew all we needed, probably more, in my opinion.

The partnership works in a number of different ways. First, it enables us to control Wal-Mart through the family and keep it together, rather than having it sold off in pieces haphazardly. We still own 38 percent of the company's stock today, which is an unusually large stake for anyone to hold in an outfit the size of Wal-Mart, and that's the best protection there is against the takeover raiders. It's something that any family who has faith in its strength as a unit and in the growth potential of its business can do. The transfer of ownership was made so long ago that we didn't have to pay substantial gift or inheritance taxes on it. The principle behind this is simple: the best way to reduce paying estate taxes is to give your assets away before they appreciate.

It turned out to be a great philosophy and a great strategy, and I certainly wouldn't have figured it out way back then without the advice of Helen's father. It wasn't lavish or exorbitant, and that was part of the plan—to keep the family together as well as maintain a sense of balance in our standards.

HELEN WALTON:

"It was great moneywise, but there was another aspect to it: the relationship that was established among the children and with the family. It developed their sense of responsibility toward one another. You just can't beat that."

So along comes *Forbes* in 1985 and says I'm the richest man in America. Well, there's no question that if you multiply the Wal-Mart stock price by how much we own, then maybe we are worth $20 or $25 billion, or whatever they say. The family may have those kinds of assets, but I have never seen that myself. For one thing, Helen and I only own 20 percent of our family's total interest in Wal-Mart. For another, as long as I have anything to do with it—and I'm confident this attitude will last at least another generation—most of that Wal-Mart stock is staying right where it is. We don't need the money. We don't need to buy a yacht. And thank goodness we never thought we had to go out and buy anything like an island. We just don't have those kinds of needs or ambitions, which wreck a lot of companies when they get along in years. Some families sell their stock off a little at a time to live high, and then—boom—somebody takes them over, and it all goes down the drain. One of the real reasons I'm writing this book is so my grandchildren and great-grandchildren will read it years from now and know this: If you start any of that foolishness, I'll come back and haunt you. So don't even think about it.

Not that I'm trying to poor-mouth here. We certainly have had more than adequate funds in this family for a long time—even before we got Wal-Mart cranked up. Here's the thing: money never has meant that much to me, not even in the sense of keeping score. If we had enough groceries, and a nice place to live, plenty of room to keep and feed my bird dogs, a place to hunt, a place to play tennis, and the means to get the kids good educations—that's rich. No question about it. And we have it. We're not crazy. We don't live like paupers the way some people depict us. We all love to fly, and we have nice airplanes, but I've owned about eighteen airplanes over the years, and I never bought one of them new. We have our family meetings at fine places like the Ritz-Carlton in Naples, Florida, or the Del Coronado in San Diego. This house we live in was designed by E. Fay Jones, who lives down the road in Fayetteville and is a world-famous disciple of Frank Lloyd Wright. And even though I think it cost too much, I have to admit that it's beautiful—but in a real simple, natural kind of way.

We're not ashamed of having money, but I just don't believe a big showy lifestyle is appropriate for anywhere, least of all here in Bentonville where folks work hard for their money and where we all know that everyone puts on their trousers one leg at a time. I'm not sure I ever really figured out this celebrity business. Why in the world, for example, would I get an invitation to Elizabeth Taylor's wedding out in Hollywood? I still can't believe it was news that I get my hair cut at the barbershop. Where else would I get it cut? Why do I drive a pickup truck? What am I supposed to haul my dogs around in, a Rolls-Royce?

Nowadays, I'm willing to concede that some good may have come from that magazine article and all the hubbub it created, as much as I hated it for years. At first I thought it was going to be bad for my relationship with the associates in the stores. But I found out that, gosh, they almost looked at it like: "Look, we helped him get there. Good for him!" I think my coming by to visit the stores somehow means more to them now. I noticed a big difference in their reaction since that list made me into sort of a public figure. And, of course, our customers seem to get a kick out of it too—asking me to autograph dollar bills and other stuff.

CHARLIE BAUM, EARLY WAL-MART PARTNER:

"I've known Sam since his first store in Newport, Arkansas, and I believe that money is, in some respects, almost immaterial to him. What motivates the man is the desire to absolutely be on top of the heap. It is *not* money. Money drives him crazy now. His question to me at 6 A.M. not long ago was

'How do you inspire a grandchild to go to work if they know they'll never have a poor day in their life?' "

DAVID GLASS, CEO, WAL-MART:

"Does Sam have money? I've been traveling with him for thirty years, and you could never tell it by me. In fact, if I didn't read the proxy statement every year, I'd swear he was broke. I remember one time we were flying out of New York —on a commercial flight—going to see our friends at The Limited in Columbus, Ohio—and all of a sudden at the airport, Sam sort of looks startled and says, 'David, I don't have any money with me. Do you?' I reached in my wallet and pulled out two twenties. He looked at them and said, 'You won't need both of those, let me borrow one.' "

Now, when it comes to Wal-Mart, there's no two ways about it: I'm cheap. I think it's a real statement that Wal-Mart never bought a jet until after we were approaching $40 billion in sales and expanded as far away as California and Maine, and even then they had to practically tie me up and hold me down to do it. On the road, we sleep two to a room, although as I've gotten older I have finally started staying in my own room. We stay in Holiday Inns and Ramada Inns and Days Inns, and we eat a lot at family restaurants—when we have time to eat. A lot of what goes on these days with high-flying companies and these overpaid CEO's, who're really just looting from the top and aren't watching out for anybody but themselves, really upsets me. It's one of the main things wrong with American business today.

GARY REINBOTH, EARLY STORE MANAGER,
WAL-MART:

"In those days, we would go on these buying trips with Sam, and we'd all stay, as much as we could, in one room or two. I remember one time in Chicago when we stayed eight of us to a room. And the room wasn't very big to begin with. You might say we were on a pretty restricted budget."

But sometimes I'm asked why today, when Wal-Mart has been so successful, when we're a $50 billion-plus company, should we stay so cheap? That's simple: because we believe in the value of the dollar. We exist to provide value to our customers, which means that in addition to quality and service, we have to save them money. Every time Wal-Mart spends one dollar foolishly, it comes right out of our customers' pockets. Every time we save them a dollar, that puts us one more step ahead of the competition—which is where we always plan to be.

CHAPTER 2

STARTING ON A DIME

"From the time we were kids, Sam could excel at anything he set his mind to. I guess it's just the way he was born. Back when he carried newspapers, they had a contest. I've forgotten what the prizes were—maybe $10, who knows. He won that contest, going out selling new subscriptions door to door. And he knew he was going to win. It's just the makeup of the man. My only explanation is that Sam has a lot of our mother's characteristics."

—BUD WALTON

I don't know what causes a person to be ambitious, but it is a fact that I have been overblessed with drive and ambition from the time I hit the ground, and I expect my brother's probably right. Our mother was extremely ambitious for her kids. She read a lot and loved education, although she didn't have too much herself. She went to college for a year before she quit to get married, and maybe to compensate for that, she just ordained from the beginning that I would go to college and make something of myself. One of the great sadnesses in my life is that she died young, of cancer, just as we were beginning to do well in business.

Mother must have been a pretty special motivator, because I took her seriously when she told me I should always try to be the best I could at whatever I took on. So, I have always pursued everything I was interested in with a true passion—some would say obsession—to win. I've always held the bar pretty high for myself: I've set extremely high personal goals.

Even when I was a little kid in Marshall, Missouri, I remember being ambitious. I was a class officer several years. I played football and baseball and basketball with the other kids, and I swam in the summers. I was so competitive that when I started Boy Scouts in Marshall I made a bet with the other guys about which one of us would be the first to reach the rank of Eagle. Before I made Eagle in Marshall, we had moved to the little town of Shelbina, Missouri—population maybe 1,500—but I won the bet; I got my Eagle at age thirteen—the youngest Eagle Scout in the history of the state of Missouri at that time.

FROM THE *SHELBINA DEMOCRAT*, SUMMER 1932:

"Because of his training in Boy Scout work, Sammy Walton, 14-year-old son of Mr. and Mrs. Tom Walton of Shelbina, rescued Donald Peterson, little son of Prof. and Mrs. K.R. Peterson, from drowning in Salt River Thursday afternoon . . .

"Donald got into water too deep for him and called for help. Loy Jones, who had accompanied the boys, made an effort to get him out, but Donald's struggles pulled Mr. Jones down several times. Young Walton, who was some distance away, got to the pair just as Donald went down a fifth time. He grasped him from behind, as he had been taught to do, pulled him to shore and applied artificial respiration that scouts must become proficient in.

"Donald was unconscious and his whole body had turned blue. It took quite a while to bring him around."

They said I saved his life—maybe yes, maybe no. Newspapers tend to exaggerate these things. But at least I got him out of the water. Looking back on such boyhood episodes helps me to realize now that I've always had a strong bias toward action—a trait that has been a big part of the Wal-Mart story. Truthfully, though, talking about this embarrasses me a good bit because I worry that it seems like I'm bragging or trying to make myself out to be some big hero. It particularly bothers me because I learned a long time ago that exercising your ego in public is definitely not the way to build an effective organization. One person seeking glory doesn't accomplish much; at Wal-Mart, everything we've done has been the result of people pulling together to meet one common goal—teamwork—something I also picked up at an early age.

Team play began for me when I was in the fifth grade, and a friend of mine's dad organized a bunch of us into a peewee football team. We competed against other towns, like Odessa and Sedalia and Richmond. I played end, but I wanted to throw the ball or be a running back, even though I was a little guy and couldn't squeeze my way in yet. Team athletics remained a big part of my life all through high school and—at the intramural level—in college too. By the time we moved to Shelbina, I had more football experience than most of the other kids in the ninth grade, so I was able to make the team as a second-string quarterback. I was still small—only about 130 pounds—but I knew a lot about blocking and tackling and throwing the ball, and by being extremely competitive I got my letter.

Then we moved on again—this time to Columbia, Missouri. There, at Hickman High School, I got involved in just about everything. I wasn't what you'd call a gifted student, but I worked really hard and made the honor roll. I was president of the student body and active in a lot of clubs—I remember the speech club in particular—and I was voted Most Versatile Boy. I was really a gym rat. I loved hanging around that gym playing basketball, but I didn't go out for the team—maybe because I was only five nine. When I was a senior, though, they drafted me for the team, and I became a guard, sometimes a starter. I wasn't a great shot, but I was a pretty good ball handler and a real good floor leader. I liked running the team, I guess. We went undefeated—and in one of my biggest thrills—won the state championship.

My high school athletic experience was really unbelievable, because I was also the quarterback on the football team, which went undefeated too—and won the state championship as well. I didn't throw particularly well, but we were mostly a running team. And I was fairly slow for a back, but I was shifty, sometimes so shifty that I would fall down with a bunch of daylight in front of me. On defense, my favorite thing was when the coach would slip me in and let me play linebacker. I had a good sense for where the ball was going to go, and I really loved to hit. I guess I was just totally competitive as an athlete, and my main talent was probably the same as my best talent as a retailer—I was a good motivator.

This is hard to believe, but it's true: in my whole life I never played in a losing football game. I certainly can't take much of the credit for that, and, in fact, there was definitely some luck involved. I was sick or injured for a couple of games that we wouldn't have won with or without me—so I dodged the bullet on a few losses that I could have played in. But I think that record had an important effect on me. It taught me to expect to win, to go into tough challenges always planning to come out victorious. Later on in life, I think Kmart, or whatever competition we were facing, just became Jeff City High School, the team we played for the state championship in 1935. It never occurred to me that I might lose; to me, it was almost as if I had a right to win. Thinking like that often seems to turn into sort of a self-fulfilling prophecy.

Having been the quarterback for the Hickman Kewpies—the undefeated state champions—I was already pretty well known around Columbia, where the University of Missouri is located. So my high school career just merged right on into college. Most of the fraternities were really for the more well-to-do kids, and I ordinarily wouldn't have qualified for membership. But they rushed me even as a town boy, and I had my pick of the best. I chose Beta Theta Pi because they were the top scholastic fraternity and had led the intramural athletic league for a number of years.

When I was a sophomore, the Betas made me rush captain. So I bought a real old Ford, and I traveled the whole state that summer, interviewing potential Beta candidates. With all this competitive spirit and ambition I had back then, I even entertained thoughts of one day becoming President of the United States.

Closer at hand, I had decided I wanted to be president of the university student body. I learned early on that one of the secrets to campus leadership was the simplest thing of all: speak to people coming down the sidewalk before they speak to you. I did that in college. I did it when I carried my papers. I would always look ahead and speak to the person coming toward me. If I knew them, I would call them by name, but even if I didn't I would still speak to them. Before long, I probably knew more students than anybody in the university, and they recognized me and considered me their friend. I ran for every office that came along. I was elected president of the senior men's honor society, QEBH, an officer in my fraternity, and president of the senior class. I was captain and president of Scabbard and Blade, the elite military organization of ROTC.

FROM AN ARTICLE CALLED "HUSTLER WALTON" IN FRATERNITY NEWSPAPER, 1940:

"Sam is one of those rare people who knows every janitor by name, passes plates in church, loves to join organizations . . . Sam's ability to lead has been the cause of much ribbing. His military uniform has let him be called 'Little Caesar.' For his presidency of the Bible class he suffered the nickname 'Deacon.' "

Also while I was at Missouri, I was elected president of the Burall Bible Class—a huge class made up of students from both Missouri and Stephens College. Growing up, I had always gone to church and Sunday school every Sunday; it was an important part of my life. I don't know that I was that religious, per se, but I always felt like the church was important. Obviously, I enjoyed running for office during my college years. But aside from dabbling in some city council politics years later, I really left my ambitions for elected office on the college campus.

I was about to graduate from the University of Missouri in June of 1940 with a business degree, and I had been working probably as hard as I ever worked in my life. I've always had lots of energy, but I was tired. Ever since high school, I had made all my own money and paid for all my own clothes. That continued in college except I had to add tuition and food and fraternity dues and date money to my expenses. Dad and Mother would have been glad to help if they could have, but it was the Depression and they had no extra money at all. I had continued to throw a newspaper route all through high school, and in college I added a few more routes, hired a few helpers, and turned it into a pretty good business. I made about $4,000 to $5,000 a year, which at the end of the Depression was fairly serious money.

EZRA ENTREKIN, FORMER CIRCULATION MANAGER OF THE *COLUMBIA MISSOURIAN:*

"We hired Sam to deliver newspapers, and he really became our chief salesman. When school started, we had a drive to get the kids in the fraternities and sororities to subscribe. And Sam was the boy we had do that because he could sell more than anybody else. He was good. He was really good. And dedicated. And he did a lot of other things besides deliver newspapers. In fact, he was a little bit scatterbrained at times. He'd have so many things going, he'd almost forget one. But, boy, when he focused on something, that was it."

In addition to the newspapers, I waited tables in exchange for meals, and I was also the head lifeguard in charge of the swimming pool. You can see that I was a pretty busy fellow, and you can see why my notorious respect for the value of a dollar continued. But now that I was about to become a college graduate, I was ready to give up this routine, really eager to get out in the world and make something of myself in a real job.

My first exposure to the possibilities of retail had come in 1939, when our family happened to move next door to a guy named Hugh Mattingly. He had been a barber in Odessa, Missouri, before he and his brothers started a variety store chain which had grown to around sixty stores by that time. I would talk with him about merchandising, how to do it, and how well it was working out for him. He took an interest in me, and later even offered me a job.

But I never seriously considered retail in those days. In fact, I was sure I was going to be an insurance salesman. I had a high school girlfriend whose father was a very successful salesman for General American Life Insurance Company, and I had talked to him about his business. It appeared to me that he was making all the money in the world. Insurance seemed like a natural for me because I thought I could sell. I had always sold things. As a little kid I sold *Liberty* magazines for a nickel, and then switched to *Woman's Home Companion* when it came along for a dime, figuring I could make twice as much money. The girl and I broke up, but I still had big plans. I figured I would get my degree and go on to the Wharton School of Finance in Pennsylvania. But as college wound down, I realized that even if I kept up the same kind of work routine I'd had all through college, I still wouldn't have the money to go to Wharton. So I decided to cash in what chips I already had, and I visited with two company recruiters who had come to the Missouri campus. Both of them made me job offers. I accepted the one from J. C. Penney; I turned down the one from Sears Roebuck. Now I realize the simple truth: I got into retailing because I was tired and I wanted a real job.

The deal was pretty straightforward—report to the J. C. Penney store in Des Moines, Iowa, three days after graduation, June 3, 1940, and begin work as a management trainee. Salary: $75 a month. That's the day I went into retail, and—except for a little time out as an Army officer—that's where I've stayed for the last fifty-two years. Maybe I was born to be a merchant, maybe it was fate. I don't know about that kind of stuff. But I know this for sure: I loved retail from the very beginning, and I still love it today. Not that it went all that smooth right off the bat.

Like I said, I could sell. And I loved that part. Unfortunately, I never learned handwriting all that well. Helen says there're only about five people in the world who can read my chicken scratch —she's not one of them—and this began to cause some problems for me at my new job. Penney's had a fellow out of New York named Blake, who traveled around the country auditing stores and evaluating personnel and whatnot, and he would come to see us pretty regularly. I remember him as a big fellow, over six feet, who always dressed to the nines, you know, Penney's best suits and shirts and ties. Anyway, he'd get all upset at the way I would screw up the sales slips and generally mishandle the cash register part of things. I couldn't stand to leave a new customer waiting while I fiddled with paperwork on a sale I'd already made, and I have to admit it did create some confusion.

"Walton," Blake would say to me when he came to Des Moines, "I'd fire you if you weren't such a good salesman. Maybe you're just not cut out for retail."

Fortunately, I found a champion in my store manager, Duncan Majors, a great motivator, who was proudest of having trained more Penney managers than anybody else in the country. He had his own techniques and was a very successful manager. His secret was that he worked us from six-thirty in the morning until seven or eight o'clock at night. All of us wanted to become managers like him. On Sundays, when we weren't working, we would go out to his house—there were about eight of us, all men —and we would talk about retailing, of course, but we also played Ping-Pong or cards. It was a seven-day job. I remember one Sunday Duncan Majors had just gotten his annual bonus check from Penney's and was waving it around all over the place. It was for $65,000, which impressed the heck out of us boys. Watching this guy is what got me excited about retail. He was really good. Then, of course, the icing on the cake was when James Cash Penney himself visited the store one day. He didn't get around to his stores as often as I would later on, but he did get around. I still remember him showing me how to tie and package merchandise, how to wrap it with very little twine and very little paper but still make it look nice.

I worked for Penney's about eighteen months, and they really were the Cadillac of the industry as far as I was concerned. But even back then I was checking out the competition. The intersection where I worked in Des Moines had three stores, so at lunch I would always go wander around the Sears and the Yonkers stores to see what they were up to.

By early 1942, though, the war was on, and as an ROTC graduate I was gung-ho to go, ready to ship out overseas and see my share of the action. But the Army had a big surprise for me.

Because of a minor heart irregularity, I flunked the physical for combat duty and was classified for limited duty. This kind of got me down in the dumps, and since I was just waiting around to be called up anyway I quit my Penney's job and wandered south, toward Tulsa, with some vague idea of seeing what the oil business was like. Instead, I got a job at a big Du Pont gunpowder plant in the town of Pryor, outside Tulsa. The only room I could find to stay in was nearby, over in Claremore. That's where I met Helen Robson one April night in a bowling alley.

HELEN WALTON:

"I was out on a date with another fellow, and it was the first time I'd ever been bowling. I had just rolled the ball and when I came back to the seats—they were those old wooden theater chairs—Sam had his leg up over the armrest of one of them, and he smiled at me and said, corny as it was, "Haven't I met you somewhere before?" We discovered that he had dated a girl I knew in college. Later on, he called me and asked me for her number, and I think maybe he even went out with her. But pretty soon, he and I were going out together. My whole family just fell in love with him, and I always said he fell in love as much with my family as he did with me."

When Helen and I met and I started courting her, I just fell right in love. She was pretty and smart and educated, ambitious and opinionated and strong-willed—with ideas and plans of her own. Also, like me, she was an athlete who loved the outdoors, and she had lots of energy.

HELEN WALTON:

"I always told my mother and Dad that I was going to marry someone who had that special energy and drive, that desire to be a success. I certainly found what I was looking for, but now I laugh sometimes and say maybe I overshot a little."

At the same time Helen and I fell for each other, I was finally called up to the Army for active duty. Because of my heart irregularity, I couldn't see combat, but I was still able to accept my ROTC commission as a second lieutenant. By the time I went into the Army I had two things settled: I knew who I wanted to marry, and I knew what I wanted to do for a living—retailing. About a year after I went into the Army, Helen and I were married on Valentine's Day, 1943, in her hometown of Claremore, Oklahoma.

I wish I could recount a valiant military career—like my brother Bud, who was a Navy bomber pilot on a carrier in the Pacific—but my service stint was really fairly ordinary time spent as a lieutenant and then as a captain doing things like supervising security at aircraft plants and POW camps in California and around the country.

Helen and I spent two years living the Army life, and when I got out in 1945, I not only knew I wanted to go into retailing, I also knew I wanted to go into business for myself. My only experience was the Penney job, but I had a lot of confidence that I could be successful on my own. Our last Army posting was in Salt Lake City, and I went to the library there and checked out every book on retailing. I also spent a lot of my off-duty time studying ZCMI, the Mormon Church's department store out there, just figuring that when I got back to civilian life I would somehow go into the department store business. The only question left was where we were going to set up housekeeping.

HELEN WALTON:

"My father wanted us to move to Claremore, but I told him, 'Dad, I want my husband to be himself, I don't want him to be L. S. Robson's son-in-law. I want him to be Sam Walton.'"

As I mentioned, Helen's father was a very prominent lawyer, banker, and rancher, and she felt we should be independent. I agreed with her, and I thought our best opportunity might be in St. Louis. As it turned out, an old friend of mine, Tom Bates, also wanted to go into the department store business. I'd known Tom when we were kids in Shelbina—his father owned the biggest department store in town—and Tom and I were roommates in the

Beta Theta Pi fraternity house at Missouri. When I got out of the Army, I caught up with Tom in St. Louis. He was working in the shoe department of Butler Brothers. Butler Brothers was a regional retailer with two franchise operations: Federated Stores, a chain of small department stores, and Ben Franklin, a chain of variety stores, what we used to call "five and dimes" or "dime stores."

Tom had a great idea, I thought. He and I would become partners, each putting up $20,000, and buy a Federated department store on Del Mar Avenue in St. Louis. Helen and I had $5,000 or so, and I knew we could borrow the rest from her father, who always had a lot of faith in me and was very supportive. Man, I was all set to become a big-city department store owner. That's when Helen spoke up and laid down the law.

HELEN WALTON:

"Sam, we've been married two years and we've moved sixteen times. Now, I'll go with you any place you want so long as you don't ask me to live in a big city. Ten thousand people is enough for me."

So any town with a population over 10,000 was off-limits to the Waltons. If you know anything at all about the initial small-town strategy that got Wal-Mart going almost two decades later, you can see that this pretty much set the course for what was to come. She also said no partnerships; they were too risky. Her family had seen some partnerships go sour, and she was dead-set in the notion that the only way to go was to work for yourself. So I went back to Butler Brothers to see what else they might have for me.

What they had was a Ben Franklin variety store in Newport, Arkansas—a cotton and railroad town of about 7,000 people, in the Mississippi River Delta country of eastern Arkansas. I remember riding down there on the train from St. Louis, still wearing my Army uniform with the Sam Browne belt, and walking down Front Street to give this store—my dream—the once-over. A guy from St. Louis owned it, and things weren't working out at all for him. He was losing money, and he wanted to unload the store as fast as he could. I realize now that I was the sucker Butler Brothers sent to save him. I was twenty-seven years old and full of confidence, but I didn't know the first thing about how to evaluate a proposition like this so I jumped right in with both feet. I bought it for $25,000—$5,000 of our own money and $20,000 borrowed from Helen's father. My naïveté about contracts and such would later come back to haunt me in a big way.

But at the time I was sure Newport and the Ben Franklin had great potential, and I've always believed in goals, so I set myself one: I wanted my little Newport store to be the best, most profitable variety store in Arkansas within five years. I felt I had the talent to do it, that it could be done, and why not go for it? Set that as a goal and see if you can't achieve it. If it doesn't work, you've had fun trying.

Only after we closed the deal, of course, did I learn that the store was a real dog. It had sales of about $72,000 a year, but its rent was 5 percent of sales—which I thought sounded fine—but which, it turned out, was the highest rent anybody'd ever heard of in the variety store business. No one paid 5 percent of sales for rent. And it had a strong competitor—a Sterling Store across the street—whose excellent manager, John Dunham, was doing more than $150,000 a year in sales, double mine.

For all my confidence, I hadn't had a day's experience in running a variety store, so Butler Brothers sent me for two weeks' training to the Ben Franklin in Arkadelphia, Arkansas. After that, I was on my own, and we opened for business on September 1, 1945. Our store was a typical old variety store, 50 feet wide and 100 feet deep, facing Front Street, in the heart of town, looking out on the railroad tracks. Back then, those stores had cash registers and clerk aisles behind each counter throughout the store, and the clerks would wait on the customers. Self-service hadn't been thought of yet.

It was a real blessing for me to be so green and ignorant, because it was from that experience that I learned a lesson which has stuck with me all through the years: you can learn from everybody. I didn't just learn from reading every retail publication I could get my hands on, I probably learned the most from studying what John Dunham was doing across the street.

HELEN WALTON:

"It turned out there was a lot to learn about running a store. And, of course, what really drove Sam was that competition across the street—John Dunham over at the Sterling Store. Sam was always over there checking on John. Always. Looking at his prices, looking at his displays, looking at what was going on. He was always looking for a way to do a better job. I don't remember the details, but I remember some kind of panty price war they got into. Later on, long after we had left Newport, and John had retired, we would see him and he would laugh about Sam always being in his store. But I'm sure it aggravated him quite a bit early on. John had never had good competition before Sam."

I learned a tremendous amount from running a store in the Ben Franklin franchise program. They had an excellent operating program for their independent stores, sort of a canned course in how to run a store. It was an education in itself. They had their own accounting system, with manuals telling you what to do, when and how. They had merchandise statements, they had accounts-payable sheets, they had profit-and-loss sheets, they had little ledger books called Beat Yesterday books, in which you could compare this year's sales with last year's on a day-by-day basis. They had all the tools that an independent merchant needed to run a controlled operation. I had no previous experience in accounting—and I wasn't all that great at accounting in college—so I just did it according to their book. In fact, I used their accounting system long after I'd started breaking their rules on everything else. I even used it for the first five or six Wal-Marts.

As helpful as that franchise program was to an eager-to-learn twenty-seven-year-old kid, Butler Brothers wanted us to do things literally by the book—their book. They really didn't allow their franchisees much discretion. The merchandise was assembled in Chicago, St. Louis, or Kansas City. They told me what merchandise to sell, how much to sell it for, and how much they would sell it to me for. They told me that their selection of merchandise was what the customers expected. They also told me I had to buy at least 80 percent of my merchandise from them, and if I did, I would get a rebate at year-end. If I wanted to make a 6 or 7 percent net profit, they told me I would have to hire so much help and do so much advertising. This is how most franchises work.

At the very beginning, I went along and ran my store by their book because I really didn't know any better. But it didn't take me long to start experimenting—that's just the way I am and always have been. Pretty soon I was laying on promotional programs of my own, and then I started buying merchandise directly from manufacturers. I had lots of arguments with manufacturers. I would say, "I want to buy these ribbons and bows direct. I don't want you to sell them to Butler Brothers and then I have to pay Butler Brothers 25 percent more for them. I want it direct." Most of the time, they didn't want to make Butler Brothers mad so they turned me down. Every now and then, though, I would find one who would cross over and do it my way.

That was the start of a lot of the practices and philosophies that still prevail at Wal-Mart today. I was always looking for offbeat suppliers or sources. I started driving over to Tennessee to some fellows I found who would give me special buys at prices way below what Ben Franklin was charging me. One I remember was Wright Merchandising Co. in Union City, which would sell to small businesses like mine at good wholesale prices. I'd work in the store all day, then take off around closing and drive that windy road over to the Mississippi River ferry at Cottonwood Point, Missouri, and then into Tennessee with an old homemade trailer hitched to my car. I'd stuff that car and trailer with whatever I could get good deals on—usually on softlines: ladies' panties and nylons, men's shirts—and I'd bring them back, price them low, and just blow that stuff out the store.

I've got to tell you, it drove the Ben Franklin folks crazy. Not only were they not getting their percentages, they couldn't com-

pete with the prices I was buying at. Then I started branching out
further than Tennessee. Somehow or another, I got in touch by
letter with a manufacturer's agent out of New York named Harry
Weiner. He ran Weiner Buying Services at 505 Seventh Avenue.
That guy ran a very simple business. He would go to all these
different manufacturers and then list what they had for sale. When
somebody like me sent him an order, he would take maybe 5
percent for himself and then send the order on to the factory,
which would ship it to us. That 5 percent seemed like a pretty
reasonable cut to me, compared to 25 percent for Ben Franklin.

I'll never forget one of Harry's deals, one of the best items I
ever had and an early lesson in pricing. It first got me thinking in
the direction of what eventually became the foundation of Wal-
Mart's philosophy. If you're interested in "how Wal-Mart did it,"
this is one story you've got to sit up and pay close attention to.
Harry was selling ladies' panties—two-barred, tricot satin panties
with an elastic waist—for $2.00 a dozen. We'd been buying simi-
lar panties from Ben Franklin for $2.50 a dozen and selling them
at three pair for $1.00. Well, at Harry's price of $2.00, we could
put them out at four for $1.00 and make a great promotion for
our store.

Here's the simple lesson we learned—which others were
learning at the same time and which eventually changed the way
retailers sell and customers buy all across America: say I bought an
item for 80 cents. I found that by pricing it at $1.00 I could sell
three times more of it than by pricing it at $1.20. I might make
only half the profit per item, but because I was selling three times
as many, the overall profit was much greater. Simple enough. But
this is really the essence of discounting: by cutting your price, you
can boost your sales to a point where you earn far more at the
cheaper retail price than you would have by selling the item at the
higher price. In retailer language, you can lower your markup but
earn more because of the increased volume.

I began to mull this idea in Newport, but it would be another
ten years before I took it seriously. I couldn't follow up on it in
Newport because the Ben Franklin program was too cut-and-

dried to permit it. And despite my dealings with the likes of Harry Weiner, I still had that contract saying I was supposed to buy at least 80 percent of my merchandise from Ben Franklin. If I missed that target, I didn't get my year-end rebate. The fact of the matter is I stretched that contract every way I could. I would buy as much as I could on the outside and still try to meet the 80 percent. Charlie Baum—who was then one of the field men for Ben Franklin—would say we were only at 70 percent, and I would foam at the mouth and rant and rave about it. I guess the only reason Butler Brothers didn't give me a harder time about it all is that our store had quickly gone from being a laggard to one of the top performers in our district.

Things began to clip along pretty good in Newport in a very short time. After only two and a half years we had paid back the $20,000 Helen's father loaned us, and I felt mighty good about that. It meant the business had taken off on its own, and I figured we were really on our way now.

We tried a lot of promotional things that worked really well. First, we put a popcorn machine out on the sidewalk, and we sold that stuff like crazy. So I thought and thought about it and finally decided what we needed was a soft ice cream machine out there too. I screwed my courage up and went down to the bank and borrowed what at the time seemed like the astronomical sum of $1,800 to buy that thing. That was the first money I ever borrowed from a bank. Then we rolled the ice cream machine out there on the sidewalk next to the popcorn machine, and I mean we attracted some attention with those two. It was new and different—another experiment—and we really turned a profit on it. I paid off that $1,800 note in two or three years, and I felt great about it. I really didn't want to be remembered as the guy who lost his shirt on some crazy ice cream machine.

CHARLIE BAUM:

"Everybody wanted to go see Sam Walton's store. We never had another store that had a Ding Dong ice cream bar in it, one of those ice cream–making machines. People went there for that, and it was fantastic. But one Saturday night for some reason they forgot to clean that machine up when they closed, and I went by there the next day with some of my clients to show them Sam's front window. And I want to tell you, the flies in that window were just out of this world."

As good as business was, I never could leave well enough alone, and, in fact, I think my constant fiddling and meddling with the status quo may have been one of my biggest contributions to the later success of Wal-Mart. As I mentioned, we faced Front Street, and our biggest competitor—John Dunham's Sterling Store—was across Hazel Street on the other corner. His store was slightly smaller than ours, but he still managed to do twice as much business as our store did before we bought it. We were coming on strong, though. In our first year, the Ben Franklin did $105,000 in sales, compared to $72,000 under the old owner. Then the next year $140,000, and then $175,000.

Finally we caught, and then passed, old John over there across Hazel Street. But next door to him, on the other side from us, was a Kroger grocery store. By now, I was real involved in the community and kept my ear to the ground pretty good, and I heard that Sterling was going to buy Kroger's lease and expand John's store into that space, making their store much bigger than mine. So I hustled down to Hot Springs, to find the landlady of that Kroger building. Somehow, I convinced her to give me the lease, instead of giving it to Sterling. I didn't have any idea what I was going to do with it, but I sure knew I didn't want Sterling to have it. Well, I decided to put in a small department store. Now Newport already had several department stores, one of which happened to be owned by my store's landlord, P. K. Holmes. That may or may not have had something to do with the trouble which was going to come soon. But we didn't think anything about it.

I drew up a plan, bought a sign, bought new fixtures from a company up in Nebraska, and bought the merchandise—dresses, pants, shirts, jackets, whatever I thought I could sell. The fixtures arrived on Wednesday by train, and Charlie Baum, who was supposed to be supervising my merchandising for Butler Brothers, offered to help me put everything together. He was the most efficient store layer-outer I've ever known. We went over to the railroad tracks and unloaded the fixtures, put them together, laid out the store, put the merchandise together—and opened six days later on Monday. We called it the Eagle Store.

So now we had two stores on Front Street in Newport. I would run up and down the alley with merchandise: if it didn't sell in one store, I would try it in the other. I guess they competed with each other, but not much. By now, the Ben Franklin was doing really well. The Eagle never made much money, but I figured I'd rather have a small profit than have my competitor over there in a big store. I had to hire my first assistant manager to help out in the Ben Franklin while I was running back and forth, and my brother Bud had come home from the war and was working with me too.

BUD WALTON

"That Newport store was really the beginning of where Wal-Mart is today. We did everything. We would wash windows, sweep floors, trim windows. We did all the stockroom work, checked the freight in. Everything it took to run a store. We had to keep expenses to a minimum. That is where it started, years ago. Our money was made by controlling expenses. That, and Sam always being ingenious. He never stopped trying to do something different. One thing, though: I never forgave him for making me clean out that damned ice cream machine. He knew I'd hated milk and dairy products ever since we were kids. He used to squirt me when he milked the cows. I always thought he gave me that job because he knew I didn't like milk. He still laughs about it."

We couldn't have felt better about our situation down there. Helen and I both have the kinds of personalities that make us want to participate in community life, and we had become deeply involved. We had joined the Presbyterian church there, and even though I was a Methodist, it worked out real well. Just as Helen and I were raised in the church, we felt that our kids would benefit from a church upbringing. Church is an important part of society, especially in small towns. Whether it's the contacts and associations you make or the contributions you might make toward helping other folks, it all sort of ties in together. Helen was very active in her churchwork, which she still is today, and in PEO, an international women's organization. Our four children had come along by now, and Helen really loved Newport. I was a member of the church's board of deacons, was active in the Rotary Club, and had become president of the Chamber of Commerce as well as head of its industrial committee. I was pretty much involved in everything around town.

It so happened that on the other side of our store, also on Front Street, was a J. C. Penney. We didn't compete much, and I was friendly with the manager. So one day this dapper supervisor from New York named Blake came to town to audit that store and got to chatting with the manager.

"Say," the manager told Blake, "we've got an ex-Penney man right here in Newport. He came in a few years ago and really made a big success of it. He doubled sales in his Ben Franklin, he's got two stores, and he's the president of the Chamber of Commerce." And when the manager told him it was Sam Walton, old Blake almost fell over. "It can't be the same one I knew in Des Moines," he said. "That fellow couldn't have amounted to anything." He came next door and we both had a big laugh about it when he saw that I really was that kid who couldn't write so you could read it.

By now, my five years in Newport were about up, and I had met my goal. That little Ben Franklin store was doing $250,000 in sales a year, and turning $30,000 to $40,000 a year in profit. It was the number-one Ben Franklin store—for sales or profit—not only in Arkansas, but in the whole six-state region. It was the largest variety store of any sort in Arkansas, and I don't believe there was a bigger one in the three or four neighboring states.

Every crazy thing we tried hadn't turned out as well as the ice cream machine, of course, but we hadn't made any mistakes we couldn't correct quickly, none so big that they threatened the business. Except, it turned out, for one little legal error we made right at the beginning. In all my excitement at becoming Sam Walton, merchant, I had neglected to include a clause in my lease which gave me an option to renew after the first five years.

And our success, it turned out, had attracted a lot of attention. My landlord, the department store owner, was so impressed with our Ben Franklin's success that he decided not to renew our lease —at any price—knowing full well that we had nowhere else in town to move the store. He did offer to buy the franchise, fixtures, and inventory at a fair price; he wanted to give the store to his son. I had no alternative but to give it up. But I sold the Eagle Store lease to Sterling—so that John Dunham, my worthy competitor and mentor, could finally have that expansion he'd wanted.

It was the low point of my business life. I felt sick to my stomach. I couldn't believe it was happening to me. It really was like a nightmare. I had built the best variety store in the whole region and worked hard in the community—done everything right—and now I was being kicked out of town. It didn't seem fair. I blamed myself for ever getting suckered into such an awful lease, and I was furious at the landlord. Helen, just settling in with a brand-new family of four, was heartsick at the prospect of leaving Newport. But that's what we were going to do.

I've never been one to dwell on reverses, and I didn't do so then. It's not just a corny saying that you can make a positive out of most any negative if you work at it hard enough. I've always thought of problems as challenges, and this one wasn't any different. I don't know if that experience changed me or not. I know I read my leases a lot more carefully after that, and maybe I became a little more wary of just how tough the world can be. Also, it may have been about then that I began encouraging our oldest boy—six-year-old Rob—to become a lawyer. But I didn't dwell on my disappointment. The challenge at hand was simple enough to figure out: I had to pick myself up and get on with it, do it all over again, only even better this time.

Helen and I started looking for a new town.

CHAPTER 3

BOUNCING BACK

"When we left Newport, it was a thriving cotton town, and I
hated to leave. We had built a life there, and it was so disturbing
to have to walk away from it. I have said that time and time
again. I still have good friends there from those days."

—HELEN WALTON

I came out of that Newport experience with my pride a
little damaged, but I had made money on the sale of the Ben
Franklin—more than $50,000. The whole thing was probably a
blessing. I had a chance for a brand-new start, and this time I
knew what I was doing. Now, at the age of thirty-two, I was a
full-fledged merchant; all I needed was a store. Helen and the kids
and I started driving around in the spring of 1950 hunting in
earnest for one, and northwest Arkansas appealed to us for several
reasons. First, for Helen it was a whole lot closer to her folks in
Claremore than Newport had been. And it was good for me
because I wanted to get closer to good quail hunting, and with
Oklahoma, Kansas, Arkansas, and Missouri all coming together
right there it gave me easy access to four quail seasons in four
states.

We tried to buy a store in Siloam Springs, on the Oklahoma
border, but we couldn't come to terms with the owner, Jim Dod-

son, who later became a friend of ours. So one day Helen's father and I drove into Bentonville and had a look around the square. It was the smallest of the towns we considered, and it already had three variety stores, when one would have been enough. Still, I love competition, and it just struck me as the right place to prove I could do it all over again. We found an old store willing to sell—Harrison's Variety Store—but we needed to double its size, and to do that we had to get a ninety-nine-year lease on the barbershop next door (no more five-year leases for me). These two old widows from Kansas City who owned it wouldn't budge, and, frankly, if Helen's father hadn't gone up there—unbeknownst to me—and negotiated a deal, I'm not sure where the Waltons would have ended up.

HELEN WALTON:

"Bentonville really was just a sad-looking country town, even though it had a railroad track to it. It was mostly known for apples, but at the time chickens were beginning to come on. I remember I couldn't believe this was where we were going to live. It only had 3,000 people, compared to Newport, which was a thriving cotton and railroad town of 7,000 people. The store was a small old country town store with cans of lace, boxes of hats, sewing patterns, everything you can imagine just stored around everywhere. But I knew right after we got here that it was going to work out."

Now I had a store to run again, and even though it didn't do but $32,000 the year before I bought it—compared to $250,000 at Newport—it didn't matter that much because I had big plans. We tore the wall out between the barbershop and the old store, put in brand-new fluorescent fixtures instead of the few low-watt bulbs they had hanging from the ceiling, and basically built a new store in there. It was a huge store for Bentonville at the time—50 feet by 80 feet, or 4,000 square feet. Charlie Baum of Ben Franklin came to my rescue again. This time he helped me break down all those fixtures he had helped me put up in my old Eagle Store. We loaded them onto a big truck, which I drove over to Bentonville from Newport. We had to get on an old dirt road to bypass a weigh station over at Rogers because I knew our load was illegal several different ways. Bouncing on that old road tore up half the fixtures. Anyway, Charlie and I installed them again. Around this time, I read an article about these two Ben Franklin stores up in Minnesota that had gone to self-service—a brand-new concept at the time. I rode the bus all night long to two little towns up there —Pipestone and Worthington. They had shelves on the side and two island counters all the way back. No clerks with cash registers around the store. Just checkout registers up front. I liked it. So I did that too.

CHARLIE BAUM:

"As soon as Sam moved the store from Newport to Benton-ville, he had a nice big sale, and we put barrels full of stuff all around the floor. Those elderly ladies would come in and bend way down over into those barrels. I'll never forget this. Sam takes a look, frowns, and says: 'One thing we gotta do, Charlie. We gotta be real strong in lingerie.' Times had been hard, and some of those underthings were pretty ragged."

So when Charlie and I laid out that store in Bentonville it became only the third self-service variety store in the whole country and the first in our eight-state area. Maybe nobody here knew it, but it was a big deal. We've got our first ad from the July 29, 1950, *Benton County Democrat* on display today down at our Wal-Mart Visitors Center. It's for the Grand Remodeling Sale of Walton's Five and Dime, promising a whole bunch of good stuff: free balloons for the kids, a dozen clothespins for nine cents, iced tea glasses for ten cents apiece. The folks turned out, and they kept coming. Although we called it Walton's Five and Dime, it was a Ben Franklin franchise, and that store took off just like Newport had and turned into a good business right away. It really was an A-1 store for these parts back then.

INEZ THREET, CLERK, WALTON'S FIVE AND DIME,
BENTONVILLE:

"I guess Mr. Walton just had a personality that drew people in. He would yell at you from a block away, you know. He would just yell at everybody he saw, and that's the reason so many liked him and did business in the store. It was like he brought in business by his being so friendly.

"He was always thinking up new things to try in the store. I remember one time he made a trip to New York, and he came back a few days later and said, 'Come here, I want to show you something. This is going to be the item of the year.' I went over and looked at a bin full of—I think they called them zori sandals—they call them thongs now. And I just laughed and said, 'No way will those things sell. They'll just blister your toes.' Well, he took them and tied them together in pairs and dumped them all on a table at the end of an aisle for nineteen cents a pair. And they just sold like you wouldn't believe. I have never seen an item sell as fast, one after another, just piles of them. Everybody in town had a pair."

Right away I started looking around for store opportunities in other towns. Maybe it was just my itch to do more business, and maybe, too, I didn't want all my eggs in one basket again. By 1952 I had driven down to Fayetteville and found an old grocery store that Kroger was abandoning because it was falling apart. It was right on the square, only 18 feet wide and 150 feet deep. Our main competitor was a Woolworth's on one side of the square, and a Scott Store on the other side of the square. So here we were challenging two popular stores with a little old 18-foot independent variety store. It wasn't a Ben Franklin franchise; we just called it Walton's Five and Dime like the store in Bentonville. I remember sitting on the square right after I bought it listening to a couple of the local codgers say: "Well, we'll give that guy sixty days, maybe ninety. He won't be there long."

But this store was ahead of its time too, self-service all the way, unlike the competition. This was the beginning of our way of operating for a long while to come. We were innovating, experimenting, and expanding. Somehow over the years, folks have gotten the impression that Wal-Mart was something I dreamed up out of the blue as a middle-aged man, and that it was just this great idea that turned into an overnight success. It's true that I was forty-four when we opened our first Wal-Mart in 1962, but the store was totally an outgrowth of everything we'd been doing since Newport—another case of me being unable to leave well enough alone, another experiment. And like most other overnight successes, it was about twenty years in the making.

Of course I needed somebody to run my new store, and I didn't have much money, so I did something I would do for the rest of my run in the retail business without any shame or embarrassment whatsoever: nose around other people's stores searching for good talent. That's when I made my first real hire, the first manager, Willard Walker.

WILLARD WALKER—FIRST MANAGER, WALTON'S
FIVE AND DIME, FAYETTEVILLE:

"The first time I ever saw Sam Walton was when he and his brother-in-law, Nick Robson, dropped into a TG&Y dime store I was managing in Tulsa. He visited with me for about an hour, asking a lot of questions, and left, and I never thought anything about it. Later on he called me and said he was opening a new store in Fayetteville and wondered if I'd be interested in interviewing for the manager's job. I had to move myself over there, work half days for free until the store opened, and I remember sleeping on a cot in the storeroom. But he said I would get a percentage of the profits, and that appealed to me. When I went to quit TG&Y, the vice president said, 'Remember, Willard, a percentage of nothing is still nothing.' But I went ahead and took the job. Sam was down there every day from the time we started until the time we left. He rolled up his sleeves and worked every day until we built that store from scratch.

"Sam would haul in all kinds of merchandise that he bought from these friends of his over in Tennessee—haul it in by station wagon. It worked real good. The first year that store was open, I believe Bentonville did $95,000 and we did $90,000.

"Well, later on, when we had Wal-Marts and went public, I went out and borrowed what seemed like an awful lot of money at the time and bought stock with it. Bud and Sam came down to the store one day, and Bud said: 'Willard, I sure hope you know what you're doing.' He told me I had more faith than he did. I always knew it was going to be successful. The philosophy made sense, and you couldn't help but believe in the man."

In the years to come, that lure of partnership helped us attract a lot of good managers, but I don't believe we ever had one who bought more stock than Willard. And of course he feels pretty good about it today.

I remember those days mostly as a time of always looking around for ideas and items that would make our stores stand out. Sometime in there the Hula Hoop fad hit real big, and they were flooding the big-city stores. But the genuine articles, which were made of plastic hose, were pricey and hard for us to get. Jim Dodson—the fellow who wouldn't sell me the Siloam Springs store—called me and said he knew a manufacturer who could make hose the same size as the Hula Hoop's. He thought we should go in fifty-fifty and make our own Hula Hoops. We did. We made them up in his attic, and sold a ton of them at his stores and mine. Every kid in northwest Arkansas had to have one. Later Jim ended up managing a Wal-Mart for us up in Columbia, Missouri, for about fifteen years.

Also at that time, I had been buying all my fixtures from Ben Franklin. They were wooden standards, which was par for the course in those days, with wooden shelf brackets to hold the merchandise. Then I went somewhere to look at what Sterling Stores was doing—most everything I've done I've copied from somebody else—and saw these all-metal fixtures. I met a guy named Gene Lauer here in Bentonville and persuaded him to build us some for the Fayetteville store, which became, I'm sure, the first variety store in the country to use 100 percent metal standards, like the ones you see in stores today. Gene built the fixtures for the first Wal-Mart and stayed with us for twenty-one years before retiring a few years ago. Today he works here in Bentonville at the Wal-Mart Visitors Center, which is sort of a museum located on the site of that first store.

CHARLIE CATE, STOCKBOY IN FAYETTEVILE STORE, NOW RETIRED WAL-MART STORE MANAGER:

"Sam used to come down to our Fayetteville store driving an old fifty-three Plymouth. He had that car so loaded up he barely had enough room to drive. And would you like to guess what he had in it? Ladies' panties. Three for $1.00 and four for $1.00 and nylon hose. He would come in and take an end counter, and say, 'Now, Charlie, here's what you do: on this feature bin you put three for $1.00 panties, and on this one you put four for $1.00. And you put these nylons right in between the two of them. And then watch 'em sell.' And they did. Like crazy."

While I was doing all this running around between Bentonville and Fayetteville and Tennessee and the Ben Franklin regional office in Kansas City, my brother Bud had borrowed some money and bought a Ben Franklin of his own up in the little town of Versailles, Missouri, population 2,000. He and I kept in touch, but we weren't really doing any business together, and he had started a family and was doing pretty well on his own. Well, one time when I was up in Kansas City I heard about this big subdivision going up there—Ruskin Heights. In the middle of the subdivision would be a 100,000-square-foot shopping center—a whole new concept at that time. It was going to have an A&P store and a Ben Franklin store in the middle, a Crown drugstore on the end, and small shops in between. So I called Bud and told him to meet me up there right away. I said, "You want to gamble and go into this thing?" And he said, "Might as well." And we did. We borrowed all the money we could and went into that Ben Franklin fifty-fifty.

BUD WALTON:

"In the early days of the variety store business out here, there were some conventions among competitors. Each chain more or less controlled its own state. Oklahoma was TG&Y. Kansas was Alco, Texas was Mott's, Missouri was Mattingly. Nebraska was Hested's. Indiana was Danners. They were locally based and developed, and they'd say, 'Well, you don't cross my border, and I won't cross your border.' Ben Franklin franchises were for little independent operators who wanted to fit a store or two somewhere in the cracks between those guys. Of course, Sam changed all that. Borders didn't mean much to my brother. He thought nothing of doing business in four states—all in one day."

If I ever had any doubts about the potential of the business we were in, Ruskin Heights ended them. That thing took off like a house afire. The first year we made about $30,000 profits on sales of $250,000, which went up to $350,000 in no time. When I saw that shopping center catch on the way it did I thought, "Man, this is the forerunner of many, many things to come." And I decided —with no money to amount to anything—to go into the shopping center development business myself back in Arkansas. I went down to Little Rock just on fire with the idea of being the pioneer shopping center developer there. I tried to get one real good corner, but a big wheeler-dealer with Sterling Stores bought it out from under me and put in what became the town's first shopping center, which featured a Sterling Store and an Oklahoma Tire and Supply.

I kept at it. I probably spent two years going around trying to sell people on the idea of shopping centers in Arkansas in the middle fifties—which was about ten years too early. I finally got an option on one piece of property and talked Kroger and Woolworth into signing leases, based on us getting this one street paved. I started raising money for the pavement, but it got real complicated, and in the end I decided I had better take my whipping, so I backed out of the whole deal and went back to concentrating on the retail business. I probably lost $25,000, and that was at a time when Helen and I were counting every dollar. It was probably the biggest mistake of my business career. I did learn a heck of a lot about the real estate business from the experience, and maybe it paid off somewhere down the line—though I would rather have learned it some cheaper way. Incidentally, after I dropped my option on that last piece of land, a well-known young fellow named Jack Stephens—who had a whole lot more money than I did—went on to develop a successful shopping center that's still there.

DAVID GLASS:

"Two things about Sam Walton distinguish him from almost everyone else I know. First, he gets up every day bound and determined to improve something. Second, he is less afraid of being wrong than anyone I've ever known. And once he sees he's wrong, he just shakes it off and heads in another direction."

All during that real estate fiasco, I was, of course, still trying to run these variety stores, and everything was going along great until May 20, 1957—I'll never forget the day. Bud called me from Versailles and said a tornado had hit the Ruskin store. "Ah, it probably shook up a little glass," I said. But later I got to worrying about it, and I couldn't get through to anybody up there so I went on up to Kansas City to see for myself. I got there about two in the morning and saw that the whole shopping center was practically leveled. None of our people were seriously hurt, but the store was about gone. And even though the merchandise and the fixtures were insured, it was still a big blow to Bud and me. This was our best store, the one we were really excited about. It was there one minute and gone the next. We just rebuilt it and got back at it. By now, though, with all the places I had to visit, I was driving too much to have time for anything else. So I began to wonder if maybe flying wouldn't be the way to go.

BUD WALTON:

"One day I got a call from Sam, and he said, 'Meet me in Kansas City, I want to buy an airplane.' Boy, it took me by such surprise. I always thought he was the world's worst driver and even my father wouldn't ever let Sam drive him. I thought, 'He will kill himself the first year.' So I did everything in the world to try and talk him out of that first airplane. He just said, 'Whether you meet me or not, I'm going to look at this airplane.' And I did not go because I knew he would kill himself in that plane. He called me later and said he hadn't bought that particular plane, but he'd gone to Oklahoma City and bought this Air Coupe for $1,850, and I had to come see it. I'll never forget going out to the Bentonville airport and seeing what he called an airplane. It had a washing machine motor in it, and it would putt-putt, and then miss a lick, then putt-putt again. It didn't even look like an airplane, and I wouldn't go near it for at least two years. But then we were putting some more stores in around Little Rock, and one day he says, 'Let's go to Little Rock.' I hadn't flown since the Navy in the Pacific, and I was always used to water. Here we were with Sam at the stick going over all these trees and mountains. It was the longest trip I ever took. That was the start of the Wal-Mart aviation era."

In spite of what Bud says, I loved that little two-seat plane because it would go 100 miles an hour—if you didn't have the wind against you—and I could get to places in a straight line. In all the years and thousands of hours I've been flying, I've only had one engine failure, and it came in that Air Coupe. I was taking off from Fort Smith and was just over the river when an exhaust stack blew. It sounded like the end of the world. The motor hadn't quite quit, but I had to cut it off. For a minute there I thought that might be it for me, but I was able to circle back and land with a dead engine.

Once I took to the air, I caught store fever. We opened variety stores, many of them Ben Franklin franchises, in Little Rock, Springdale, and Siloam Springs, Arkansas, and we had a couple more in Neodesha and Coffeyville, Kansas. All these stores were organized as separate partnerships between Bud and me, along with other partners, including my dad, Helen's two brothers— Nick and Frank—and even the kids, who invested their paper route money.

JOHN WALTON, SECOND SON OF SAM AND HELEN:
"This is hard to believe, but between my paper route money and the money I made in the Army—both of which I invested in those stores—that investment is worth about $40 million today."

Whatever money we made in one store, we'd put it in another new one, and just keep on going. Also, from Willard Walker on, we would offer to bring the managers we hired in as limited partners. If you had, say, a $50,000 investment in a store, and the manager put in $1,000, he'd own 2 percent.

GARY REINBOTH:
"He would never let us buy more than $1,000 per store. I think $600 of it was a loan, and $400 of it was four shares of privately owned stock at $100 a share. All he would guarantee was that he would pay us interest every year, which at that time was 4½ percent. I remember one guy who ran a store would call and say, 'Are you going to buy into store so-and-so?' And I'd say, 'I think so.' Later, he would say, 'I'm not going to loan it to Sam and let him expand on *my* money.' Then I'd pick up the phone and call Mr. Walton and say, 'So-and-so isn't going to buy his share of that store, can I buy his share?' He'd say, 'Sure.' So I'd get a double share."

That whole period—which scarcely gets any attention from most people studying us—was really very, very successful. In fifteen years' time, we had become the largest independent variety store operator in the United States. But the business itself seemed a little limited. The volume was so little per store that it really didn't amount to that much. I mean, after fifteen years—in 1960 —we were only doing $1.4 million in fifteen stores. By now, you know me. I began looking around hard for whatever new idea would break us over into something with a little better payoff for all our efforts. Our first big clue came in Saint Robert, Missouri —near Fort Leonard Wood—where we learned that by building larger stores, which we called family centers—we could do un- heard-of amounts of business for variety stores, over $2 million a year in sales per store, just unthinkable for small towns. The same thing proved true to a lesser degree in Berryville, Arkansas, and right here in Bentonville too.

I began to hear talk of the early discounters—companies like Ann & Hope, whose founder, Marty Chase, is generally consid- ered the father of discounting. Spartan's and Mammoth Mart and Two Guys from Harrison and Zayre and Arlan's were all starting up in the Northeast, and I remembered that lesson I'd learned a long time ago in Newport with the panties selling in such huge volume when they were priced at $1.00, instead of $1.20. So I started running all over the country, studying the concept from the mill stores in the East to California, where Sol Price started his Fed-Mart in 1955.

Then closer to home, Herb Gibson—a barber from over at Berryville—started his stores with a simple philosophy: "Buy it low, stack it high, sell it cheap." He sold it cheaper than anybody ever had before, and he sold more of it. He did it in Abilene, he did it in Amarillo, and he surrounded Dallas with stores. Then in 1959 he came to northwest Arkansas with a franchiser named Howard's and did so well in Fort Smith that he branched out to the square in Fayetteville and started competing with our variety stores. We knew we had to act. He was the only one discounting out this way, and, because I had made all those trips back East, I was probably one of the few out here who understood what he was up to.

By then, I knew the discount idea was the future. But I was used to franchising, and I liked the mind-set. I generally liked my experience with Ben Franklin, and I didn't want to get involved in having to build a company with all that support apparatus. So, first I went up to Butler Brothers in Chicago armed with my usual yellow legal pad full of notes and made a big pitch for them to back me in a discounting venture. I wanted them to be our wholesale arm, our merchandiser. If they had agreed, our family could have continued our fairly normal lifestyle. In those days, I wasn't as fully committed with my time to the business, and it wouldn't have been all that difficult to put together an organization with them. But they weren't interested. Then I approached Gibson, but he already had his franchiser so we couldn't get together either. We really had only two choices left: stay in the variety store business, which I knew was going to be hit hard by the discounting wave of the future; or open a discount store. Of course I wasn't about to sit there and become a target. Now, right down the road from Bentonville sits Rogers, Arkansas, which was a good bit bigger town, but I never could operate there because Max Russell owned the Ben Franklin franchise. I tried to talk him into going in with me as a partner and building a big store there. But he wasn't interested.

I went ahead and started building a store in Rogers. It was a big commitment on the family's part. We couldn't use Ben Franklin at all for that store, so I had made some arrangements with a distributor in Springfield, Missouri.

Nobody wanted to gamble on that first Wal-Mart. I think Bud put in 3 percent, and Don Whitaker—whom I had hired to manage the store from a TG&Y store out in Abilene, Texas—put in 2 percent, and I had to put up 95 percent of the dollars. Helen had to sign all the notes along with me, and her statement allowed us to borrow more than I could have alone. We pledged houses and property, everything we had. But in those days we were always borrowed to the hilt. We were about to go into the discount business for real now. And from the time those doggone Wal-Marts opened until almost today, it has been a little challenging.

"We were flying to Fort Smith in the spring of 1962, and Sam was piloting the plane over the Boston Mountains. It was that Tri-Pacer by then, not the original plane that we had made a lot of trips in. Sam pulled this card out of his pocket, on which he had written down three or four names, and he handed it to me and asked me which one I liked best. They all had three or four words in the title, and I said, 'Well, you know, Scotch as I am, I'd just keep the Walton name and make it a place to shop.' I scribbled 'W-A-L-M-A-R-T' on the bottom of the card and said, 'To begin with, there's not as many letters to buy.' I had bought the letters that said 'Ben Franklin,' and I knew how much it cost to put them up and to light them and repair the neon, so I said, 'This is just seven letters.' He didn't say anything, and I dropped the subject. A few days later I went by to see when we could start setting the fixtures in the building, and I saw that our sign maker, Rayburn Jacobs, already had the 'W-A-L' up there and was headed up the ladder with an 'M.' You didn't have to be a genius to figure out what the name was going to be. I just smiled and went on."

Something else about that sign that's worth mentioning. On one side of it, I had Rayburn put "We Sell for Less," and on the other, "Satisfaction Guaranteed," two of the cornerstone philosophies that still guide the company.

After years and years of studying the discount business and experimenting with it sort of halfheartedly, we were finally getting ready to jump into it whole hog. On July 2, 1962, we finally opened Wal-Mart No. 1, and not everybody was happy about it.

"Because there was a Ben Franklin store in Rogers, run by somebody else, we really stirred up a hornet's nest when we opened that first store. I vividly remember opening day.

Along with the crowds of shoppers, a group of 'officials' from Ben Franklin in Chicago—all dressed in pin-striped suits—showed up. They marched in like a military delegation, and in the front of the store asked me, just as cold as they could be, 'Where is Mr. Walton?' They marched on back to Sam's office without a word.

"They were back there about a half hour, and then they marched out without so much as a good-bye. A few minutes later, Sam came down and told Whitaker and me that they had issued an ultimatum: Don't build any more of these Wal-Mart stores. We knew he felt threatened because he had all those Ben Franklin franchises. But we also knew Sam Walton wasn't the kind of guy you issued ultimatums to."

To tell the truth, though, that first Wal-Mart in Rogers wasn't all that great. We did a million dollars in a year, a lot more than most of our variety stores, which did $200,000 to $300,000 a year. But remember, Saint Robert—up there in that Army town—was doing $2 million in sales. Once we opened Rogers, we sat there and held our breath for two years. Then we put stores up in Springdale, a bigger town near Rogers, and Harrison, a smaller town. Here, of course, I have to let David Glass tell his now-famous story about coming to Harrison to see what a Wal-Mart was, and being so horrified at the sight.

DAVID GLASS:

"In those days, word was starting to get out that a guy named Sam Walton had some interesting retailing ideas, so I drove down from Springfield, where I was with Crank Drugs at the time, to see a Wal-Mart opening. It was the worst retail store I had ever seen. Sam had brought a couple of trucks of watermelons in and stacked them on the sidewalk. He had a donkey ride out in the parking lot. It was about 115 degrees, and the watermelons began to pop, and the donkey began to do what donkeys do, and it all mixed together and ran all over the parking lot. And when you went inside the store, the mess just continued, having been tracked in all over the floor. He was a nice fellow, but I wrote him off. It was just terrible."

I guess it really was about as bad as David describes it, but he just happened to hit it on its worst day. The store was only 12,000 square feet, and had an 8-foot ceiling and a concrete floor, with bare-boned wooden plank fixtures. Sterling had a huge variety store in downtown Harrison, with tile on the floor, nice lights, really good fixtures, and good presentations. Ours was just barely put together—highly promotional, truly ugly, heavy with merchandise—but for 20 percent less than the competition. We were trying to find out if customers in a town of 6,000 people would come to our kind of a barn and buy the same merchandise strictly because of price. The answer was yes. We found out they did, and they wanted it. Today, we have a 90,000-square-foot store in Harrison. Down the road in Springdale, we were trying to learn something else: would a really big, nice store work in a larger town? We opened a 35,000-square-foot Wal-Mart there, and it quickly became our number-one store in sales. Just to give you some idea of how the whole concept has changed over the years, we recently opened a gigantic 185,000-square-foot store in Springdale, and the store in Rogers today is 135,000 square feet compared to 18,000 for the original old number one.

Maybe a lot of people saw the same things David Glass observed that day out there in Harrison, but I was feeling pretty good. After we got those first three stores up and running, I knew it would work.

Wal-Mart was off to a good start, and we saw lots of potential. But now Gibson's and other folks were beginning to look at the smaller towns and say, "Hey, maybe there is something out there that we ought to look into." We figured we'd better roll the stores out just as quickly as we could.

CHAPTER 4

SWIMMING UPSTREAM

"From day one of Wal-Mart, Mr. Walton made it clear that this wasn't just Ben Franklin with low prices on some items. He wanted real discounting. He said, 'We want to discount everything we carry.' When the other chains around us weren't discounting, he said, 'We advertise that we sell for less, and we mean it!' So whatever else we did, we always had to sell for less. If an item came in and everybody else in town was selling it for twenty-five cents, we'd go with twenty-one cents."

—CHARLIE CATE,
store manager

As I said earlier, once we opened that Wal-Mart in Springdale, I knew we were on to something. I knew in my bones it was going to work. But at the time, most folks—including my own brother, Bud—were pretty skeptical of the whole concept. They thought Wal-Mart was just another one of Sam Walton's crazy ideas. It was totally unproven at the time, but it was really what we'd been doing all along: experimenting, trying to do something different, educating ourselves as to what was going on in the retail industry and trying to stay ahead of those trends. This is a big contradiction in my makeup that I don't completely understand to this day. In many of my core values—things like church and family and civic leadership and even politics—I'm a pretty conservative guy. But for some reason in business, I have always been driven to buck the system, to innovate, to take things beyond where they've been. On the one hand, in the community, I really am an establishment kind of guy; on the other hand, in the marketplace, I have always been a maverick who enjoys shaking things up and creating a little anarchy. And sometimes the establishment has made me mad. The truth is, when those Butler Brothers folks turned down my discounting idea, I got a little angry, and maybe that helped me decide to swim upstream on my own.

DON SODERQUIST, FORMER PRESIDENT OF BEN FRANKLIN, NOW VICE CHAIRMAN AND CHIEF OPERATING OFFICER, WAL-MART:

"I first met Sam in 1964, when I was in charge of data processing at Ben Franklin, and he was our biggest franchisee. He had already opened the Rogers Wal-Mart and he was up in Chicago trying to convince our officers to franchise his discount stores in small towns. They gave him a flat no. After the meeting he came back to see me and moved right on to the subject of computers. He wanted to know all about how we were using them, and how we were planning to use them. And he took everything I said down on this yellow legal pad.

"The next day was Saturday, and I went shopping—dressed in a pair of mangy cutoff jeans—at the Kmart near my house. I walked over into the apparel section and saw this guy talking to one of the clerks. I thought, 'Jeez, that looks like that guy I met yesterday. What the heck is he doing way out here?' I strolled up behind him, and I could hear him asking this clerk, 'Well, how frequently do you order? . . . Uh-huh. . . . How much do you order? . . . And if you order on a Tuesday, when does the merchandise come in?' He's writing everything she says down in a little blue spiral notebook. Then Sam gets down on his hands and knees and he's looking under this stack table, and he opens the sliding doors and says, 'How do you know how much you've got under here when you're placing that order?'

"Finally, I said, 'Sam Walton, is that you?' And he looked up from the floor and said, 'Oh, Don! Hi! What are you doing here?' I said, 'I'm shopping. What are *you* doing?' And he said, 'Oh, this is just part of the educational process. That's all.' Of course, he's still doing the same thing today, except he uses his little tape recorder."

I guess everybody who knew I was going ahead with the discounting idea on my own really did think I'd completely lost my mind. I laugh now when I look back on Wal-Mart's beginning. In 1962, the discount industry was fairly young and full of high-living, big-spending promoters driving around in Cadillacs —guys like Herb Gibson—who had the world by the tail. But it had very few of what you'd call good operators—until 1962, the year which turned out to be the big one for discounting. In that year, four companies that I know of started discount chains. S. S. Kresge, a big, 800-store variety chain, opened a discount store in Garden City, Michigan, and called it Kmart. F. W. Woolworth, the granddaddy of them all, started its Woolco chain. Dayton-Hudson out of Minneapolis opened its first Target store. And some independent down in Rogers, Arkansas, opened something called a Wal-Mart. At the time, and for quite a while after that, I can guarantee you that hardly anybody noticed that last guy. Heck, within five years, Kmart had 250 stores to our 19, and sales of more than $800 million to our $9 million. Here's what makes me laugh today: it would have been absolutely impossible to convince anybody back then that in thirty years most all of the early discounters would be gone, that three of these four new chains would be the biggest, best-run operators in the business, that the one to fold up would be Woolco, and that the biggest, most profitable one would be the one down in Arkansas. Sometimes even I have trouble believing it.

I can tell you this, though: after a lifetime of swimming upstream, I am convinced that one of the real secrets to Wal-Mart's phenomenal success has been that very tendency. Many of our best opportunities were created out of necessity. The things that we were forced to learn and do, because we started out underfinanced and undercapitalized in these remote, small communities, contributed mightily to the way we've grown as a company. Had we been capitalized, or had we been the offshoot of a large corporation the way I wanted to be, we might not ever have tried the Harrisons or the Rogers or the Springdales and all those other little towns we went into in the early days. It turned out that the first big lesson we learned was that there was much, much more business out there in small-town America than anybody, including me, had ever dreamed of.

CLARENCE LEIS, SECOND MANAGER,
WAL-MART NO. 1:

"When we opened Wal-Mart No. 3 in Springdale, Sam wanted a red-hot price on antifreeze. So he got two or three truckloads of Prestone and priced it at $1.00 a gallon. Then he priced Crest toothpaste at 27 cents a tube. Well, we had people come from as far as Tulsa to buy toothpaste and antifreeze. The crowd was so big that the fire department made us open the doors for five minutes, then lock them until shoppers left. Sam grabbed a tackle box and started using it as a cash register, checking people out as fast as he could."

We stuck with what we had learned in the variety store business about customer service and satisfaction guaranteed, but I have to admit that in those days we did not have anywhere near the emphasis on quality that we have today. What we were obsessed with was keeping our prices below everybody else's. Our dedication to that idea was total. Everybody worked like crazy to keep the expenses down. We tried to build decent buildings, but we had to keep the rent down—we never liked to pay more than $1.00 a square foot. Our stores really didn't look that good—they weren't professional at all. We opened one, store number 8 in Morrilton, Arkansas, that was really a sight. We rented this old Coca-Cola bottling plant. It was all broken up into five rooms, and we bought some old fixtures from a failing Gibson's store for $3,000. We hung them by baling wire from the ceiling. We had clothes hanging in layers on conduit pipe all the way to the ceiling, and shelves wired into the walls. But this was really a small, small town, so number 8 was another experiment.

We didn't have systems. We didn't have ordering programs. We didn't have a basic merchandise assortment. We certainly didn't have any sort of computers. In fact, when I look at it today, I realize that so much of what we did in the beginning was really poorly done. But we managed to sell our merchandise as low as we possibly could, and that kept us right-side-up for the first ten years—that and consistently improving our sales in these smaller markets by building up our relationship with the customers. The idea was simple: when customers thought of Wal-Mart, they should think of low prices and satisfaction guaranteed. They could be pretty sure they wouldn't find it cheaper anywhere else, and if they didn't like it, they could bring it back.

CLARENCE LEIS:

"Rogers had been open about a year, and everything was just piled up on tables, with no rhyme or reason whatsoever. Sam asked me to kind of group the stuff by category or department, and that's when we began our department system. The thing I remember most, though, was the way we priced goods. Merchandise would come in and we would just lay it down on the floor and get out the invoice. Sam wouldn't let us hedge on a price at all. Say the list price was $1.98, but we had only paid 50 cents. Initially, I would say, 'Well, it's originally $1.98, so why don't we sell it for $1.25?' And he'd say, 'No. We paid 50 cents for it. Mark it up 30 percent, and that's it. No matter what you pay for it, if we get a great deal, pass it on to the customer.' And of course that's what we did."

It was a little frustrating there for a while, being out on our own. In addition to no basic merchandise assortment, we had no real replenishment system. We didn't even have inventory books like we had with the Ben Franklin stores, where if necessary you could simply look over what you needed and order it from Butler Brothers, then price it accordingly. We had no established distributors. No credit. Salesmen would just show up at our door, and we would try to get the best deals we could. Sometimes it was difficult getting the bigger companies—the Procter & Gambles, Eastman Kodaks, whoever—to call on us at all, and when they did they would dictate to us how much they would sell us and at what price. P&G gave a 2 percent discount if you paid within ten days, and if you didn't, man, they took that discount right off. I don't mind saying that we were the victims of a good bit of arrogance from a lot of vendors in those days. They didn't need us, and they acted that way. I never could understand it. To me, it always seemed like a customer was a customer, and you ought to try to sell them what you could.

The biggest challenge was buying health and beauty aids at low cost and staying stocked up on them because those items were really at the heart of almost every early discounter's strategy. I figured that out after I went into the first Gibson's store. His whole concept was to buy direct at a lower cost than individual stores could buy, then charge $300 a month to run one of his franchises, and he would act as the store's buying agent. The basic discounter's idea was to attract customers into the store by pricing these items—toothpaste, mouthwash, headache remedies, soap, shampoo—right down at cost. Those were what the early discounters called your "image" items. That's what you pushed in your newspaper advertising—like the twenty-seven-cent Crest at Springdale—and you stacked it high in the stores to call attention to what a great deal it was. Word would get around that you had really low prices. Everything else in the store was priced low too, but it had a 30 percent margin. Health and beauty aids were priced to give away.

As far as building the company up, we simply had no time for it. We were too busy concentrating on day-to-day operations. I had moved my office from the Ben Franklin on the Bentonville square to an old garage nearby, where I worked with three ladies who helped out with the bookkeeping. By the early sixties, we had eighteen variety stores and a handful of Wal-Marts. (For a time in there, we owned a mix of several different types of stores. We had variety stores under both the Ben Franklin and Walton names as well as our Wal-Mart discount stores. For years, while we were building Wal-Marts, we continued to run our various Ben Franklin and Walton variety stores. But we gradually phased them out, usually replacing them with Wal-Marts.) We kept a little pigeonhole on the wall for the cash receipts and paperwork of each store. I had a blue binder ledger book for each store. When we added a store, we added a pigeonhole. I know we did that at least up to twenty stores. Then once a month, Wanda Wiseman and I would close those books—enter the merchandise, enter the sales, enter the cash, balance it, and close them. Nowadays, you hear a lot about fancy accounting methods, like LIFO and FIFO, but back then we were using the ESP method, which really sped things along when it came time to close those books. It's a pretty basic method: if you can't make your books balance, you take however much they're off by and enter it under the heading ESP, which stands for Error Some Place.

Then we would come up with a profit and loss sheet, a p&l for each store, and get it out to that store manager as quickly as we could—something we still do today. If there was a problem, I would get with that manager immediately. But most of them owned a piece of their stores, so they were likely to be as concerned as I was. I had a big ledger sheet pasted together to make room for everything I wanted on it, probably fifteen different columns, for every store. It had columns for sales, expenses, net profit, markdowns—everything—utilities, postage, insurance, taxes. I entered the numbers myself each month with a pen, which helped me remember them better. It became a habit with me, and I carried this ledger sheet in my pocket when I went to the stores so everybody always knew exactly where they stood.

For several years the company was just me and the managers in the stores. Most of them came to us from variety stores, and they turned into the greatest bunch of discount merchants anybody ever saw. We all worked together, but each of them had lots of freedom to try all kinds of crazy things themselves.

The closest thing we had to an operations manager was Don Whitaker, the guy I hired from TG&Y out in Abilene to be our first Wal-Mart manager. After that, he became our first regional manager. Don had barely finished high school, if that, and he had terrible grammar. He threw people off sometimes because he only had one eye, and he looked at you sort of funny. But he was one of the finest people I have ever known in my life. Everybody called him Whitaker, and he was a hard-working, practical, smart fellow. He had a great big heart, but he was gruff and he scared all the young folks to death. There was never any question that he was the boss, and when he wanted something done, believe me it got done. I single him out here because Don Whitaker was very, very important in the early development of the company, establishing the philosophy of Let's be out front. Let's do it right. Let's get it done now and get on with it.

CLAUDE HARRIS, WAL-MART'S FIRST BUYER:
"Sam is very sharp on being able to read people and their personalities, and their integrity, and he didn't make any mistakes back there picking people, if I do say so myself. Really, back early, one bad manager could have pulled us under. When you're only making $8,000 or maybe $12,000 a year net in a store, it would have only taken one or two managers who were dishonest to lose the whole company. Sam would meet them in the stores where they worked, and invite them down to look at his stores. You know, he's a very persuasive man; he could charm a bird out of a tree. And he and Helen would have you out to the house and serve ice cream, and they'd always ask if you and your family went to church. He was so good at evaluating and selecting these fellows. He wasn't just looking for store managers. I think he was selecting people he thought he could go forward with. He was progressive. He knew that he needed something, and he was looking for it, and he was getting it every step of the way."

We found Claude over in Memphis running a Woolworth store. He was from Muskogee, Oklahoma, and about one-quarter Indian, and he had started with Woolworth out of high school. None of these fellows like Don or Claude had any college, and they didn't want me hiring any college men. They had the idea that college graduates wouldn't get down and scrub floors and wash windows. The classic training in those days was to put a two-wheeler—you know, a cart that you carry merchandise on—

into a guy's hands within the first thirty minutes he came to work and get him pushing freight out of the back room. They all came out of these variety stores with the same background and the same kind of philosophy and education. And we looked for the action-oriented, do-it-now, go type of folks.

Claude had four or five kids and was probably making $12,000 a year, maybe $10,000. I hauled up in front of his soda fountain one day and started talking to him. I found out that he had been able to save on his salary, and I usually felt that if a fellow could manage his own finances, he would be more successful managing one of our stores. We put him into our variety store on the east side of the square in Fayetteville, so he had to compete against our other store on the west side of the square, which was run by Charlie Cate, and supervised by Charlie Baum at the time. That was a real test because nobody was more competitive than Charlie Baum—he would compete with a buzzsaw. But Claude was so skillful and nice that Charlie had to get along with him to some degree.

CLAUDE HARRIS:

"My store wasn't making much money, and we were starting to get competition from Gibson's, which also had a little store on the square down there. It was obvious that their discount-ing thing was working, and they were pulling everybody in with their health and beauty aids—HBA we call it. So I thought, 'Well, why don't I try that in my variety store?' I changed the whole store around and got McKesson-Robbins down in price and put in a bunch of over-the-counter drugs. It was the first discount department in our company, the health and beauty aids department at the east side of the square in Fayetteville. But I liked to have lost my best friend over that one. Charlie Baum liked to have had a heart attack. He thought I was trying to undercut him. You got to under-stand that Charlie is one of the most competitive people who ever lived. He'll fight you tooth and toenail at bridge, or anything. I was just trying to see where it might lead us. Anyway, Sam knew all about it, and he said, 'Go ahead and try it.' He would always try things like that. He was always open to suggestions, and that's one reason he's been such a success. He's still that way."

When I started buying for Wal-Mart, I would often take Claude along with me. Pretty soon, we made him Wal-Mart's general merchandise manager. He didn't have any more experience at being a general merchandise manager than the guy off the street. He was a store manager, but we didn't have anybody else so he became general merchandise manager. I don't even know when we finally brought our first professional buyer, or even someone who had ever had any buying experience, into the company, but it was years later.

I guess the thing those early managers and I all had the most in common was that we all loved merchandising. Don't get me wrong. Our early stores weren't all that well merchandised. By that, I mean we didn't necessarily have the best assortment of merchandise available, all displayed seductively. Because remember, we didn't have any real distribution system, and we had to buy where we could. But we all loved to find unusual items and the store managers had a lot of freedom to try different things.

CHARLIE CATE:

"Sam had us send our sales report in every week, and along with it we had to send in a Best Selling Item. I mean we *had to*. What he was doing was teaching us to look for what's selling all the time. You had to look because you had to send in this report every week, and if you reported that nothing was selling well, Mr. Walton would not be happy. He would think you weren't studying your merchandise, and in that case he'd come study it for you. He's been that way ever since I first met him in 1954."

It's almost embarrassing to admit this, but it's true: there hasn't been a day in my adult life when I haven't spent some time thinking about merchandising. I suspect I have emphasized item merchandising and the importance of promoting items to a greater degree than most any other retail management person in this country. It has been an absolute passion of mine. It is what I enjoy doing as much as anything in the business. I really love to pick an item—maybe the most basic merchandise—and then call attention to it. We used to say you could sell anything if you hung it from the ceiling. So we would buy huge quantities of something and dramatize it. We would blow it out of there when everybody knew we would have only sold a few had we just left it in the normal store position. It is one of the things that has set our company apart from the very beginning and really made us difficult to compete with. And, man, in the early days of Wal-Mart it really got crazy sometimes.

PHIL GREEN, EARLY WAL-MART MANAGER:

"Me and Sam used to have a big time picking items. We'd go buy a Dallas newspaper and a Little Rock newspaper and a Fort Smith newspaper, and he'd say, 'Well now, Phil, let's make us up some kind of an ad for this weekend.' So we'd look around the store and find a big display of socks or a big display of panties, or a wastebasket, or a broom, or a big old stack of motor oil. We'd pick out, say, twenty items, and then we'd sit down on the floor with a pair of scissors and go through those newspapers until we found some store that had run oil, and we'd just cut out the oil can and paste it on there and write 'Pennzoil 30W' and stick our price on it. And we'd do the same thing for the socks and the panties and the wastebasket—just make up our own ad out of everybody else's ads in those newspapers. But it worked! Because we made real hot prices. He'd say there was no use running an ad everybody else was running for the same price, or why would they come in? Sam was a dime store man so at first he wanted to make a certain percentage of profit on everything. But he came around to the idea that a real hot item would really bring them in the store so we finally started running things like toothpaste for sixteen cents a tube. Then we'd have to worry about getting enough of it in stock."

A little later on, Phil ran what became one of the most famous item promotions in our history. We sent him down to open store number 52 in Hot Springs, Arkansas—the first store we ever opened in a town that already had a Kmart. Phil got there and decided Kmart had been getting away with some pretty high prices in the absence of any discounting competition. So he worked up a detergent promotion that turned into the world's largest display ever of Tide, or maybe Cheer—some detergent. He worked out a deal to get about $1.00 off a case if he would buy some absolutely ridiculous amount of detergent, something like 3,500 cases of the giant-sized box. Then he ran it as an ad promotion for, say, $1.99 a box, off from the usual $3.97. Well, when all of us in the Bentonville office saw how much he'd bought, we really thought old Phil had completely gone over the dam. This was an unbelievable amount of soap. It made up a pyramid of detergent boxes that ran twelve to eighteen cases high —all the way to the ceiling, and it was 75 or 100 feet long, which took up the whole aisle across the back of the store, and then it was about 12 feet wide so you could hardly get past it. I think a lot of companies would have fired Phil for that one, but we always felt we had to try some of this crazy stuff.

PHIL GREEN:

"Mr. Sam usually let me do whatever I wanted on these pro-motions because he figured I wasn't going to screw it up, but on this one he came down and said, 'Why did you buy so much? You can't sell all of this!' But the thing was so big it made the news, and everybody came to look at it, and it was all gone in a week. I had another one that scared them up in Bentonville too. This guy from Murray of Ohio called one day and said he had 200 Murray 8 horsepower riding mowers available at the end of the season, and he could let us have them for $175. Did we want any? And I said, 'Yeah, I'll take 200.' And he said, 'Two hundred!' We'd been selling them for $447, I think. So when they came in we unpacked every one of them and lined them all up out in front of the store, twenty-five in a row, eight rows deep. Ran a chain through them and put a big sign up that said: '8 h.p. Murray Tractors, $199.' Sold every one of them. I guess I was just always a promoter, and being an early Wal-Mart manager was as good a place to promote as there ever was."

I'll tell you, Phil not only liked to swim upstream, he liked to do it with weights strapped on just to show he could do it. Things may not be quite as wild today as they once were, but being a Wal-Mart manager is *still* a great place to promote items because it is such a part of our heritage, and it is a part we had better always hold on to. Over the years, I've had so much fun with this, and it really is amazing how much merchandise you can move with just a little promotion. Folks always ask me what are some of the big moments I remember in the history of Wal-Mart, and I usually say, oh, when we passed a billion dollars in sales, or 10 billion, or whatever. But the truth is, some of my fondest memories are of plain old everyday items that we sold a ton of by presenting nicely on endcaps (displays at the end of aisles)—or on tables out in action alley (the big horizontal aisle running across a store just behind the checkout counters). I guess real merchants are like real fishermen: we have a special place in our memories for a few of the big ones.

I realize this may sound boring to most of you, but one of my best items ever was a mattress pad called a Bedmate. I think I picked this one up one day by going out and talking to one of those salesmen waiting in the lobby—which is something I like to do from time to time just to keep in touch. At the time I don't think we even carried mattress pads, but somehow or another I felt it was an unexplored item or an item we should have. So we bought a bunch of the pads, lowered the price and the margin a little bit, displayed them prominently, and it has become one of the most fantastic items we have ever had in our stores. I had somebody check for me the other day, and since we introduced the Bedmate in 1980, we've sold over five and a half million of those doggoned things.

Another day I walked out into the lobby and began talking with this salesman from the Aladdin Company, the folks who make Thermos bottles. He had his samples with him, and I asked him the usual question, what do you have that is real hot that we could promote successfully? And he had a half-gallon red and blue Thermos bottle that looked real handsome and he said, "This will make a great special. We'll give you this kind of price and you can sell it for such-and-such." I said, "Let's talk about it." So I got him down a little more, ran it at an even lower price, and we went crazy with that thing. We sold carloads of that Thermos by shooting it into the stores.

For a while there I got to thinking that maybe I was just a genius at picking these items, they all did so well. But I finally realized that because I was the chairman, and because they knew I'd be coming into their stores sooner or later, our associates would get at it on those items I chose and move those things right on out. I learned I had to be careful the time we promoted the Moon Pies. These gooey marshmallow snacks, which are real popular in the South, were another one of my great items. I got on to them in Tennessee, where I ran into a department head, a woman who had been selling Moon Pies in an unbelievable way just by putting them out where folks would notice them. Well, I knew they weren't being pushed across Wal-Mart because I hardly ever saw them around in the stores. So I took her idea, came back, got with the buyer, called the company, and said, "Hey, what if I make the Moon Pie my item, ship it to all our stores, and sell it five for $1.00 instead of 23 cents apiece?" They went for it and came down in their price to 12½ cents apiece. We charged 20 cents and sold 500,000 Moon Pies, or $100,000 worth, in one week. Company-wide, it was a real winner. The problem was everybody got carried away with my item and we shipped them to Wisconsin. Those people up there never heard of Moon Pies before, and they weren't too interested in learning about them. It was the kind of mistake we had to watch out for once we got so big.

DAVID GLASS:

"We have this executive VPI (Volume Producing Item) contest, you know, but it's really hard to compete with Sam on it because it is just unbelievable the compliance he gets. I think the Chattanooga Bakery, which makes Moon Pies, made him their man of the year. If they didn't, they should have. No one in history has ever even dreamed you could sell Moon Pies like that. But see, if he picks an item, he'll say he wants a table in front of the check stands, and he wants fifteen cases of Moon Pies there broken down into vanilla, chocolate, and caramel, in whatever ratios he decides they're going to sell. That Bedmate thing was ordinarily a side-counter item—maybe you stock four on a side counter and they sell a few a month. Well, Sam takes a table in action alley, designs the sign himself, and makes a rule that you have to keep the thing full of Bedmates. Of course, it just exploded. Ask him about his minnow bucket, though. That was his worst item ever. That was the same year I won the contest with Seneca Apple Juice. It was just sensational. It sold tons. So I would go to the stores, and get them to take that minnow bucket up front to the people greeter at the door, put ice in it, ice down the apple juice, and give away samples out of his minnow bucket. I particularly did it in stores I knew he was going to visit. It drove him crazy, and he got off that minnow bucket pretty quick.

"We have a lot of fun with all this item promotion, but here's what it's really all about. The philosophy it teaches, which rubs off on all the associates and the store managers and the department heads, is that your stores are full of items that can explode into big volume and big profits if you are just smart enough to identify them and take the trouble to promote them. It has been a real key to helping this company dramatically increase its sales per square foot. If you are going to show the kind of double-digit comparable store sales increases that we show every year, and grow a company the way we've grown ours, you have to be merchandise driven. Otherwise, you become like everybody else. I can name you a lot of retailers who were originally merchandise driven, but somehow lost it over the years. In retail, you are either operations driven—where your main thrust is toward reducing expenses and improving efficiency—or you are merchandise driven. The ones that are truly merchandise driven can always work on improving operations. But the ones that are operations driven tend to level off and begin to deteriorate. So Sam's item promotion mania is a great game and we all have a lot of fun with it, but it is also at the heart of what creates our extraordinary high sales per square foot, which enable us to dominate our competition."

By the way, I'm promoting an item in the stores this year that I think is a real winner: a halogen car headlight for only $10.94. I teamed up on it with Jack Welch, the CEO of General Electric. It's a good example of how we're cooperating with our big vendors these days at the highest levels.

In the early days of Wal-Mart, this period we've been talking about, I really believe our emphasis on item promotion helped us to make up for a lot of shortcomings we had—an unsophisticated buying program, a less than ideal merchandise assortment, and practically no back-office support. It was another way of swimming upstream. We made up for what we didn't have by being merchants.

The only other reason the thing held together back then is that from the very start we would get all our managers together once a week and critique ourselves—that was really our buying organization, a bunch of store managers getting together early Saturday morning, maybe in Bentonville, or maybe in some motel room somewhere. We would review what we had bought and see how many dollars we had committed to it. We would plan promotions and plan the items we intended to buy. Really, we were planning our merchandising programs. And it worked so well that over the years, as we grew and built the company, it just became part of our culture. I guess that was the forerunner of our Saturday morning meetings. We wanted everybody to know what was going on and everybody to be aware of the mistakes we made. When somebody made a bad mistake—whether it was myself or anybody else—we talked about it, admitted it, tried to figure out how to correct it, and then moved on to the next day's work.

Another way we tried hard to make up for our lack of experience and sophistication was to spend as much time as we could checking out the competition. It's something I did from the beginning, and it's something I insisted all our managers do.

CHARLIE CATE:

"I remember him saying over and over again: go in and check our competition. Check *everyone* who is our competition. And don't look for the bad. Look for the good. If you get one good idea, that's one more than you went into the store with, and we must try to incorporate it into our company. We're really not concerned with what they're doing wrong, we're concerned with what they're doing right, and everyone is doing something right."

CLARENCE LEIS:

"When Gibson's first came into Rogers, we practically lived between the two stores. My assistants, John Jacobs and Larry English, would go over there and walk through their store trying to memorize prices. Then they would come out and write them all down. But there was a great big open trash bin out behind that store, and at night, after both stores were closed, John and Larry would go over to Gibson's and get down in their trash and check as many prices as they could find."

I guess we had very little capacity for embarrassment back in those days. We paid absolutely no attention whatsoever to the way things were supposed to be done, you know, the way the rules of retail said it had to be done. You should have seen us on some of those early buying trips to New York. We had hired this wholesaler from Springfield, Missouri, a guy named Jim Haik, to work with us as sort of an agent. We had bought goods from him, so we said we needed someone to hold our hand and take us around New York to get some merchandise. Jim was a good guy, a straight guy. He took Don Whitaker and me around and introduced us to his sources. He would say, 'These are guys from a little chain down in Arkansas, and they are good people.' We bought dresses and blouses and girls' and infants' and, again, we were mostly item buyers. We didn't buy like other chains, where a buyer specializes in one line of merchandise and just buys that one line. I don't think any of those guys in New York really understood our thinking, but we were a store whose profit and volume had to be driven by finding real bargains on things we could promote out in the sticks. And we did. I usually found my best buys in men's shirts from a guy named Harry Criss at Colonial Manufacturing. He would give us special treatment, meeting us at his showrooms by seven in the morning so we would have extra time to work the street. I always appreciated that, and I bought a lot of shirts from Harry Criss over the years.

BUD WALTON:

"I'll never forget those buying trips. Four, five, six of us might go at a time: Sam, me, Don Whitaker, Phil Green, Claude Harris, Gary Reinboth. We had this budget, and we knew we could spend X amount of dollars, whatever it was. We would have $10,000 for this department, or $20,000 for that one, right on down the line. So here we were, a bunch of guys from Arkansas wandering around New York City. It was all new to me. I had never been to New York City. Sam would split us up into pairs—some would buy domestics, others ladies' tops and bottoms, whatever.

"So one day he says, 'Bud, you and Don Whitaker go buy men's department.' Well, neither one of us had ever bought men's before. We were mostly hardlines merchants, who didn't know much about clothes. We went down to the Empire State Building where all the men's clothes manufacturers were, and I will never forget that day as long as I live. I had never seen anything like it. We got real carried away and just bought sweaters, pants, all kinds of stuff. Then at night we would get together back at our hotel room and see what we'd spent. Most of the time we would have overbought and somebody would have to go back the next day and cancel a few orders."

GARY REINBOTH:

"From the very beginning, Sam was always trying to instill in us that you just didn't go to New York and roll with the flow. We always walked everywhere. We never took cabs. And Sam had an equation for the trips: our expenses should never exceed 1 percent of our purchases, so we would all crowd in these little hotel rooms somewhere down around Madison Square Garden.

"He was always trying to get somebody to work with us early in the morning or late at night. To get New Yorkers to do that is something really difficult, you know, because they all catch the train and they've got their rules about everything. But Sam would always find somebody to visit with us at night. For one thing, he wanted the trips to be as short as possible. For another, he wanted to make sure we were working all the time.

"Anyway, we would split up and go to all these different showrooms. We'd walk in, and they'd say, 'Who are you with?'

"And we'd say, 'We're with Walton's.'

" 'Oh yeah, where are you located?'

" 'Arkansas.'

" 'What town?'

" 'Bentonville, Arkansas.'

"Then they'd always say, 'Where in the world is Bentonville, Arkansas?'

"And Don Whitaker, with a straight face, would always say, 'Next to Rogers.'

"Then, the guy would say, 'Excuse me, I need to get something out of the back room.'

"And old Whitaker would say, 'You don't need to check us out with Dun and Bradstreet. We're the same as General Motors.'

"Then the guy would come back and say, 'Well, I found you in there, and you do have good credit. So what can I show you?'

"We never finished up until about twelve-thirty at night,

and we'd all go out for a beer except Mr. Walton. He'd say, 'I'll meet you for breakfast at six o'clock.' And we'd say, 'Mr. Walton, there's no reason to meet that early. We can't even get into the buildings that early.' And he'd just say, 'We'll find something to do.'

"The next morning he would talk some janitor or somebody into letting us in the building, and we'd be sitting there outside the showroom when those folks started coming in to work. Like I said, I think he was trying to make a point: just because we're in New York doesn't mean we have to start doing things their way."

I expect Gary's right about my trying to make a point. Because wherever we've been, we've always tried to instill in our folks the idea that we at Wal-Mart have our own way of doing things. It may be different, and it may take some folks a while to adjust to it at first. But it's straight and honest and basically pretty simple to figure out if you want to. And whether or not other folks want to accommodate us, we pretty much stick to what we believe in because it's proven to be very, very successful.

We started out swimming upstream, and it's made us strong and lean and alert, and we've enjoyed the trip. We sure don't see any reason now to turn around and join the rest of the pack headed downcurrent.

CHAPTER 5

RAISING A FAMILY

"As kids, we all worked for the company in one way or another. I got to work behind the candy counter or run the popcorn stand when I was five years old. The business was part of life, and it was always included in the dinner conversation. We heard a lot about the debt it took to open new stores, and I worried about it. I remember confiding to my girlfriend one time—crying—and saying, 'I don't know what we're going to do. My daddy owes so much money, and he won't quit opening stores.'"

—ALICE WALTON

In the early years, before Wal-Mart, I don't think our family was much different from most other families of that era. Helen and I had made pretty deliberate plans; we wanted four kids, and Helen said she'd like to have them all by the time she was thirty so she could enjoy her grown children and her grandkids. Sure enough, by the time we left Newport, we had four kids: three boys—Rob, John, and Jim—and a baby girl, Alice.

One of the reasons Helen insisted all along on our living in a small town, I'm sure, is so we could raise the kids with the same values she and I had been exposed to in our youth. And we did, except it wasn't the Depression, and we never had to worry about having enough to go around at the dinner table. Another goal of ours was to create the kind of family togetherness Helen had grown up with. I've already told you how much the Robsons influenced Helen and me in the organization of our finances, but really I think their successful, happy, prosperous family was just an all-round inspiration for the kind of family I wanted as a young man, and, of course, it was the only kind of family Helen ever considered.

I have fond memories of my own boyhood, yet it pains me to talk about one part of it. But because Helen thinks it had an important influence on me, I'll mention it briefly. The simple truth is that Mother and Dad were two of the most quarrelsome people who ever lived together. I loved them both dearly, and they were two wonderful individuals, but they were always at odds, and they really only stayed together because of Bud and me. After we were grown, they even split up and went their separate ways for a while. During the war, for example, Mother moved to California to work in the defense plants. But growing up as the oldest child, I felt like I took a lot of the brunt of this domestic discord. I'm not exactly sure how this situation affected my personality—unless it was partly a motivation to stay so busy all the time—but I swore early on that if I ever had a family, I would never expose it to that kind of squabbling.

So Helen and I did the best we could to promote a sense of togetherness in the family, and we made sure our children had a chance to participate in the same sorts of things we did as kids. They were in Scouts, and for a time I was a scoutmaster. All the boys played football and did well. In fact, they each made the all-state team, and when Jim was about to graduate I remember the coach being quoted around town to the effect that he couldn't face the prospect of a team without a Walton, so he was trying to talk Alice into going out for football. She probably wouldn't have been half bad either. I always tried to be home on Friday nights so I would miss very few of their games. They threw paper routes; you know how strongly I felt about that experience as training. Alice was involved with horse shows at a very early age. And, of course, we all went to church and Sunday school. I was a Sunday school teacher there for a while too.

HELEN WALTON:

"Sam did teach Sunday school for a while, but even then he had unusual work habits. During one period in Newport, he would work until ten on Saturday night, and then he'd get up and go right back in Sunday morning. We were supposed to be taking turns about getting the kids to Sunday school, and to get four little kids dressed for church with nobody to help me was a little unreal. It's true that we had less time with Sam after Wal-Mart, but don't get the idea that he wasn't working most of the time before that."

Through our combined efforts the kids received your everyday heartland upbringing, based on the same old bedrock values: a belief in the importance of hard work, honesty, neighborliness, and thrift. Helen bore more than her share of raising the kids, and I worked long hours, at least six days a week. Saturday was our big store day, and I worked all day Saturday and Saturday night too. As far as I'm concerned, our values really took. The only thing that might have made our family different was that, as Alice said, everybody was involved in working around the stores.

ROB WALTON:

"We always worked in the stores. I would sweep the floors and carry boxes after school, and even more in the summer. I remember just barely having a driver's license and driving a truckload of merchandise one night up to that Ben Franklin in Saint Robert, which we all knew to be the best Ben Franklin in the world. In those days, we all got an allowance too, and it was less than some of our friends. I don't know that we particularly felt deprived, but we didn't have a lot of money. Dad was always—frugal is probably a good word for it. But he always let us invest in those stores, and I had an investment in that Saint Robert store so I came out real well on that. It paid for my house and various other—Dad would call them—extravagances."

I guess the kids thought of themselves as slave labor back then, but we didn't work them that hard. We just taught them the value of work. And besides, I needed the help—at the store and at home. I didn't have time to mow the lawn, and why should I anyway, with three strapping boys and a healthy girl available for chores. And it wasn't all work. Helen and I made it a point to take the whole family out and spend time traveling or camping together. Sometimes the kids thought of these trips as forced marches, but I think that time we spent together has had a lot to do with our close relationship as a family today. We have a lot of good memories of traveling all over the country, especially in this one fine old DeSoto station wagon.

JIM WALTON:

"Dad always said you've got to stay flexible. We never went on a family trip nor have we ever heard of a business trip in which the schedule wasn't changed at least once after the trip was underway. Later, we all snickered at some writers who viewed Dad as a grand strategist who intuitively developed complex plans and implemented them with precision. Dad thrived on change, and no decision was ever sacred."

HELEN WALTON:

"Sam wasn't so tied up year-round until Wal-Mart started. During the Ben Franklin days, we took a month off every year. In fifty-six, I remember we did the whole state of Arkansas. We went to the parks, camped out, and we all fell in love with this state because we really got to know it. That was a marvelous, wonderful time. Then one year we took a long trip to Yellowstone, another year we went to Mesa Verde and the Grand Canyon, and another time we took a long journey up the East Coast. We took a car full of kids and all our camping equipment strapped on everywhere, and I loved it. Camping was really important in our lives. Of course, we always had to stop and look at stores—any kind of stores—on the way to wherever we were headed. You know, we would go through a good town, and he knew about some store there. I would sit in the car with the kids, who, of course, would say, 'Oh no, Daddy, not another store . . .' We just got used to it. Later on, Sam never went by a Kmart that he didn't stop and look at it."

ALICE WALTON:

"It was great. We would get in the station wagon—four brats and the dog—strap the canoe on top and hitch up a home-made trailer behind, and take off for a different part of the country every summer. We would always do it as long as Dad could stop and see his stores along the way. He would usually get us situated, set up camp, and then Mother would stay at camp with us while he took off to look at stores. We learned to work together, and everybody had their chores, and at night we prayed together.

"You know, it's interesting. I know Dad worked incredible hours, and I know he traveled a lot, but I never really felt like he was gone much. He went out of his way to spend time with us, and he was fun to be with. He loved to play baseball with us. I tagged along with him on his trips a good bit, and I still visit stores because of it. When I got into junior high and high school, he would take me to my horse shows. Mother thought he was staying and watching, but Dad and I had a pact. He would drop me off, and I would show my horses, while he would go look at stores. The store thing was always a part of it. It wasn't that he wasn't supportive or fair. It was just something he had to do, and we understood it."

ROB WALTON:

"I remember Dad visiting stores, but I don't remember the store visits as imposing or interfering with the trips because mostly I remember the trips as being really good times.

"On the trip to the Grand Tetons, we had an opportunity to take what was a very expensive—for that time—pack trip up into the mountains to a fishing camp and stay there for a few days. But that was going to use up all our money, and we had to take a family vote to decide whether to do that or not. We decided to do it, and it was fun. But after we had spent all our money on the big trip, we made a quick stop in the Black Hills and hiked it on home in a hurry.

"I especially remember the trip East. We went through the Carolinas and headed up the coast. It was Mother and Dad and all four kids and one scroungy dog named Tiny. We rolled into New York City in a station wagon with a canoe on top and a camping trailer on the back—that was the first time any of us kids had ever been there. I have one really special memory of that trip. We went to see *Camelot,* with the original cast—Julie Andrews, Richard Burton, Roddy McDowall, and Robert Goulet—and we were all wearing Bermuda shorts."

Of course, what they say is true. I was visiting stores all the time, and I still do it today. In fact, we've visited them all over the world, and gotten some great ideas that way—as well as a few that didn't work out so well. Like working weekends, it's just something you have to do if you want to be successful in the retail business. I'm glad my kids remember the good times and don't seem to resent me too much for my absences and distractions over the years. I think maybe one reason they don't have too much resentment is that Helen and I always involved them in the business and kept them informed right from the start—I had no idea, incidentally, that Alice was so frightened of debt as a little girl, but there are certainly more irrational things she could have feared. They may not have wanted to go visit all those stores while we were on vacation, but they had some idea why I was doing it. They worked in the stores, invested in the stores, and shopped in the stores.

HELEN WALTON:

"At that first Bentonville store I was part of the shrinkage [unaccounted-for inventory losses usually caused by theft]. If I needed something, I just got it and took it home with me. I didn't even think about paying for it. It wasn't good business at all. I mean, people would see me picking up things and they probably thought, well, I'll pick up some too. I remember it was difficult for me when we went into the Wal-Mart business from the Five and Dime. I had to start paying for things, and it was a real shock.

"Also, at Christmastime, we would get a list from the

welfare office of some children who weren't going to have Santa Claus. We'd get the ages and sizes and that sort of thing. I remember one night we took our children into the store after it was closed and gave them that list and told them to go around and pick out things for them because we wanted them to have some sense of what was going on outside our privileged little family. It was a small town, and we were a real small-town kind of operation."

One thing I never did—which I'm really proud of—was to push any of my kids too hard. I knew I was a fairly overactive fellow, and I didn't expect them to try to be just like me. Also, I let them know they were welcome to come into our business, but that they would have to work as hard as I did—they would have to commit to being merchants. Rob went to law school and became our first company lawyer. He did most of the work to take us public, and has been involved with the senior management of the company ever since—as an officer and board member.

Jim learned a lot about real estate—and the art of negotiation —from his uncle Bud. After Bud sort of stepped back from his involvement with locating and buying store sites, Jim took over. He was really good at it, and they still tell stories about him flying into some small town, unfolding his bicycle, and pedaling around looking for a good site. He never told anybody who he was, and he got some great deals. Now he's running Walton Enterprises, the family partnership, and I think he's almost as tight with a dollar as I am.

Among other things, Walton Enterprises owns banks in several towns around here. Jim and a partner own the local newspaper, the *Daily Record*. The story of buying the *Record* shows just how far we've come from those days when Helen could just sashay through the store and pick up what she wanted—a practice, by the way, that I always frowned on. Back before we went public with Wal-Mart, I bought the newspaper figuring that we would have a cheap place to print our circulars. I think I only paid $65,000 for that old paper. When we went public, though, some New York lawyers came down and told us we had to sell the paper to Wal-Mart because otherwise we would be taking advantage of the public company if we continued to print the circulars. So we sold it to Wal-Mart at cost, about $110,000 by then. Well, years later, Jim decides he wants to buy the paper. So we had an outside consultant come in and tell Wal-Mart what it was worth. Jim and his partner paid $1.1 million for that darned paper. It's been marginally profitable at best, and it quit printing Wal-Mart circulars years ago. The point I'm trying to make is that we as a family have bent over backward not to take advantage of Wal-Mart, not to press our ownership position unfairly, and everybody in the company knows it.

Alice and John worked for a little while at Wal-Mart, but have both branched out into independent businesses of their own. Alice tried her hand as a buyer, but didn't care for it too much, and now she's got her own investment company, The Llama Company, down in Fayetteville. In some ways, I believe she's the most like me—a maverick—but even more volatile than I am. John, who was a Green Beret medic in Vietnam, became our second company pilot—I was the first. He's the most independent of the bunch and the only one who doesn't live here in Arkansas, and he's a tremendous individual. He and his family live out West, where he designs and builds sailboats, and he also runs a large crop-dusting business, which is owned by Walton Enterprises. We're all pilots, so it's real easy for us to get together on a moment's notice.

HELEN WALTON:

"One way in which Sam and my dad were really different. My dad was always talking to me about how I should live, how I should work, and challenging me to do this and that. I don't know that Sam did that very much with our children. I probably did it, and they got enough from me. He probably saw that and kept his mouth shut."

ALICE WALTON:

"When we were growing up, Dad was really very accepting. If you made A's and B's, Mother was the one who would press us with, 'I made all A's, and I know you can do it.' Dad was more, well, 'This is what I made. A's and B's are pretty good.' "

JOHN WALTON:

"I remember asking Dad for permission to climb a bluff overlooking the Buffalo River. He said, 'Do anything you're big enough to do.' What an exhilarating challenge of judgment and confidence booster for a twelve-year-old. Later, when I was a young man trying to find my way in the world, he gave me an open invitation to join the Wal-Mart team, but never a hint of pressure. What a wonderful way to grow up."

Now, as I said, one of the reasons I fell for Helen in the first place was that she was her own woman—and she has not proved a disappointment in that category. For example, one of the things I'm famous for around our company is absolutely insisting that all our executives and managers here in Bentonville attend our Saturday morning meeting. One of the reasons I like it is that if all our folks out there in the stores have to work on Saturday, I think those of us back here in the general office should show up on Saturday too. Plus, as I've said, if you don't want to work weekends, you shouldn't be in retail.

But Helen will tell anybody who asks her what she thinks of the Saturday morning meeting.

HELEN WALTON:

"I think it is a shame that a lot of those fathers and mothers who have children involved in things like athletic programs can't be there to support them because they have to go to the Saturday morning meeting. I don't blame people at all for complaining about them."

As a merchant, I've always tried to stay fairly neutral publicly on controversial political issues, even though I obviously have opinions, but Helen is one who's going to answer bluntly about what she believes in if questioned. Really, she's a bit of a feminist,

I think, not unlike my mother. And I guess we've caught a little heat from time to time. Some of her causes aren't all that popular with some of these fairly extreme groups. But I'll tell you this: she doesn't ask me what she should think, and I'd be the last person on earth to try to tell her. We had one really ugly fight in our marriage—early on—over what kind of car to buy. I was a Chevy man, and she was from a Ford family. Nobody won that one, but we both learned how stubborn we could be, and we haven't gotten into anything like that since. We have been happy together, but we've stayed independent to pursue our own interests as well.

One big strain on the family that I've already talked about was this whole richest man in America business. I don't know if Helen ever really forgave me for putting us in the position to be dragged into that.

HELEN WALTON:

"What I hate is being the object of curiosity. People are so curious about everything, and so we are just public conversation. The whole thing still makes me mad when I think about it. I mean, I hate it."

Helen's right, of course, but I think we've mostly come to terms with all the commotion caused by our unwillingly becoming a semipublic family. And we've enjoyed a few of the things it's enabled us to do. Our kids just shrug it off. I don't think it has affected our kids too much because it all happened gradually to them, and they were raised so basically, with good fundamental values.

I do admit to worrying sometimes about future generations of the Waltons. I know it's unrealistic of me to expect them all to get up and throw paper routes, and I know it's something I can't control. But I'd hate to see any descendants of mine fall into the category of what I'd call "idle rich"—a group I've never had much use for. I really hope that somehow the values both Helen and I, and our kids, have always embraced can be passed on down through the generations. And even if these little future Waltons don't feel the need to work from dawn on into the night to stay ahead of the bill collector, I hope they'll feel compelled to do something productive and useful and challenging with their lives. Maybe it's time for a Walton to start thinking about going into medical research and working on cures for cancer, or figuring out new ways to bring culture and education to the underprivileged, or becoming missionaries for free enterprise in the Third World. Or maybe—and this is strictly my idea—there's another Walton merchant lurking in the wings somewhere down the line.

CHAPTER 6

RECRUITING
THE TEAM

"I kept saying, Sam, we're making a good living. Why go out,
why expand so much more? The stores are getting farther and
farther away. After the seventeenth store, though, I realized
there wasn't going to be any stopping it."

—HELEN WALTON

As much as we must have looked like promoters in the early
going—with our donkey rides and riding mowers out in the
parking lots, and mountains of Tide, or whatever, piled up inside
the stores—what nobody realized, including a few of our own
managers at the time, was that we were really trying from the
beginning to become the very best operators—the most professional managers—that we could. There's no question that I have
the personality of a promoter. That personality, and our somewhat unorthodox style at Wal-Mart, probably confused people at
the outset. In fact, I have occasionally heard myself compared to
P. T. Barnum because of the way I love to get in front of a crowd
and talk something up—an idea, a store, a product, the whole
company—whatever I happen to be focused on right then. But
underneath that personality, I have always had the soul of an
operator, somebody who wants to make things work well, then
better, then the best they possibly can. So I guess when folks saw

me walking around scribbling notes on my coffee-stained yellow legal pad, or hauling boxes of ladies' lingerie into the stores out of my station wagon, maybe they didn't take me that seriously. They assumed we couldn't be in it for the long haul. Some folks no doubt figured we were a little fly-by-night—you know, in the discount business today but out selling cars or swampland tomorrow. I think that misunderstanding worked to our advantage for a long time, and enabled Wal-Mart to fly under everybody's radar until we were too far along to catch.

Truth be told, discounting attracted mostly promoters in the beginning—people who had been in the distribution center business or who were real estate promoters, guys who weren't really even aspiring merchants but who saw a huge opportunity. You didn't have to be a genius to see discounting as a new trend that was going to sweep the country, and all kinds of folks came jumping into it with all four feet—wherever they could arrive first—Cedar Rapids, Iowa, or Springfield, Missouri, it didn't matter. They would take a carbon copy of somebody's store in Connecticut or Boston, hire some buyers and some supervisors who were supposed to know the business, and start opening up stores. From about 1958 until around 1970, it was phenomenally successful.

Anybody who has ever known anything about me knows I was never in anything for the short haul; I always wanted to build as fine a retailing organization as I could. But in those early days —before, and just after, we opened the first Wal-Mart—I got to know a lot of those promoters. As I told you, I ran the country studying the discounting concept, visiting every store and company headquarters I could find. The first ones I saw were the mill stores in the East, where the whole thing started. Ann & Hope was in Providence, Rhode Island, and there were others in Massachusetts and across New England. I went all over up there looking at Giant stores and Mammoth Mart and Arlan's. Another one I learned a lot from was Sol Price, a great operator who had started Fed-Mart out in southern California in 1955. I made friends with Sol's son-in-law, who was running a distribution center in Houston, and talking with him helped me sort out some of my thinking on distribution—which would eventually become another key to Wal-Mart's success. I guess I've stolen—I actually prefer the word "borrowed"—as many ideas from Sol Price as from anybody else in the business. For example, it's true that Bob Bogle came up with the name Wal-Mart in the airplane that day, but the reason I went for it right away wasn't that the sign was cheaper. I really liked Sol's Fed-Mart name so I latched right on to Wal-Mart. I do not believe Kmart existed at that time.

I read in some trade publication not long ago that of the top 100 discounters who were in business in 1976, 76 of them have disappeared. Many of these started with more capital and visibility than we did, in larger cities with much greater opportunities. They were bright stars for a moment, and then they faded. I started thinking about what really brought them down, and why we kept going. It all boils down to not taking care of their customers, not minding their stores, not having folks in their stores with good attitudes, and that was because they never really even tried to take care of their own people. If you want the people in the stores to take care of the customers, you have to make sure you're taking care of the people in the stores. That's the most important single ingredient of Wal-Mart's success.

Most of these early guys were very egotistical people who loved to drive big Cadillacs and fly around in their jets and vacation on their yachts, and some of them lived in houses like I'd never even thought about before. I remember going to dinner at one of their houses, and we got picked up by this limousine that must have had room for fourteen people. Man, they were living high. And they could afford to back then because this discounting thing was working so well. Customers just flocked to their stores, and these fellows were covered up in cash. Most of them could still be around today if they had followed some basic principles about running good stores. There are a lot of ways to build strong companies. They don't have to be done the Wal-Mart way, or my way, or anybody else's way. But you do have to work at it. And somewhere along the line, these folks stopped short of setting the goals and paying the price that needed to be paid. Maybe it wasn't the Cadillacs and the yachts, maybe they just decided it wasn't

My grandfather, Samuel Walton.

My grandmother, Clara Etta
Layton Walton.

My mother, Nannia Lee
Lawrence Walton.

My father, Thomas Gibson Walton.

Me at ten months, 1919.

Main Street in the town of Kingfisher,
Oklahoma, around the time of my birth.

My brother Bud and me atop
my horse Trix, accompanied
by Dad and Mother.

Bud looks on with his usual
patience as I explain something or other to him.

My 1936 graduation photo from Hickman High School in Columbia, Missouri. My classmates voted me Most Versatile Boy.

Feeling real proud of my first *real* car. It was used, of course, but took a nice shine.

That's me behind and to the right of the youngster in the front center. These fellas and myself worked our way through school delivering the *Columbia Missourian* on the University of Missouri campus.

Helen and I on our wedding day—Valentine's Day 1943. The happiness we share together has only deepened over our forty-nine years of marriage.

Mr. and Mrs. Leland Stanford Robson
request the honor of your presence
at the marriage of their daughter
Helen Alice
to
Samuel Moore Walton
Lieutenant United States Army
on Sunday the fourteenth of February
at five o'clock
First Presbyterian Church
Claremore, Oklahoma

Reception
immediately following the ceremony
Hotel Will Rogers

Our wedding invitation.

We are a "family" with Rob's birth in 1944.

Oldest son Rob and his proud dad enjoying some quiet time together.

Always game, Helen invites a crowd of Rob's young friends to celebrate his fourth birthday.

A rare moment of quiet in our busy household as we hold still for this family picture in 1950. (The children are, left to right: Jim, Rob, John, and Alice.)

The first store: a Ben Franklin franchise in Newport, Arkansas, that we took over in 1945 when I was discharged from the Army.

Santa Claus arrives on the square in Bentonville outside our Walton's Five and Dime in 1951.

We could all breathe a bit easier when we saw the crowds line up for the grand opening of the first Wal-Mart in Rogers, Arkansas, on July 2, 1962.

. . . and the customers kept coming. It was particularly satisfying to return to Newport, Arkansas, in 1969 and open Wal-Mart No. 18.

This group of ladies was real influential in getting us set up and started.

worth it. But whatever it was, they just didn't stay close enough to their business, they sort of chose to get over on the other side of the road.

They expanded quickly without building the organizations and the support—such as distribution centers—needed to expand those companies. They didn't get out into their stores to see what was going on. Then Kmart got their machine in gear and began to do it better and better. I remember going in their stores—I'll bet I've been in more Kmarts than anybody—and I would really envy their merchandise mix and the way they presented it. So much about their stores was superior to ours back then that sometimes I felt like we couldn't compete. Of course that didn't stop us from trying. And Target came along and did a fine job, taking the whole idea a little more upscale. As these big operators became more organized, the competition grew a lot more difficult. That's when all those guys who were failing to meet their customers' needs and who didn't build strong organizations—all those promoters—started to fall apart and, eventually, fall out.

Actually, during this whole early period, Wal-Mart was too small and insignificant for any of the big boys to notice, and most of the promoters weren't out in our area so we weren't competitive. That helped me get access to a lot of information about how they were doing things. I probably visited more headquarters offices of more discounters than anybody else—ever. I would just show up and say, "Hi, I'm Sam Walton from Bentonville, Arkansas. We've got a few stores out there, and I'd like to visit with Mr. So-and-So"—whoever the head of the company was—"about his business." And as often as not, they'd let me in, maybe out of curiosity, and I'd ask lots of questions about pricing and distribution, whatever. I learned a lot that way.

KURT BARNARD, RETAILING CONSULTANT:
"I was executive vice president of the discounters' trade association, working in my New York office one day in 1967. My secretary said there was a man out front who wanted to join our group. I said I would give him ten minutes. So in comes

this short, wiry man with a deep tan and a tennis racket under his arm. He introduced himself as Sam Walton from Arkansas. I didn't know what to think. When he meets you, he looks at you—head cocked to one side, forehead slightly creased—and he proceeds to extract every piece of information in your possession. He always makes little notes. And he pushes on and on. After two and a half hours, he left, and I was totally drained. I wasn't sure what I had just met, but I was sure we would hear more from him."

Looking at everybody else's companies made me feel we were definitely headed in the right direction. But as we developed, we began to feel a little out of control. In the late sixties, we had more than a dozen Wal-Marts and fourteen or fifteen variety stores, which is a pretty good-sized company to be running with three ladies, myself, and Don Whitaker in the office, and a manager in each store. I already told you what scrubby buyers we were. We had a lot of people with little or no experience, or not enough knowledge of how bigger operations actually worked. I made up my mind that we had to get somebody with management under his belt. I had hired Gary Reinboth from J. J. Newberry, a big variety chain that was having some problems at the time, so I asked him if he knew anybody, and he told me about this guy up in Omaha named Ferold Arend. He was Newberry's district manager and head of merchandise for the whole Midwest, so Bud and I flew out to see him. We talked him and his wife into coming down and looking at our operation.

FEROLD AREND,
WAL-MART'S FIRST VICE PRESIDENT
OF OPERATIONS, AND LATER ITS PRESIDENT:
"In the middle of 1966, Wal-Mart No. 5 was under construction in Conway, Arkansas, and Sam was all excited and said, 'I've got to show you these plans.' So he loaded my wife and me in his plane and we flew down there. The store had a cotton mill on one side and a stockyard on the other, and it

was in a terrible neighborhood. My first thought was: 'This is not a very good place for a store.' I also thought the Bentonville store didn't seem to have any organization to the way it was run. Let's just say I wasn't very impressed with the whole Sam Walton operation at that time. I told him I wasn't interested.

"Later on, after that Conway Wal-Mart opened up, Sam called me and told me what the sales were. I thought, 'My gosh, that store did as much in one day as some of our bigger stores do in a month.' And then he told me he was only paying ninety cents a square foot. And I thought, 'He must have something there.' About that time, Newberry's decided to reorganize and I was going to have to move to a new division. So I thought, 'Well, if I'm going to have to start over in a company where I've worked for twenty-one years, why not look at something I'm really interested in'—and that was discounting and Sam Walton.

"Here I was coming in as vice president, and it took some getting used to. The offices were still up on the square in Bentonville, and Sam had just got through remodeling them —which I'm sure was a great improvement—but in my opinion they weren't much. The offices were in an old narrow hallway upstairs—some were over the barbershop and others were over an attorney's office. The floor sagged up there, about four inches from the wall to the center. And they had some partitions and some wood paneling, and they were real little offices. It was very close-knit up there."

Even if he couldn't tell it by the office we gave him, bringing Ferold in was an important step for our company. I knew we had to get better organized than we were. We still had to build a basic merchandise assortment, and a real replenishment system. We had lists of items we were supposed to carry, and we were dependent on the people in the stores to keep good records of everything manually—this was at a time when quite a few people were beginning to go into computerization. I had read a lot about that, and I was curious. I made up my mind I was going to learn something about IBM computers. So I enrolled in an IBM school for retailers in Poughkeepsie, New York. One of the speakers was a guy from the National Mass Retailers' Institute (NMRI), the discounters' trade association, a guy named Abe Marks.

ABE MARKS, HEAD OF HARTFIELD ZODY'S, AND
FIRST PRESIDENT, NMRI:

"I was sitting there at the conference reading the paper, and I had a feeling somebody was standing over me, so I look up and there's this grayish gentleman standing there in a black suit carrying an attaché case. And I said to myself, 'Who is this guy? He looks like an undertaker.'

"He asks me if I'm Abe Marks and I say, 'Yes, I am.'

" 'Let me introduce myself, my name is Sam Walton,' he says. 'I'm only a little fellow from Bentonville, Arkansas, and I'm in the retail business.'

"I say, 'You'll have to pardon me, Sam, I thought I knew everybody and every company in the retail business, but I never heard of Sam Walton. What did you say the name of your company is again?'

" 'Wal-Mart Stores,' he says.

"So I say, 'Well, welcome to the fraternity of discount merchants. I'm sure you'll enjoy the conference and getting acquainted socially with everyone.'

" 'Well, to be perfectly honest with you, Mr. Marks, I didn't come here to socialize, I came here to meet you. I know you're a CPA and you're able to keep confidences, and I really wanted your opinion on what I am doing now.' So he opens up this attaché case, and, I swear, he had every article I had ever written and every speech I had ever given in there. I'm thinking, 'This is a very thorough man.' Then he hands me an accountant's working column sheet, showing all his operating categories all written out by hand.

"Then he says: 'Tell me what's wrong. What am I doing wrong?'

"I look at these numbers—this was in 1966—and I don't believe what I'm seeing. He's got a handful of stores and he's doing about $10 million a year with some incredible margin. An unbelievable performance!

"So I look at it, and I say, 'What are you doing wrong? Sam—if I may call you Sam—I'll tell you what you are doing wrong.' I handed back his papers and I closed his attaché case, and I said to him, 'Being here is wrong, Sam. Don't unpack your bags. Go down, catch a cab, go back to the airport and go back to where you came from and keep doing exactly what you are doing. There is nothing that can possibly improve what you are doing. You are a genius.' That's how I met Sam Walton."

Abe invited me to join the NMRI and it turned out to be quite a valuable association for me. I was on the board for about fifteen years, and made some terrific contacts and generous friends. I visited with Abe a number of times at his New York offices, and he was a very open guy. He shared with me how he used computers to control his merchandise.

ABE MARKS:

"Our system was rudimentary by today's standards, but it was very advanced for the 1960s. Very few companies controlled their merchandise the way we did. Sam spent a lot of time reviewing these operations and he brought some of his people up to review them. He has just been a master of taking the best out of everything and adapting it to his own needs.

"What we helped him with in the early days was really logistics. It's like in the Army. You can move troops all over the world, but unless you have the capacity to supply them with ammunition and food, there's no sense putting them out there. Sam understood that. He knew that he was already in what the trade calls an 'absentee ownership' situation. That just means you're putting your stores out where you, as management, aren't. If he wanted to grow he had to learn to control it. So to service these stores you've got to have timely information: How much merchandise is in the store? What is it? What's selling and what's not? What is to be ordered, marked down, replaced? To get more technical, that helps you control what we call turn, or inventory turnover—the ratio of sales to inventory. That's a key. The more you turn your inventory, the less capital is required. And all this involves getting the merchandise to the store at the right time, communicating how it's being priced and how it's being marked down, whatever. Logistics.

"Anyway, the man's a genius. He realized—even at the rudimentary level he was on in 1966, operating those few stores that he had—that he couldn't expand beyond that horizon unless he had the ability to capture this information on paper so that he could control his operations, no matter where they might be. He became, really, the best utilizer of information to control absentee ownerships that there's ever been. Which gave him the ability to open as many stores as he opens, and run them as well as he runs them, and to be as profitable as he makes them.

"You've got to realize this too. By being at that conference, he was absolutely in the right place at the right time. There were no such things in those days as minicomputers and microcomputers. He was really ten years away from the computer world coming. But he was preparing himself. And this is a very important point: without the computer, Sam Walton could not have done what he's done. He could not have built a retailing empire the size of what he's built, the way he built it. He's done a lot of other things right, too, but he could not have done it without the computer. It would have been impossible."

Much as I hate to admit to something like that, I expect Abe is probably right. His memory's pretty good about why I was at that conference, too. I wanted to show him my books, and I wanted to ask him about merchandise control. But I knew I'd never be any whizbang computer guy myself, so I had another reason for going to that school: I was looking to hire a good, bright systems person, and I figured I might find one there. As it happened, there were all sorts of bright people in that school.

Dale Worman—a very astute retailer from the Fred Meyer company out in Portland and now a good friend—was there, as was Arlie Lazarus, who became president of Herb Fisher's Jamesway Corp. And, of course, that's where I first met Ron Mayer, then the smart young chief financial officer at Duckwall Stores in Abilene, Kansas. I targeted him as the guy we needed at Wal-Mart, and started wooing him right there. Like so many of them, he wasn't interested just then in moving to Bentonville, Arkansas, to work for somebody he knew next to nothing about. Later on, we changed his mind.

But I had another problem on my mind when I went up there: distribution. All these other guys, like Abe Marks, were in large urban markets, and their stores were being supplied by big distributors. Kmart and Woolco were using the same distribution system that was supplying their thousands of variety stores. So here we were out in the sticks with nobody to distribute to our stores, which meant basically that our managers would order from salesmen and then some day or other a truck from somewhere would come along and drop off the merchandise. Even at the stage we were in, this was totally unworkable. A lot of our stores weren't big enough to order whole pallets of merchandise, so we had rented that old garage in downtown Bentonville as our warehouse. We would have big shipments delivered there, then unpack them and repack them into smaller quantities. Then we'd call the trucklines to come get them and take them to the stores. It was expensive and inefficient. Somewhere in that period, Ferold and I had hired another fellow from Newberry's, Bob Thornton, who had been running a distribution center for them in Omaha, with the promise that we were going to build a distribution center for him to run.

BOB THORNTON:

"He hired me with the full understanding that I was going to put together a warehouse and distribution system. I accepted the job, moved down here, and started drawing some plans. Then one day he proceeds to tell me he doesn't know for sure whether we really need a warehouse yet or not. It upset me to no end because that was really the only field I wanted to be into. I said, 'Gee, Sam, I want to run a warehouse.' For about six months to a year there, I just worked doing various things around the company, and in my spare time I drew up plans for a distribution center. There wasn't room for me in the office so they knocked a hole through the wall and went into the upstairs of the shoe store next door. It was kind of like an attic, my office, with no heat or air conditioning in it. We had one old toilet for a rest room, with a screen-door hook on the door. And there were about twenty-five people working there by now. Sam would come by every so often and tell me to keep working on drawing those warehouse plans, but I could see he wasn't sure about it at all."

I knew we needed a warehouse. I just wanted to make sure we got the kind we needed, and at this time too, remember, we were financing everything ourselves. We were borrowing heavily to open new stores. But anyway, there was one guy at that same IBM school—a fellow up in Green Bay, Wisconsin—who was the only one who had a warehouse, a distribution center. He invited me to go look at it. So when I got home from the school, I threw Don Whitaker and Ferold and Bob Thornton and some other folks—there were six of us, I remember—into a Beechcraft Baron I was flying in those days, and hauled us up to Green Bay, Wisconsin. We went through this warehouse, saw how they did it, took a lot of notes on everything. It was computerized, one of the first computerized warehouses I know anything about.

After that trip, I knew we had to build one, and everybody was pressuring me for a new general office, so we bought fifteen acres on a farm right outside Bentonville, where we still are today, for about $25,000. Bob was in charge of building us a new 15,000-foot general office, which I thought would last us forever, and a 60,000-foot warehouse, which I thought was too big, but Ferold convinced me we needed it.

BOB THORNTON:

"As I recall, my blueprint for the warehouse called for 100,000 square feet, which to me was very minimal. Then Sam decided to get an architect involved. When I got to look at the drawing, I thought, 'Well, this can't be right. It's only 60,000 square feet.' So I went to tell Sam about it, and he said, 'Well, I called the architect and told him to cut it back. I just don't think we need that 100,000 square feet, Bob.'

"Another thing. I had designed that distribution center around an in-floor towline system, you know, a track that moves carts around the floor. Sam says, 'Well, Bob, I just don't think we can do that. We can't spend that kind of money.' At that point, I literally didn't know how to run a warehouse without one so I just said, 'Hey, Sam, if we don't have a towline system, then you don't need me because I don't know what to do without it.' So he gave in to that. The truth is, Sam never did *anything* in size or volume until he actually had to. He always played it close to the belt."

It's true enough that I was nervous about spending any unnecessary money in those days. We were generating as much financing for growth as we could from the profits of the stores, but we were also borrowing everything we could. I was taking on a lot of personal debt to grow the company—it approached $2 million, which was a lot of money at the time. The debt was beginning to weigh on me.

By now I no longer had any doubt that we were really on to something. We had expanded to Missouri—Sikeston was our first store there. And we'd put stores in Neosho and West Plains. We'd gone to Claremore, Oklahoma—Helen's hometown. Our first seven or eight Wal-Marts were showing spectacular results. Once we got it going, it was hard to see why we should quit. The thing was, you could see the potential so clearly. The profits and the sales were there but we needed to get better organized and come up with a more sensible way to finance the growth. I needed someone to help me with systems and distribution.

I had stayed in touch with Ron Mayer, and I kept after him to work for us. Finally, I talked him into coming down to look over our operations, and then darned near killed him before he ever had a chance to sign on. We were flying around in my Beech Baron, looking at stores, and we were on our way in to land at Carthage, Missouri—headed for store number 12. There are two intersecting runways at Carthage, and as I touched down on one of them, all of a sudden up ahead we saw this plane on the other runway, right at the intersection, and we were headed straight at him. I hadn't seen him or heard him on the radio. I didn't know where he came from. I gave that Baron all the power it had and we just barely made it over the top of the other plane. Then we circled around and landed. This was Ron's first trip with me, and who knows what he must have thought. But somehow, I talked him into coming to work with us anyway. He joined Wal-Mart in 1968 as vice president for finance and distribution.

Even though it may surprise some people, I have to say that I consider the time Ron was at the company, from 1968 until 1976 (when he left under some fairly unpleasant circumstances for both of us), to be the most important period of development in Wal-Mart's history. We had a good thing going before Ron arrived, but he, and some of the people he brought on board, like Royce Chambers, our first data processing manager, gave the company its first sophisticated systems. And those systems were the beginnings of a management method which allowed us to stay real close to our stores even as our growth exploded.

We were forced to be ahead of our time in distribution and in communication because our stores were sitting out there in tiny little towns and we had to stay in touch and keep them supplied. Ron started the programs that eventually improved our in-store communications system. Building on the groundwork already laid by Ferold Arend, Ron also took over distribution and began to design and build a system that would enable us to grow as fast as we could come up with the money. He was the main force that moved us away from the old drop shipment method, in which a store ordered directly from the manufacturer and had the merchandise delivered directly to the store by common carrier. He pushed us in some new directions, such as merchandise assembly, in which we would order centrally for every store and then assemble their orders at the distribution center, and also cross-docking, in which preassembled orders for individual stores would be received on one side of our warehouse and leave out the other.

From Ron Mayer's arrival on, we as a company have been ahead of most other retailers in investing in sophisticated equipment and technology. The funny thing is, everybody at Wal-Mart knows that I've fought all these technology expenditures as hard as I could. All these guys love to talk about how I never wanted any of this technology, and how they had to lay down their life to get it. The truth is, I did want it, I knew we needed it, but I just couldn't bring myself to say, "Okay, sure, spend what you need." I always questioned everything. It was important to me to make them think that maybe the technology wasn't as good as they thought it was, or that maybe it really wasn't the end-all they promised it would be. It seems to me they try just a little harder and check into things a little bit closer if they think they might have a chance to prove me wrong. If I really hadn't wanted the technology, I wouldn't have sprung the money loose to pay for it.

By the late sixties, we were really well positioned for serious growth. We had a retail concept we believed in, the core of a professional management team, and the foundations of systems which would support growth. In 1968, we had fourteen variety stores and thirteen Wal-Marts. In 1969, we had fourteen variety stores and eighteen Wal-Marts. And we were raring to go. I couldn't resist taking that next step to see how far we could go. And I always figured we would slow down or stop when we weren't as profitable as we should be.

It was around that time that Bud and I—very quietly—began to think about taking the company public.

CHAPTER 7

TAKING THE COMPANY PUBLIC

"When we went on the stock market, it didn't mean anything to some of us country boys. The chairman always said I came across the Red River barefooted and hunting a job, which is almost the way it was. I didn't even know what stock was. But I bought some, thank God, because Phil Green said, 'Hey, you buy some of that stock, boy.' I bought it and I kept it because I believed in Mr. Walton, and I believed in my store. It's real simple. I believed him when he said we could do all these things with the company. And we did."

—AL MILES,
first assistant manager, store number 6,
Fayetteville, Arkansas,
now a retired Wal-Mart executive

From the time I took out my first bank loan—the $1,800 to buy that ice cream machine for the Ben Franklin down in Newport—I was never really comfortable with debt. But I recognized it as a necessity of doing business, and I had gotten pretty good at accumulating it. For a while, I would just go down to the local bank and borrow whatever I could to build a store or buy something we needed to grow the business. That practice had gotten me in debt to practically every bank in Arkansas and southern Missouri. They believed in what we had done up to that point, and they believed we would pay them off. I always did pay them off on time, but sometimes I would borrow from one to pay the other. I had bought a bank in Bentonville, for about $300,000, just a little old bank with only about $3.5 million in deposits. But it really helped me learn a lot about financing things. I made some new acquaintances and began to study more about bankers and how they liked to do business.

I struck up a relationship with a guy named Jimmy Jones at Republic Bank down in Dallas, and he loaned us a million dollars. And, of course, I had tried all along to attract some equity investment from our store managers and a few relatives. So by 1970, we had seventy-eight partners invested in our company, which really wasn't one company, but thirty-two different stores owned by a combination of different folks. My family owned the lion's share of every store, but Helen and I were also in debt up to our eyeballs—several million dollars' worth. I never dwell on the negative, but that debt weighed heavy on me. If something happened and everybody decided to call their notes, I kept thinking, we would be sunk. Maybe that's what being raised in the Depression does to you, but I wanted out of that debt in the worst way.

I had talked a little bit about the idea of taking the company public, seeking advice from people like Abe Marks and some of those other discounters in that association we all belonged to, but I really hadn't pursued anything seriously. One day in 1969 we got a call from Mike Smith, who said he wanted to come up and talk to us. Mike worked for Witt and Jack Stephens in Little Rock. Today, Stephens Inc. is the largest investment banking firm west of the Mississippi, and one of the most respected in the country. Back then it was mostly a bond house. Jack, by the way, was the fellow who had come in and successfully developed that Little Rock shopping center after I failed. So Mike Smith drove up to Bentonville. We were still in those old three rooms of offices over the lawyer's office and the barbershop on the square. I remember Mike climbing those stairs. He is a bit of a renegade himself—he has a lot of original ideas—and during our conversation that day, he planted the seed that maybe we really were doing well enough to go public, that is, to issue stock in the company and sell it to the public.

MIKE SMITH, STEPHENS INC.:

"I went up there to see them in the fall of 1969, and it was really the height of ambition. We had only done one public offering, and I had done it, so I thought I was an expert. Sam was eager to talk because he had borrowed all the money he possibly could. I stopped at every Wal-Mart between Little Rock and Bentonville so I would know something about his stores. Of course the first thing he did was throw me in that plane of his and fly us all over Oklahoma and Missouri looking at stores."

Not long after that, Bud and I went quail hunting up on the Robson ranch in Oklahoma, and the hunting was really good. We spent most of that day talking about our options. We wanted to expand, and we realized we weren't generating enough profits both to expand and to pay off our debts. In fact, our cash shortage had forced us to give up five land sites where we had already planned to build new stores, so we knew we had to do something. Driving back that night, we agreed to seriously explore the possibilities of going public. It was a huge step for us, and we were concerned about losing control of the company. My son Rob had graduated from Columbia University law school the year before and had gone to work at the biggest law firm in Tulsa. We, the Walton family, were his first client. As our lawyer, he also kept track of the various Wal-Mart store partnership agreements, so I asked him to start looking at all our options.

We still weren't sure we could take the company public. Meanwhile, money was getting tight, and some of our creditors were pressuring us. I flew to Dallas and tried to borrow some more from Republic Bank, whose officers were getting nervous about what they'd already loaned us. They made it clear we had all of their money we were likely to see, and that ended our relationship. By then, Jimmy Jones had moved to a bank in New Orleans, First Commerce, so I flew down there from Dallas to see if he could help us. Jimmy came up with a $1.5 million loan, which helped us out in the short term, but it really wasn't the answer to our long-term problem.

For various reasons, including taxes, Rob recommended restructuring our debt, consolidating it into one big loan for the company. Ron Mayer and I had heard that the Prudential was making loans to a lot of small retail chains, so we made an appointment with one of their loan officers and flew to New York.

By now we really needed the money, pure and simple. I went to Prudential. I had my predictions all spelled out on my yellow legal pad, and I was sure they were going to loan us the money. I went through my five-year plan—my sales, profits, number of stores— and talked about our strategy of going to the small towns where there was no competition and told the loan officer how much business we thought there was out there waiting to be plucked. He didn't buy it at all, told us he didn't think a company like the Prudential could afford to gamble with us. I saved those projections for a long time, and they were all exceeded by 15 to 20 percent in the years to come.

Somehow we had a contact at another insurance company, Mass Mutual, so we went to see them. They agreed to lend us a million dollars, and, in turn, we agreed to give them our right arm and our left leg. We didn't just pay interest, we had to give them all sorts of stock options in case we did go public. By now they had us over a barrel. I had no choice: we had to have the money. When we went public they made millions and millions on that deal.

By then, I was tired of owing money to people I knew, and I was even more tired of begging money from strangers. I made up my mind for sure that we were going to take Wal-Mart to the stock market. I let Mike Smith and Jack Stephens know we wanted to go ahead with the idea, but I also let them know they were going to have to compete for our business, just like I've always made everybody else compete for business with us. Also, I let them know I didn't feel comfortable going with a Little Rock firm; I thought we needed a Wall Street underwriter. Maybe that was right, and maybe it wasn't. I know Mike and Jack didn't feel too good about it. But I went running off to New York to see what I could find out.

MIKE SMITH:

"Obviously, we wanted to handle the whole offering, but Sam was always one to shop around. Here's what happened the way I remember it: Sam was up in New York on a buying trip, and he decided to go down to Wall Street and hear what some of those guys had to say, just cold calling—right off the street. He knew that White, Weld had taken public a retail chain called Pamida up in Omaha, so he went to visit them. He introduced himself to the receptionist as Sam Walton of Wal-Mart stores—like he always does—and said, 'I want to talk to somebody about taking my company public.' She said, 'Oh really, where are you from?' And when he told her Bentonville, Arkansas, she said, 'Well, we have a Mr. Remmel here, and he's from Arkansas. Perhaps he could help you.' And she introduced him to Buck Remmel, who was from Little Rock."

I don't really remember how I met Buck, but Mike might have it right. I remember introducing myself to him and saying something like, "What are the chances that you folks would be interested in backing us on this offering?" Well, he said he would look at it, and, sure enough, they decided they were interested. I still think that's one reason the offer was so successful, because at the time White, Weld was one of the leading institutional investment banking firms. Not everyone around here agrees with me, but I'm sticking to my opinion.

MIKE SMITH:

"Sam decided—correctly at the time—that White, Weld knew more about public offerings than we did, so he let them have the business. But he told them, 'I hope you'll include the folks at Stephens, because they're good friends, and they're good people.' White, Weld asked us if we wanted to take a third of the deal to their two-thirds. I talked it over with Jack, and he asked me what I thought of the company. I said I thought we ought to do it. And we did. Later on, in other offerings, we got a fifty-fifty piece of the deal along with White, Weld."

So Rob started to work on the plan, which was to consolidate all these partnerships into one company and then sell about 20

percent of it to the public. At the time, our family owned probably 75 percent of the company, Bud owned 15 percent or so,
some other relatives owned a percentage, Charlie Baum owned
some, Willard Walker owned some, Charlie Cate owned some,
Claude Harris owned some. All those early managers would borrow money from our bank to buy stock in the stores. Willard was
the most skillful at getting money. He would cultivate the guys
who ran the banks and they'd let him have what he wanted.
Consequently, he realized fabulous returns on it. He had more
ownership than any of the managers.

ROB WALTON:

> "Dad had a spread sheet listing all the minority ownerships in
> the various companies, and the problem was figuring out on
> what basis to value them all for the initial offering. As I recall,
> we basically proposed using book value. We did not do any
> kind of sophisticated relative evaluation of the companies
> which would have taken into account earnings and growth
> projections and all that sort of stuff. But everybody signed
> right up. And as far as I know, everybody's happy today with
> the way it worked out."

We were all ready to go at the beginning of 1970, and Ron
Mayer and I did a dog and pony show all over the place—Los
Angeles, San Francisco, Chicago—telling everybody how great
we were going to be. But before we got the stock issued, the
market fell out on us, and we had to postpone the offering. We
were already having unusual managers' meetings in those days.
We would all go fishing together, without wives, for four or five
days at a time and talk about the business. I remember we were on
one of those trips to Table Rock Dam, and I had to tell everybody that we were pulling back on the deal. But the market
recovered some, and on October 1, 1970, Wal-Mart became a
public company, traded over the counter. Our prospectus offered
300,000 shares at a price of $15, but it sold for $16.50. It was well
received, though not widely held; we only had about 800 share-

holders, most of them either institutions or folks we knew. Those who bought in that offering, or who owned some of those early partnerships and had them converted in that offering, made an absolute killing.

As everybody today knows, Wal-Mart's stock performance, and the wealth it has created, is a story in itself. Just fifteen years ago, the market value of the company was around $135 million; today it's over $50 billion. But here's a better way to look at it: let's say you bought 100 shares back in that original public offering, for $1,650. Since then, we've had nine two-for-one stock splits, so you would have 51,200 shares today. Within the last year, it's traded at right under $60 a share. So your investment would have been worth right around $3 million at that price. Obviously, our stock has made a lot of folks happy over the years, and—pure and simple—that's where the Walton family net worth has been created. It's paid off beyond any of our dreams.

Here's a chart that shows the course over the years of that 100 shares:

SHARES	100% SPLITS	MKT. PRICE ON SPLIT DATE
100		
200	May 1971	$46/47 OTC
400	March 1972	46/47 OTC
800	August 1975	23 NYSE
1,600	November 1980	50 NYSE
3,200	June 1982	497/8 NYSE
6,400	June 1983	815/8 NYSE
12,800	September 1985	493/4 NYSE
25,600	June 1987	665/8 NYSE
51,200	June 1990	621/2 NYSE

One funny memory about that public offering. The day it went through Ron and I were leaving New York, and at the airport we met a guy from T. Rowe Price, a money management firm in Baltimore. We were so full of ourselves that somehow we made him believe we were going to do well. He went back to Baltimore and bought a pretty large share of that stock for his firm. They held it for ten or fifteen years and became the star of their industry. We would split and split, and they would sell and sell. I don't know how many millions they made on that stock.

HELEN WALTON:

"I realized before we went public that I didn't want it to happen. I guess if I were going to be mad with Sam about anything, it would be over the fact that I always felt we could have gotten by without going public. Nothing about the company ever affected me as deeply, and it was at that point that I decided I had to pursue my other interests outside the company. I just hated the idea that we were going to put all our financial interests out there for everybody to see. When you go public, they can ask all kinds of questions, and the family gets involved. We just became an open book, and I hated it."

Helen's right, of course, about the downside of taking the company public. It did end up bringing us a lot of unwanted attention. But coming back from New York that day, I experienced one of the greatest feelings of my life, knowing that all our debts were paid off. The Walton family only owned 61 percent of Wal-Mart after that day, but we were able to pay off all those bankers, and from that day on, we haven't borrowed one dime personally to support Wal-Mart. The company has rolled along on its own and financed itself. Going public really turned the company loose to grow, and it took a huge load off me. We had another offering later on, trying to get broader ownership of the stock so we could be traded on the New York Stock Exchange, but as a family we've only sold very limited amounts of Wal-Mart stock outside of those offerings. I think that has really set us apart, and, as I said, that's the source of our net worth. We just kept that stock. Most families somewhere along the line would have said, We don't want this rat race. We don't need to do what we are doing. Let somebody else have it. And then either I would have retired and backed out of the company and sold it to some Dutch investor or to Kmart or Federated, or somebody like that. But I enjoyed doing what I was doing so much and seeing the thing grow and develop, and seeing our associates and partners do so well, that I never could quit.

It was always interesting to me that, except for those folks who worked in our company, our stock got very little support early on from the folks right here in northwest Arkansas. I always had the feeling that the people around here who remembered us when we had one store and three stores, or remembered me when I was president of the Rotary or the Chamber of Commerce, somehow thought we were doing it with mirrors. They couldn't help but think we were just lucky, that we could not continue long term to do as well as we have done. I don't think it was anything peculiar to this part of the country or me or anything like that. I think it must be human nature that when somebody homegrown gets on to something, the folks around them sometimes are the last to recognize it.

Like any other company, we obviously wanted to keep our stock price up and attract as many new investors as we could. And the way we went at that early on was about as unorthodox as everything else we've done. Most public companies hold annual stockholders' meetings, and many hold sessions for Wall Street stock analysts, where they tell their company story and try to drum up support for their stock. As I told you, Mike Smith is an off-the-wall guy with good ideas and suggestions that are somewhat unorthodox. So right after we went public, Mike suggested that we might want to turn our stockholders' meeting into an event, and we went along with him.

Most meetings are held in some hotel ballroom in a big city, and are pretty quick, formal affairs with the reading of the minutes and the passing of a few shareholder motions. A lot of them, I understand, are held in places like Wilmington, Delaware, where the companies are incorporated, in the hope that a whole lot of people won't show up. We took the opposite approach. We figured we were already out of the way enough to discourage anybody from coming, but since we wanted to encourage folks to attend, we scheduled a whole weekend of events for them. We invited folks down from New York, Chicago, or wherever. They

paid their own way down and back, but we really showed them a
time.

MIKE SMITH:

"It's true that I came up with the idea of making the annual
meeting more of an event, but Sam didn't tell you the whole
reason why. I'll never forget Wal-Mart's first annual meeting,
or I should say, meetings. I went up a day early to help prepare for it, but this friend of Sam's—Fred Pickens from Newport—got confused on the dates and showed up a day early.
So Sam decided to go ahead and hold the meeting for Fred,
right there in his office. The next day we had the official
annual meeting: six of us met around a table of the coffee shop
there by the warehouse.

"The next year I said, 'Sam, you're a public company, and
we ought to have a real meeting and try to get some folks to
come. Let's do it in Little Rock. You're from Arkansas, and
Little Rock is the capital of Arkansas and people can get there
a lot easier than they can to Bentonville.' He didn't like it
much, but he agreed to it. So we held the second meeting at a
motel, the Coachmen's Inn, in Little Rock. Nobody came.
And he said, 'So much for your idea, Mike.' Well, I was
getting desperate to get some analysts down to really start
following the company, so I came up with the idea of bringing them all in for a weekend at Bella Vista, which is this nice
development in the hills just north of Bentonville, with lots of
golf courses, tennis courts, and lakes. I still remember Sam's
response to the idea when I brought it up: 'Sounds like a big
waste of money to me.' But he decided to give it a try."

It turned out to be a really good idea. These folks would
come down, and we would assign a manager from the company
to meet them at the airport and drive them around for the weekend. We wanted these investment types from the cities, including
a lot of the bankers who were lending money to our company at
the time, to see firsthand what we do and how we do it. We
wanted them to get to know our managers as individuals and

come to understand our company's principles. And we felt like to do that they really had to come to Bentonville and see what kind of people we were, understand our integrity, our dedication, our work ethic, all the ingredients that were enabling us to out-perform our competitors. They couldn't do that back in New York. The values and the approach of most retailers were entirely different from what this crazy bunch in Arkansas was doing, and we wanted them to see it for themselves. So they would come down and we would have the stockholders' meeting on Friday, followed by a big picnic that night. I remember one lady wore a formal gown to one of our dinners. It got quite a few curious looks. Then we would get them up early on Saturday morning and have them come to our meeting and listen to us talk mer-chandising and finance and distribution, or whatever we were dealing with at the time.

In the early days, it wasn't anything like what it's turned into now, which is the largest, most raucous stockholders' meeting in the world. But it was different. After the meeting on Saturday, we always had a special event. One year it was a golf tournament, which is not all that unusual, I guess. But another year we went fishing on Bull Shoals Lake. And another year we took everybody on a float trip down Sugar Creek. The wildest event I remember was when we all went camping overnight in tents on the banks of Sugar Creek. That was a real fiasco. Remember now, these are a bunch of investment analysts from the big cities. Well, a coyote started howling, and hoot owls hooting, and half of these analysts stayed up all night around the campfire because they couldn't sleep. We decided it wasn't the best idea to try something like this with folks who weren't accustomed to camping on the rocks in sleeping bags.

MIKE SMITH:

"These get-togethers became a big hit. The Wal-Mart folks would stay up all night barbecuing, and the analysts or other big shareholders would stay up with them to 'help.' But after a while, things got a little out of hand for Sam's taste. Some of those Yankees got so drunk floating down Sugar Creek they

couldn't stay in the boat. And some of those fellows barbecuing had a few too many beers. Well, Sam isn't a Puritan or a
strict teetotaler or anything, but he can't stand for people to
get drunk. So he banned alcohol completely from the events,
and, of course, they were never quite the same after that."

They did get a little wild for me, I guess. But if nothing else,
our meetings generated a lot of talk about us back on Wall Street
—not all of it good, I'm sure—but the ones who paid attention
understood that we were serious operators who were in it for the
long haul, that we had a disciplined financial philosophy, and that
we had growth on our minds. They also knew we liked to have
fun, and a few of them probably thought maybe we were a little
nuts.

Those meetings are just one example of how, in the early days
of being a public company, we really did have to go to greater
lengths than most companies to let Wall Street get to know us and
understand us. Partly that was because we operated so differently
from everybody else, and partly it was because we were so isolated
from New York, where a lot of folks seem to think you have to be
to do business on the scale and size that we are. And in the process
of wooing Wall Street, we met all kinds. We've been blessed and
appreciated by some analysts and dismissed by others who have
believed all along that we are just a house of cards waiting to fall
down any second.

One of our most loyal followers has been Maggie Gilliam, an
analyst for First Boston who has believed in us for years, and she's
made her clients an awful lot of money by sticking to those be-
liefs. Here's an excerpt from a report, one of my favorites, that she
wrote:

MARGARET GILLIAM, FIRST BOSTON:
   Wal-Mart is the finest-managed company we have ever
followed. We think it is quite likely the finest-managed company in America, and we know of at least one investor who
thinks it is the finest-managed company in the world. We do
not expect to find another Wal-Mart in our lifetime . . .

On the other hand, I remember another analyst who came down here in the mid-seventies. I'll never forget her visit. I had been out hunting all day, and I was pretty grubby when I came in to go out to dinner with her. My son Jim, who was head of the real estate department in those days, joined us. And he was never one for dressing up. Really, he always looks pretty grubby. We took her out, and we were extremely honest with her. We told her what we felt our weaknesses were at that time, and what some of our problems were. But we tried to explain our philosophy too, and to get her excited about all the potential we felt we had. She went back and wrote probably the darkest report on Wal-Mart that has ever been written. The impression you got from reading it was that if you hadn't already sold your stock, it was probably too late.

Over the last ten or fifteen years, most of the analysts who've followed our stock have been consistent in their support, although they'll go off us temporarily for one reason or another. By and large, though, they've stayed with us.

I don't subscribe much to any of these fancy investing theories, and most people seem surprised to learn that I've never done much investing in anything except Wal-Mart. I believe the folks who've done the best with Wal-Mart stock are those who have studied the company, who have understood our strengths and our management approach, and who, like me, have just decided to invest with us for the long run.

We have a group of longtime investors in Scotland who have done it better maybe than anybody. Back in the early days of our growth, the Stephens people took us to London, where we first attracted the interest of these folks. They told us right off that they believed in investing for the long term. They said that as long as they felt good about the basics of the company, and had confidence in the management, they wouldn't be buying and selling the way many of these fund managers do. Man, they were talking my language. Years after that first trip, we visited with them in Edinburgh, and they really laid it on for us. We have a similar group out in California.

And we also have an investor in France—his name is Pierre,

and he's done exactly the same thing. We almost drowned him that first year we floated down Sugar Creek, and I was afraid we'd never see him again. But Pierre started believing, and he started acquiring our stock and recommending it to his French fund members. He's been with us for about fifteen years, and he's had exceptionally good success with our company.

Our long-term investors are happy because we have consistently rewarded them with one of the highest returns on equity in American business. From 1977 to 1987, our average annual return to investors was 46 percent. And even in the middle of the recession, in 1991, we reported a return on equity of more than 32 percent.

I guess what's annoying to executives—to anybody who tries to spend their time managing a company as big as this—is these money managers who're always churning their investors' accounts. You know, the stock will get to $40 or $42, and they'll rush in there and say, "Hey, let's sell this thing because it's just too high. It's an overvalued stock." Well, to my mind, that doesn't make much sense. As long as we're managing our company well, as long as we take care of our people and our customers, keep our eye on those fundamentals, we are going to be successful. Of course, it takes an observing, discerning person to judge those fundamentals for himself. If I were a stockholder of Wal-Mart, or considering becoming one, I'd go into ten Wal-Mart stores and ask the folks working there, "How do you feel? How's the company treating you?" Their answers would tell me much of what I need to know.

On this same subject, I have frequently been asked if being a widely followed stock has forced us to manage differently, to think more short term at the expense of long-term strategic planning. The answer is that we've always had to do a good bit of both. When you're opening 150 stores a year the way we do these days, a lot of your planning is necessarily short term. But to sustain that kind of growth, you constantly have to consider what you're going to be doing five years out. I think that the stock market pressure has driven us to plan further out so that there will be some consistency next year, and the year after—not only to our profitability but to our operating sales, our gross margins, and those sorts of things.

I've never let myself fret too much about that. We've had some tremendous fluctuations of our stock over time. Sometimes it will shoot up because retailing has become a fashionable sector with the investment community. Or it will plunge because somebody writes a report saying that Wal-Mart's strategy is all wrong. When we bought a chain of stores called Kuhn's Big K in 1981— which took us east of the Mississippi for the first time in a significant way—several reports said we were taking on more than we could handle, and that we would never make it once we got to Atlanta or New Orleans. We've had reports predicting that when we got to St. Louis, or wherever, and met some *real* competition, we would never be able to stay profitable. Our demise has been predicted ever since we hit the stock market. And whenever one of these big institutional investors reads something like that, and decides he believes it, he unloads a million shares, or 500,000 shares, and in the past that has created some fluctuations in the price of our stock.

Just a couple of years ago, we had some retail analysts worrying that we couldn't sustain a 20 percent annual growth rate because we were getting so big. At the time, I said I would be tickled to death with 20 percent. I mean, when we were doing $25 billion a year in sales, 20 percent was $5 billion, which is bigger in itself than most retailers. But these folks thought a $5 billion increase would be a disaster for us. In the meantime, look what's happened to the industry. Nowadays, we're heroes because we're still showing double-digit growth. If we do 20 percent, it's the lead item on the national news broadcasts because they view it as an economic indicator. The point is, all those analysts may have had perfectly logical theories about why a 20 percent increase would be a disaster for us. But they failed to see that in a big economic downturn, when everybody is suffering, Wal-Mart's fundamental strengths would keep us going strong. And we would look great compared to everybody else.

As companies get larger, with a broader following of investors, it becomes awfully tempting to get into that jet and go up to Detroit or Chicago or New York and speak to the bankers and the people who own your stock. But since we got our stock jump-started in the beginning, I feel like our time is better spent with our own people in the stores, rather than off selling the company to outsiders. I don't think any amount of public relations experts or speeches in New York or Boston means a darn thing to the value of the stock over the long haul. I think you get what you're worth. Not that we don't go out of our way to keep Wall Street up to date on what's going on with the company. For the last few years, in fact, a group called the United Shareholders Association has voted us the number-one company in the U.S. based on our responsiveness to shareholders.

What's really worried me over the years is not our stock price, but that we might someday fail to take care of our customers, or that our managers might fail to motivate and take care of our associates. I also was worried that we might lose the team concept, or fail to keep the family concept viable and realistic and meaningful to our folks as we grow. Those challenges are more real than somebody's theory that we're headed down the wrong path.

As business leaders, we absolutely cannot afford to get all caught up in trying to meet the goals that some retail analyst or financial institution in New York sets for us on a ten-year plan spit out of a computer that somebody set to compound at such-and-such a rate. If we do that, we take our eye off the ball. But if we demonstrate in our sales and our earnings every day, every week, every quarter, that we're doing our job in a sound way, we will get the growth we are entitled to, and the market will respect us in a way that we deserve. Our associates and our customers— many of whom are now stockholders too—will all be better served if we perform consistently over the next ten years, whether it is at a 15 percent rate or a 20 percent rate or a 25 percent rate.

If we fail to live up to somebody's hypothetical projection for what we should be doing, I don't care. It may knock our stock back a little, but we're in it for the long run. We couldn't care less about what is forecast or what the market says we ought to do. If we listened very seriously to that sort of stuff, we never would have gone into small-town discounting in the first place.

CHAPTER 8

ROLLING OUT THE FORMULA

"Sam hired me in 1970 as district manager in charge of new store openings. He had eighteen Wal-Marts and some variety stores doing about $31 million a year. I moved my family, and as the van was unloading the furniture into our rented house, they called from the office and said, 'Can you go set up this new store in Missouri?' My wife, who had three babies and a moving van to deal with, helped me find some clothes, and I left. I didn't see her again for two weeks. Then there was a managers' meeting so I didn't see her for two more weeks. It would be safe to say that in those days we all worked a minimum of sixteen hours a day."

—JACK SHEWMAKER,
former president and COO of Wal-Mart

Now that we were out of debt, we could really do something with our key strategy, which was simply to put good-sized discount stores into little one-horse towns which everybody else was ignoring. In those days, Kmart wasn't going to towns below 50,000, and even Gibson's wouldn't go to towns much smaller than 10,000 or 12,000. We knew our formula was working even in towns smaller than 5,000 people, and there were plenty of those towns out there for us to expand into. When people want to simplify the Wal-Mart story, that's usually how they sum up the secret of our success: "Oh, they went into small towns when nobody else would." And a long time ago, when we were first being noticed, a lot of folks in the industry wrote us off as a bunch of country hicks who had stumbled onto this idea by a big accident.

Maybe it was an accident, but that strategy wouldn't have worked at all if we hadn't come up with a method for implementing it. That method was to saturate a market area by spreading out, then filling in. In the early growth years of discounting, a lot of national companies with distribution systems already in place—Kmart, for example—were growing by sticking stores all over the country. Obviously, we couldn't support anything like that.

But while the big guys were leapfrogging from large city to large city, they became so spread out and so involved in real estate and zoning laws and city politics that they left huge pockets of business out there for us. Our growth strategy was born out of necessity, but at least we recognized it as a strategy pretty early on. We figured we had to build our stores so that our distribution centers, or warehouses, could take care of them, but also so those stores could be controlled. We wanted them within reach of our district managers, and of ourselves here in Bentonville, so we could get out there and look after them. Each store had to be within a day's drive of a distribution center. So we would go as far as we could from a warehouse and put in a store. Then we would fill in the map of that territory, state by state, county seat by county seat, until we had saturated that market area.

We saturated northwest Arkansas. We saturated Oklahoma. We saturated Missouri. We went from Neosho to Joplin, to Monett and Aurora, to Nevada and Belton, to Harrisonville, and then on to Fort Scott and Olathe in Kansas—and so on. Sometimes we would jump over an area, like when we opened store number 23 in Ruston, Louisiana, and we didn't have a thing in south Arkansas, which is between us and Ruston. So then we started back-filling south Arkansas. In those days we didn't really plan for the future. We just felt like we could keep rolling these stores out this way, and they would keep working, in Tennessee, or Kansas, or Nebraska—wherever we decided to go. But we did try to think ahead some when it came to the cities. We never planned on actually going into the cities. What we did instead was build our stores in a ring around a city—pretty far out—and wait for the growth to come to us. That strategy worked practically everywhere. We started early with Tulsa, putting stores in Broken Arrow and Sand Springs. Around Kansas City, we built in Warrensburg, Belton, and Grandview on the Missouri side of town and in Bonner Springs and Leavenworth across the river in Kansas. We did the same thing in Dallas.

This saturation strategy had all sorts of benefits beyond control and distribution. From the very beginning, we never believed in spending much money on advertising, and saturation helped us to save a fortune in that department. When you move like we did from town to town in these mostly rural areas, word of mouth gets your message out to customers pretty quickly without much advertising. When we had seventy-five stores in Arkansas, seventy-five in Missouri, eighty in Oklahoma, whatever, people knew who we were, and everybody except the merchants who weren't discounting looked forward to our coming to their town. By doing it this way, we usually could get by with distributing just one advertising circular a month instead of running a whole lot of newspaper advertising. We've never been big advertisers, and, relative to our size today, we still aren't. Just like today, we became our own competitors. In the Springfield, Missouri, area, for example, we had forty stores within 100 miles. When Kmart finally came in there with three stores, they had a rough time going up against our kind of strength.

So for the most part, we just started repeating what worked, stamping out stores cookie-cutter style. The only decision we had to make was what size format to put in what market. We had five different store sizes—running from about 30,000 to 60,000 square feet—and we would hardly ever pass up any market because it was too small. I had traveled so much myself looking at competitors in the variety store business that I had a good feel for the kind of potential in these communities. Bud and I knew what we wanted in the way of locations.

Like so many of the ideas that have made our company work from the beginning, we're still more or less following this same strategy, although today we've moved into some cities outright. But I think our main real estate effort should be directed at getting out in front of expansion and letting the population build out to us. Just like in the beginning, we start around these small towns, people drive past our stores, get to know us, and become customers. The amazing thing to me is how quickly it works. We have created so many new friends down in Florida—Yankee friends, folks who live up North—who see our stores in Florida while they're down there for the winter, and they can't wait for us to get up there.

Believe it or not, I get letters all the time asking us to put a store in some place up North because our customers miss us when they go back home. It's the same way in the Rio Grande Valley. All the farmers from North Dakota, South Dakota, and Minnesota go down there for the winter and get to know us. So we are presold, almost, when we go into some of these areas that are new for us. We're still spreading out and filling in, and we've got a heck of a long way to go before we saturate territory which we consider to be basically friendly to Wal-Mart.

There's no question whatsoever that we could not have done what we did back then if I hadn't had my airplanes. I bought that first plane for business, to travel between the stores and keep in touch with what was going on. But once we started really rolling out the stores, the airplane turned into a great tool for scouting real estate. We were probably ten years ahead of most other retailers in scouting locations from the air, and we got a lot of great ones that way. From up in the air we could check out traffic flows, see which way cities and towns were growing, and evaluate the location of the competition—if there was any. Then we would develop our real estate strategy for that market.

I loved doing it myself. I'd get down low, turn my plane up on its side, and fly right over a town. Once we had a spot picked out, we'd land, go find out who owned the property, and try to negotiate the deal right then. That's another good reason I don't like jets. You can't get down low enough to really tell what's going on, the way I could in my little planes. Bud and I picked almost all our sites that way until we grew to about 120 or 130 stores. I was always proud of our technique and the results we got. I guarantee you not many principals of retailing companies were flying around sideways studying development patterns, but it worked really well for us. Until we had 500 stores, or at least 400 or so, I kept up with every real estate deal we made and got to view most locations before we signed any kind of commitment. A good location, and what we have to pay for it, is so important to the success of a store. And it's one area of the company in which we've always had family involvement. Jim did it for a while. And even today, Rob goes on real estate trips and attends every real estate meeting.

Once we found a good location, we just got after it and put up a store there. We built our own fixtures then, and we still do today. We had what we called a Store Opening Plan, but basically we would call in the troops—usually we called in all the available assistant managers—and put together a store. I'll bet a guy like Al Miles has put together 100 stores and been to over 300 store openings. We had to assemble the fixtures, order the merchandise, and plan the advertising—not to mention hiring and training the folks to run the store. We just all dove in and got it done. There are all kinds of stories about those things. I remember one time I didn't want to spend any money on motels so we all slept in sleeping bags on the floor of one of our guys' houses. His furniture hadn't gotten there yet.

Ferold Arend made a big difference in the early rollout of Wal-Marts. He was a very organized person in a way that I wasn't. I always told him it was because he was German. But he was the kind of fellow who, if he had ten things to do in a day, would write them all down and then work to get them done. He would double back to see that people did what he told them to do. I never did that as a rule in those days. I just kept moving.

I think a powerful sense of needing to take off to the next town or the next store when I'm ready, without wasting any time waiting on somebody else, is probably the main reason I never was able to work real well with pilots. It seemed like they were never ready to go when I was. Anyway, I love the flying, the challenge of finding my way all over the country, evaluating the weather and making the instrument approaches and doing everything my-self. But even more than that, I love the independence of being able to go where I want to, when I want to—in a hurry. Plus, I always like to see people working, and the nature of a corporate pilot's job includes a lot of downtime. So, when we first got a few pilots around here I conceived this brilliant idea: "Okay, guys," I said. "If you want to fly airplanes, I want you to go into the stores and check on our in-stock positions in all our departments when you aren't flying." It made perfect sense to me. They needed to learn more about the business, they would be helping us, and they could have had some fun with it. My idea lasted about three months and provoked all kinds of grumbling. I heard every excuse in the book. We've got to check the weather and make sure the planes are taken care of and all that. Finally, I gave in. And today, our pilots stay in the air about as much as anybody in their business.

JACK SHEWMAKER:

"The first store we opened after I got there was number 21 in Saint Robert, Missouri. Our store opening crew was supposed to take possession of a store after construction was complete. It didn't always work out that way. When we took that store, the parking lot wasn't done. I mean, it was gravel and had no striping, no cording of cars or anything. So the store manager, Gary Reinboth, and I were trying to figure out how to avoid chaos at the opening. Our eyes lit up when we saw this snack bar vendor hauling used cooking grease in these huge yellow barrels in the back of his truck. So we made a deal with him. He could buy all our grease at a good price if we could have all his grease barrels for the grand opening. We tied flags and rope on them and made a parking lot. That's the way we thought in those days. Sam wanted a job done, and he was willing to accept creativity as long as the job got done. Our minds were freewheeling. We rushed to get things done.

"I remember another opening. We had finally built a new store in Morrilton, Arkansas, out near Interstate 40, to replace that incredible store Sam was so proud of in the old Coca-Cola plant. My boss was Ferold Arend, and he told me we were going to set a new record of opening a store in three weeks. I said okay. But he had made a mistake by a week so we really had a target date of two weeks from the day we began. We tried desperately, but we didn't quite make it. We opened on Thanksgiving Day, and the store was horrible. I

was standing out in front when Sam drove up. He saw the
disaster, but he was smart enough to know how hard we'd
been working and that if he told the truth we would have just
disintegrated. He said, 'The store looks really good, guys.'
And he drove away and left us."

Obviously, because I have spent as much time as I could out
where it counts, in the stores, seeing if we're doing the job we
should be, it has put a very heavy load on all our executives,
especially since I expect them to get out in the stores too. My
style has always been to lay off a lot of the day-to-day operating
responsibilities to folks like Ferold Arend and Ron Mayer in the
early days, later on to Jack Shewmaker, and eventually to David
Glass and Don Soderquist. So my role has been to pick good
people and give them the maximum authority and responsibility.

I've been asked if I was a hands-on manager or an arm's-
length type. I think really I'm more of a manager by walking and
flying around, and in the process I stick my fingers into everything I can to see how it's coming along. I've let our executives
make their decisions—and their mistakes—but I've critiqued and
advised them. My appreciation for numbers has kept me close to
our operational statements, and to all the other information we
have pouring in from so many different places. In that sense, I
think my style as an executive has been pretty much dictated by
my talents. I've played to my strengths and relied on others to
make up for my weaknesses.

As I mentioned, I found out early that one of my talents is
remembering numbers. I can't recall names and a lot of other
things as well as I would like to. But numbers just stick with me,
and always have. That's why I come in every Saturday morning
usually around two or three, and go through all the weekly numbers. I steal a march on everybody else for the Saturday morning
meeting. I can go through those sheets and look at a store, and
even though I haven't been there in a while, I can remind myself
of something about it, the manager maybe, and then I can remember later that they are doing this much business this week and
that their wage cost is such and such. I do this with each store

every Saturday morning. It usually takes about three hours, but when I'm done I have as good a feel for what's going on in the company as anybody here—maybe better on some days.

But if you asked me am I an organized person, I would have to say flat out no, not at all. Being organized would really slow me down. In fact, it would probably render me helpless. I try to keep track of what I'm supposed to do, and where I'm supposed to be, but it's true I don't keep much of a schedule. I think my way of operating has more or less driven Loretta Boss, and later Becky Elliott, my two secretaries, around the bend. My style is pretty haphazard.

LORETTA BOSS PARKER, PERSONAL SECRETARY
FOR TWENTY-FIVE YEARS:

"He has *always* been like this. His mind works ten times faster than everybody else's. I mean he just gets going and stays two or three jumps ahead, and he's quick to go with what's on his mind. If he gets something in his mind that needs to be done —regardless of what else might have been planned—the new idea takes priority, and it has to be done now. Everybody has their day scheduled, and then *bang!* He just calls a meeting on something.

"In the early years, this caused a number of embarrass-ments. I would make appointments for him and then tell him about them—we kept two calendars, one on his desk and one on mine—but he would just totally forget. I've had people fly in here from Dallas all set to see him. I'd come in at 8 A.M. to meet them and find out he had flown out of town at 5 A.M. without telling anybody where he was going. I would just have to look at this man from Dallas and say, 'He's gone.' So after a few times like that, I finally said, 'I'm not going to make appointments for you anymore.' And he said, 'Well, that's probably best.' Then he would make his own appoint-ments and forget about them, and I was still the one who had to give them the bad news. I couldn't organize him in a quarter of a century, and I don't think anyone else is ever going to."

Except for reading my numbers on Saturday morning and going to our regular meetings, I don't have much of a routine for anything else. I always carry my little tape recorder on trips, to record ideas that come up in my conversations with the associates. I usually have my yellow legal pad with me, with a list of ten or fifteen things we need to be working on as a company. My list drives the executives around here crazy, but it's probably one of my more important contributions.

DAVID GLASS:

"When Sam feels a certain way, he is relentless. He will just wear you out. He will bring up an idea, we'll all discuss it and then decide maybe that it's not something we should be doing right now—or ever. Fine. Case closed. But as long as he is convinced that it is the right thing, it just keeps coming up— week after week after week—until finally everybody capitulates and says, well, it's easier to do it than to keep fighting this fight. I guess it could be called management by wearing you down."

One way I've managed to keep up with everything on my plate is by coming in to the office really early almost every day, even when I don't have those Saturday numbers to look over. Four-thirty wouldn't be all that unusual a time for me to get started down at the office. That early morning time is tremendously valuable: it's uninterrupted time when I think and plan and sort things out. I write my letters and my articles for *Wal-Mart World,* our company newsletter.

A. L. JOHNSON, VICE CHAIRMAN, WAL-MART:

"I think one of Sam's greatest strengths is that he is totally unpredictable. He is always his own person, totally independent in his thinking. As a result, he is not a rubber-stamp manager. He never rubber-stamps anything for anyone.

"Back when I was general merchandise manager, we didn't have much computer support. So every Friday morning for six years, I would take my columnar pad with all the numbers on it into Sam's office for him to review. Every morning that I went through those numbers, Sam would jot them down on his own pad and work through all the calculations himself. I never felt that he didn't trust my judgment. He just felt that it was his function to make sure of everything. Sometimes he would work the numbers a little differently from the way I had, or argue with some of my conclusions, which kept me on my toes. The point is: I always knew I could not just go in there and lay a sheet of numbers in front of him and expect him to just accept it.

"As famous as Sam is for being a great motivator—and he deserves even more credit than he's gotten for that—he is equally good at checking on the people he has motivated. You might call his style: management by looking over your shoulder."

I'm always asked if there ever came a point, once we got rolling, when I knew what lay ahead. I don't think that I did. All I knew was that we *were* rolling and that we were successful. We enjoyed it, and it looked like something we could continue. We had found a concept, certainly, that the customers liked. Even back then, I always said at the first sign of it getting out of control, the first time our numbers don't come through as they should, we will pull in and put our arms around what we've built. Up to this point, of course, we haven't had to do it.

FEROLD AREND:

"The truth is, we were working with a great idea. It was really easy to develop discounting in those small communities before things got competitive. There wasn't a lot of competition for us in the early days because nobody was discounting in the small communities. So when we discounted items, it was just an unheard-of concept outside the larger towns. The customers, of course, weren't dumb. They had friends and relatives in the cities, and they had visited places where discounters were operating, so when they saw this happening in their town, well, shoot, they just *flocked* to our stores to take advantage of it."

I guess Ferold is right about the competition—if you're talking strictly about discounters. But there's a paradox here that I think confused a lot of folks about us for a long time. For twenty years back East, they always said Wal-Mart never had any competition, and that we wouldn't know what to do with it when it hit us. They forgot that we had come out of the variety store business, and that the heartland was the home ground for practically all the regional variety chains that developed in the U.S. In our Ben Franklin days, we had all the competition you could ever want from Sterling and TG&Y and Kuhn's and all those other regionals. So while we may not have had any competition for discounting in those little towns, we weren't strangers to competition. We were always looking at Gibson's and any other regionals that might decide to come our way, and we knew what to do when they did: keep our prices as low as possible by keeping our costs as low as possible.

Managing that whole period of growth was the most exciting time of all for me personally. Really, there has never been anything quite like it in the history of retailing. It was the retail equivalent of a real gusher: the whole thing, as they say in Oklahoma and Texas, just sort of blowed. We were bringing great folks on board to help make it happen, but at that time, I was involved in every phase of the business: merchandising, real estate, construction, studying the competition, arranging the financing, keeping the books—everything. We were all working untold hours, and we were tremendously excited about what was going on. I'm not sure we even had time to realize just how phenomenal our growth rate in the seventies would look on a chart years later:

	STORES	SALES
1970	32	$ 31 million
1972	51	$ 78 million
1974	78	$ 168 million
1976	125	$ 340 million
1978	195	$ 678 million
1980	276	$ 1.2 billion

In the early seventies, we had formed this cooperative research group among some of us discounters—mostly regionals—who didn't compete with one another. Comparing notes with them made me realize just what an amazing performance Wal-Mart was turning in. I remember they were just astonished. They could not believe we could be establishing the number of stores that we were. We would be putting in fifty stores a year, when most of our group would be trying to start three, four, five, or six a year. It always confounded them. They would always ask, "How do you do it? There's no way you can be doing that."

But we *were* doing it. We just stayed on top of it, and, along with increasing our sales, we increased our profitability—from $1.2 million in 1970, to $41 million in 1980. On paper, we really had no right to do what we did. We were all pounding sand, and stretching our people and our talents to the absolute maximum. And don't get me wrong: I'm not saying we didn't have our share of growing pains.

FEROLD AREND:

"More than anything else, we had manpower problems— finding good people and getting them trained in a hurry. Because we always ran a real tight organization, we had no excess people in the stores so they had to get real good real fast. Back when I had been at Hested's, and at Newberry's, too, a guy had to have ten years' experience before we'd even consider him to be what we called a manager-in-training. Down here, Sam would take people with hardly any retail experience, give them six months with us, and if he thought they showed any real potential to merchandise a store and manage people, he'd give them a chance. He'd make them an assistant manager. They were the ones who would go around and open all the new stores, and they would be next in line to manage their own store. In my opinion, most of them weren't anywhere near ready to run stores, but Sam proved me wrong there. He finally convinced me. If you take someone who lacks the experience and the know-how but has the real desire and the willingness to work his tail off to get the job done, he'll make up for what he lacks. And that proved true nine times out of ten. It was one way we were able to grow so fast."

We were trying to put in as many merchandising programs as we could and give our stores as much support as possible during all this growth, but in the early seventies, that Wal-Mart manager was still pretty much out there on his own when it came to promoting items and moving the merchandise.

THOMAS JEFFERSON, EARLY WAL-MART DISTRICT MANAGER, HIRED FROM STERLING STORES, LATER OPERATIONS MANAGER:

"Several times a year, most stores would have a big sidewalk promotion. In those days, we sold about as much merchandise off the sidewalks on weekends as we sold inside the store. You know, we'd rope off part of the parking lot, get a band, and have maybe a boatload sale. We would take our boats—we sold these John boats—put them up on sawhorses, and dump one item into each boat. We'd put big signs up calling them Boatload Sales. They still have sidewalk promotions today, but not like we once did. It doesn't work that well anymore."

While all this was going on in the early seventies, Ferold Arend and Ron Mayer and Bob Thornton and myself were still trying to get a handle on how to distribute to a growing number of stores in these small towns off the beaten path. It was one of those things that used to drive me crazy. I was always walking through the warehouse in Bentonville saying, "Where does this go?" "Who bought this?" "We've got too much of that!" Meanwhile, the guys out in the stores would be crying for this stuff, and we couldn't get it out to them. I remember being very nervous when everybody decided we needed to buy our own trucks, but we did it. We had two tractors and four trailers, and the folks in the warehouse got to where they thought we needed four tractors and six trailers. I thought that was pretty extreme. So word would get out that I was coming out to the warehouse, and if they had an extra tractor or trailer sitting idle, they would haul it around to the other side of the building and hide it so I wouldn't know we had anything empty.

THOMAS JEFFERSON:

"The faster we grew, the further behind we fell. We were always behind with our distribution. We never opened a warehouse soon enough, and we always had too many stores to service before the warehouse would get opened. Nowadays, I think they stay about one and a half distribution centers out front of demand, but back then we had a terrible time getting the freight to the stores. So we were renting outside warehouses, which were very expensive to operate, and we just had more than we could handle. Sometimes we would have five hundred trailers full of merchandise sitting around one of those warehouses. And it took time to deal with all that. We couldn't get it out. Then the next day we'd get sixty boxcar loads. We'd have to unload the doggoned boxcars, and here the merchandise they wanted in the stores would be sitting there sometimes a week or a week and a half."

It was a big problem, and one that worried me a lot, which is probably why as we moved along in the seventies, I just kept after folks like David Glass, who was still in the discount drug business up in Missouri, and Don Soderquist, who was running Ben Franklin, to come to work for us. I knew they were both big talents, and I knew we were going to need all the help we could get in all areas—but especially in the ones I wasn't all that great at, such as distribution and systems. Like I said before, Ron Mayer had worked hard on that distribution system, introducing all the concepts like merchandise assembly, cross-docking, and transship-ment. But I don't think our distribution system ever really got under complete control until David Glass finally relented and came on board in 1976. More than anybody else, he's responsible for building the sophisticated and efficient system we use today.

While Ron and Ferold were helping me run the company, and well before David joined us in the mid-seventies, Jack Shew-maker was coming on strong as a big talent. He had done a fantastic job in opening stores. Jack had been the manager of a Kroger SuperCenter which was a concept combining groceries and general merchandise not unlike our own supercenters today. So he had been a merchant, but he wasn't overly experienced when I hired him. He was in that first wave of college men I had started to hire, and, being a graduate of Georgia Tech, he had that engineer's love of systems and organization that we were still badly in need of. By now, I was really surrounding myself with guys who were good at all the things I tended to just sluff off, like organizing the company to handle the growth explosion we had started. If I hadn't gone after those folks, and kept on doing it, we would have come apart somewhere there in the seventies, or we certainly wouldn't have been able to pull off our really incredible expansion in the eighties. Getting an early start on all these sys-tems, building a foundation for our distribution center develop-ment, starting to put data processing into the stores, really saved our bacon later on.

JACK SHEWMAKER:

"Sam and Ferold called me in one day and said, 'We under-stand you've got some experience in writing policy manuals.' I had written some for both Kroger and Coast-to-Coast Hardware Stores out of Minneapolis. So they said, 'We want you to come in and write up our policies and procedures for us.' I said, 'Well, that's nice, but that's not really what I would like to do. I want to work with the merchandising people.' And Sam said, 'Well, we would kind of like you to do it anyway. How long do you think it will take to do it?' I knew from experience it would take six months to a year to properly do this job. But I said, 'I'll do it in ninety days.' Sam replied, 'You've got sixty days.' Sam never wants to wait for anything. He has no patience. That was probably the meld between us. That bias toward action. Anyway, we published it —360 pages of it—in fifty-nine days."

As you'll see later, Jack may have been the most controversial guy we ever had in senior management, but he dove right into systematizing things, and he became a great merchant too.

THOMAS JEFFERSON:

"That whole period, Mayer's time of duty, and early Shewmaker, was when we really saw the systems and computers begin to come into our lives at the operations level—the store level. We had been using Class 5 cash registers in all our stores, old hand-crank jobs, you know, which were very slow. Ron talked Sam into buying Singer electric cash registers for the stores, which was a great idea because you couldn't really have run a business much longer without electric registers. Only trouble was those Singer registers turned out to be temperamental as hell. Al Miles was the only manager we had who ever really figured out how to work one. So Mayer had the right idea but the wrong register.

"As for in-store computers, you'd have to give Shewmaker the credit for that. Not many of us gave in-store computers much thought. But Shewmaker studied all that stuff, and we would run with whatever he talked Sam into putting in the stores. It seems like we tried to better ourselves with some new gadget every year. That was the beginning of what turned into Wal-Mart's communications system, I guess. But most of us were too busy in the stores to even think about where it was all leading."

As we moved along in the seventies, we had very definitely become an effective retail entity, and we had set the stage for the even more phenomenal growth that was going to follow. It's amazing that our competitors didn't catch on to us quicker and try harder to stop us. Whenever we put a Wal-Mart store into a town, customers would just flock to us from the variety stores. It didn't take those stores long to figure out that if they were going to stay in business against this thing Wal-Mart had created, they were going to have to go into it themselves. And most of them did eventually convert to discounting. Kuhn's Big K became a discount chain. Sterling launched its Magic Mart discount chain. And Duckwall went into discounting.

Now, most of these guys already had distribution centers and systems in place, while we had to build one from scratch. So on paper we really didn't stand a chance. What happened was that they didn't really commit to discounting. They held on to their old variety store concepts too long. They were so accustomed to getting their 45 percent markup, they never let go. It was hard for them to take a blouse they'd been selling for $8.00, and sell it for $5.00, and only make 30 percent. With our low costs, our low expense structures, and our low prices, we were ending an era in the heartland. We shut the door on variety store thinking.

CHAPTER 9

BUILDING THE PARTNERSHIP

"What you've created here is better than communism, better than socialism could ever be, better even than capitalism. I like to call what you've got here 'enlightened consumerism,' where everybody works together as a team and the customer is finally king again."

—PAUL HARVEY,
radio commentator and guest
at a Wal-Mart year-end meeting

As much as we love to talk about all the elements that have gone into Wal-Mart's success—merchandising, distribution, technology, market saturation, real estate strategy—the truth is that none of that is the real secret to our unbelievable prosperity. What has carried this company so far so fast is the relationship that we, the managers, have been able to enjoy with our associates. By "associates" we mean those employees out in the stores and in the distribution centers and on the trucks who generally earn an hourly wage for all their hard work. Our relationship with the associates is a partnership in the truest sense. It's the only reason our company has been able to consistently outperform the competition—and even our own expectations.

Now, I would love to tell you that this partnership was all part of my master plan from the beginning, that as a young man I had some sort of vision of a great retailing company in which all the employees would be awarded a stake in the business. That I saw them having the opportunity to participate in many of the decisions that would determine the profitability of that business. I would love to tell you that from the very beginning we always paid our employees better than anyone else paid theirs, and treated them as equals. I would love to tell you all that, but unfortunately none of it would be true.

In the beginning, I was so chintzy I really didn't pay my employees very well. The managers were fine. From the time we started branching out into more stores, we always had a partnership with the store managers. Those guys I've already told you about, like Willard Walker and Charlie Baum and Charlie Cate, all had a piece of their stores' profits from the beginning. But we really didn't do much for the clerks except pay them an hourly wage, and I guess that wage was as little as we could get by with at the time. In fairness to myself, though, that was pretty much the way retail was in those days, especially in the independent variety store part of the business.

CHARLIE BAUM:

"When I took over the store in Fayetteville, which would have been May of 1955, Sam was paying the girls fifty cents an hour. After that first paycheck went out, I thought about it and decided, 'This is for the birds.' So the next week I raised them to seventy-five cents an hour, and I got a telephone call from Sam. He said, 'Charlie, we don't give raises of a quarter an hour. We give them a nickel an hour.' But I didn't cut back. I stayed with the seventy-five cents because those girls were earning it. We were a high-volume store for those days, making pretty good money."

I don't remember being *that* tight, but I guess Charlie's got it about right. We didn't pay much. It wasn't that I was intentionally heartless. I wanted everybody to do well for themselves. It's just that in my very early days in the business, I was so doggoned competitive, and so determined to do well, that I was blinded to the most basic truth, really the principle that later became the foundation of Wal-Mart's success. You see, no matter how you slice it in the retail business, payroll is one of the most important parts of overhead, and overhead is one of the most crucial things you have to fight to maintain your profit margin. That was true then, and it's still true today. Back then, though, I was so obsessed with turning in a profit margin of 6 percent or higher that I ignored some of the basic needs of our people, and I feel bad about it.

The larger truth that I failed to see turned out to be another of those paradoxes—like the discounters' principle of the less you charge, the more you'll earn. And here it is: the more you share profits with your associates—whether it's in salaries or incentives or bonuses or stock discounts—the more profit will accrue to the company. Why? Because the way management treats the associates is exactly how the associates will then treat the customers. And if the associates treat the customers well, the customers will return again and again, and *that* is where the real profit in this business lies, not in trying to drag strangers into your stores for one-time purchases based on splashy sales or expensive advertising. Satisfied, loyal, repeat customers are at the heart of Wal-Mart's spectacular profit margins, and those customers are loyal to us because our associates treat them better than salespeople in other stores do. So, in the whole Wal-Mart scheme of things, the most important contact ever made is between the associate in the store and the customer.

I didn't catch on to that idea for quite a while. In fact, the biggest single regret in my whole business career is that we didn't include our associates in the initial, managers-only profit-sharing plan when we took the company public in 1970. But there was nobody around preaching that philosophy in those days, and I guess I was just too worried about my own debt, and in too big a hurry to get somewhere fast. Today, some of our company's critics would like everybody to believe we started our profit-sharing program and other benefits merely as a way to stave off union organizing. The traditional version of what happened is that the Retail Clerks Union organized a strike against us when we opened store number 20 in Clinton, Missouri, and another one when we opened store number 25 in Mexico, Missouri, and that in response to those troubles we started all these programs to keep the unions out.

That story is only partly true. We did have labor trouble in those two stores, and we did fight the unions—legally and above-board—and we won. In fact, we've never lost a union organizing election. But the idea for sharing profits and benefits had come up even before we went public, not from me, but from Helen.

HELEN WALTON:

"We were on a trip, driving someplace, and we were talking about the high salary that Sam was earning, and about all the money and benefits that he was paying the officers of the company in order to keep his top people. He explained that the people in the stores didn't get any of those benefits, and I think it was the first time I realized how little the company was doing for them. I suggested to him that unless those people were on board, the top people might not last long either. I remember it because he didn't really appreciate my point of view at that time. Later on, I could tell he was thinking about it, and when he bought it, he really bought it."

It may be true that our skirmishes with the Retail Clerks and some other unions along the way—construction unions at our building sites, and the Teamsters at our distribution centers—helped hurry along our thinking in this direction. The unions, who don't seem to like our company much—maybe because they've never had any luck organizing us—want everyone to believe they're the only reason we've ever done anything good for any of our associates. The truth is, once we started experimenting with this idea of treating our associates as partners, it didn't take long to realize the enormous potential it had for improving our business. And it didn't take the associates long to figure out how much better off they would be as the company did better.

I have always believed strongly that we don't need unions at Wal-Mart. Theoretically, I understand the argument that unions try to make, that the associates need someone to represent them and so on. But historically, as unions have developed in this country, they have mostly just been divisive. They have put management on one side of the fence, employees on the other, and themselves in the middle as almost a separate business, one that depends on division between the other two camps. And divisiveness, by breaking down direct communication, makes it harder to take care of customers, to be competitive, and to gain market share. The partnership we have at Wal-Mart—which includes profit sharing, incentive bonuses, discount stock purchase plans, and a genuine effort to involve the associates in the business so we can all pull together—works better for both sides than any situation I know of involving unions. I'm not saying we pay better than anybody, though we're certainly competitive in our industry and in the regions where we're operating; we have to be if we want to attract and keep good people. But over the long haul, our associates build value for themselves—financially and otherwise— by believing in the company and keeping it headed in the right direction. Together, we have ridden this thing pretty darned far.

On the other hand, let me say this: anytime we have ever had real trouble, or the serious possibility of a union coming into the company, it has been because management has failed, because we have not listened to our associates, or because we have mistreated them. I think anytime the employees at a company say they need a union, it's because management has done a lousy job of managing and working with their people. Usually, it's directly traceable to what's going on at the line supervisor level—something stupid that some supervisor does, or something good he or she doesn't do. That was our problem at Clinton and at Mexico. Our managers didn't listen. They weren't as open with their folks as they should have been. They didn't communicate with them, they didn't share with them, and consequently, we got in trouble.

We fought those situations using pretty traditional methods. We hired a good labor lawyer, John Tate, who has won a lot of organizing battles over the years, and who has since joined our company. His advice helped me become even more determined to change the relationship between management and the associates at Wal-Mart: take care of your people, treat them well, involve them, and you won't spend all your time and money hiring labor lawyers to fight the unions. Right after those confrontations, John helped us conduct a management seminar down at Tan-Tar-A resort in Missouri, and soon thereafter we launched a program called "We Care" designed to let the associates know that when they had problems, we wanted them to come to management and give us a chance to solve them. Our message became "Sure, we are a nonunion company, but we think we are stronger because of it. And because you are our partner, we have an open door, and we listen to you, and together we can work out our problems." The union, of course, would argue more along the line of "Hey, we can get you a $3.00-an-hour raise. Why don't you strike?"

There's been all sorts of debate over why we chose to call our employees "associates," and everybody and his brother takes credit for it. I don't know. Maybe they're right. But the way I remember it is pretty simple. First of all, in my day, James Cash Penney had called his hourly employees "associates," and I guess I always had that idea in the back of my head. But the idea to try it at Wal-Mart actually occurred to me on a trip to England.

HELEN WALTON:

"We were on a tennis vacation to England. We were there to see Wimbledon. One day, we were walking down a street in London, and Sam, of course, stopped to look at a store—he always stopped to look in stores wherever we went—anywhere in the world, it didn't matter. On that same trip, we lost a lot of our things in Italy when thieves broke into the car while he was looking at a big discount store. Anyway, he stopped at this one English retailing company, and I remember him saying, 'Look at that sign. That is great. That's what we should do.' "

It was Lewis Company, J. M. Lewis Partnership. They had a partnership with all their associates listed up on the sign. For some reason that whole idea really excited me: a partnership with all our associates. As soon as we got home, we started calling our store workers "associates" instead of employees. That may not sound like any big deal to some folks, and they're right. It wouldn't have meant a thing if we hadn't taken other actions to make it real, to make it something other than window dressing. The decision we reached around that time, to commit ourselves to giving the associates more equitable treatment in the company, was without a doubt the single smartest move we ever made at Wal-Mart.

In 1971, we took our first big step: we corrected my big error of the year before, and started a profit-sharing plan for all the associates. I guess it's the move we made that I'm proudest of, for a number of reasons. Profit sharing has pretty much been the carrot that's kept Wal-Mart headed forward. Every associate of the company who has been with us at least a year, and who works at least 1,000 hours a year, is eligible for it. Using a formula based on profit growth, we contribute a percentage of every eligible associate's wages to his or her plan, which the associate can take when they leave the company—either in cash or Wal-Mart stock. There's nothing that unusual about the structure of the plan. It's the performance I'm so proud of. For the last ten years, the company contributed an average of 6 percent of wages to the plan. Last year, for example, Wal-Mart's contribution was $125 million. Now, the folks who administer profit sharing—and this includes a committee of associates—have chosen year after year to keep the plan invested mostly in Wal-Mart stock, so the thing has grown beyond belief, collectively, and in the individual accounts of a lot of associates. Today, as I write this, profit sharing has around $1.8 billion in it—equity in the company that belongs to our associate partners.

BOB CLARK, WAL-MART TRUCK DRIVER,
BENTONVILLE, ARKANSAS:

"I went to work for Mr. Walton in 1972, when he only had sixteen tractors on the road. The first month, I went to a drivers' safety meeting, and he always came to those. There were about fifteen of us there, and I'll never forget, he said, 'If you'll just stay with me for twenty years, I guarantee you'll have $100,000 in profit sharing.' I thought, 'Big deal. Bob

Clark never will see that kind of money in his life.' I was worrying about what I was making right then. Well, last time I checked, I had $707,000 in profit sharing, and I see no reason why it won't go up again. I've bought and sold stock over the years, and used it to build on to my home and buy a whole bunch of things. When folks ask me how I like working for Wal-Mart, I tell them I drove for another big company for thirteen years—one they've all heard of—and left with $700. Then I tell them about my profit sharing and ask them, 'How do you think I feel about Wal-Mart?' "

GEORGIA SANDERS, RETIRED HOURLY ASSOCIATE, WAL-MART NO. 12, CLAREMORE, OKLAHOMA:

"I started out in April 1968, and worked as a department head in cameras, electronics, and small appliances. In the beginning, I made $1.65 an hour, minimum wage. In 1989, when I retired, I was making $8.25 an hour. I took $200,000 in profit sharing when I left, and we invested it pretty well, I think. We've done a lot of traveling, bought a new car, and we still have more money than we started with. Over the years, I bought and sold some Wal-Mart stock, and it split a lot. I bought my mom a house off some of that money. For me, Wal-Mart was just a great place to work."

JOYCE MCMURRAY, DISTRICT OFFICE TRAINER AT WAL-MART STORE NO. 54 IN SPRINGDALE, ARKANSAS:

"I live and breathe Wal-Mart. Sam always gives so much to the associates, I want to give as much as I can back in return. I got my fifteen-year pin from him personally. I've had the maximum taken out of my check for stock purchases, and I've bought some on the outside too. You cannot imagine how my profit sharing has increased. This year my profit sharing amounts to $475,000. I had originally planned to retire this year, take my bundle and bail out. But I'm only forty, and I've decided to hang in here for a while. I'm not sure what we'll do with the money. It's for retirement, of course. But I think we'll also buy a piano and maybe someday build our dream house. But I'm keeping this stock a long time."

JEAN KELLEY, ASSOCIATE IN THE GENERAL OFFICE, WHERE SHE SUPERVISES CARGO CLAIMS:

"I grew up on a farm in Mexico, Missouri, and went to work in store number 25 there when I was twenty years old. When I came to Bentonville, there were nine people in the traffic department, and now there are sixty-one of us. My brother tried to talk me into quitting back in the beginning. He said I could go anywhere other than Wal-Mart and make more an hour. Well, in 1981 I had $8,000 in profit sharing. In 1991, I had $228,000. I told my brother to show me anywhere else I could go and do that, and I would change jobs. If you have faith in this company, it's amazing how your loyalty pays off. I'm so glad I stuck to it. My money is going to send my daughter, Ashley, to college."

Those are some of my partners, and we've come a long way together. About the same time we started profit sharing, we cranked up a lot of other financial partnership programs. We've got an employee stock purchase plan so associates can buy stock through payroll deductions at a discount of 15 percent off market value. Today, more than 80 percent of our associates own Wal-Mart stock, either through profit sharing or on their own, and personally I figure most of the other 20 percent either haven't qualified for profit sharing yet, or haven't been with us long enough to catch on. Over the years, we've also had a variety of incentive and bonus plans to keep every associate involved in the business as partners.

One of the most successful bonuses has been our shrink incentive plan, which demonstrates the partnership principle as well as any I know beyond just straight profit sharing. As you may know, shrinkage, or unaccounted-for inventory loss—theft, in other words—is one of the biggest enemies of profitability in the retail business. So in 1980, we decided the best way to control the problem was to share with the associates any profitability the company gained by reducing it. If a store holds shrinkage below the company's goal, every associate in that store gets a bonus that could be as much as $200. This is sort of competitive information, but I can tell you that our shrinkage percentage is about half the industry average. Not only that, it helps our associates feel better about each other, and themselves. Most people don't enjoy stealing, even the ones who will do it if given the opportunity. And most associates don't want to think that they're working alongside anyone who does enjoy stealing. So under a plan like this, where you're directly rewarded for honesty, there's a real incentive to keep from ignoring any customers who might want to walk off with something, or, worse, to allow any of your fellow associates to fall into that trap. Everybody working in that store becomes a partner in trying to stop shrinkage, and when they succeed, they —along with the company in which they already hold stock— share in the reward.

It all sounds simple enough. And the theories really are pretty basic. None of this leads to a true partnership unless your managers understand the importance of the associates to the whole process and execute it sincerely. Lip service won't make a real partnership—not even with profit sharing. Plenty of companies offer some kind of profit sharing but share absolutely no sense of partnership with their employees because they don't really believe those employees are important, and they don't work to lead them. These days, the real challenge for managers in a business like ours is to become what we call servant leaders. And when they do, the team—the manager and the associates—can accomplish anything.

Many people have predicted for years that Wal-Mart would lose its way once we got to the tough challenges of real urban environments. Supposedly, our approach just won't work in neighborhoods with disenfranchised citizens and underprivileged people who have never been winners. The Wal-Mart way can't reach folks who have been thieves, and who for the most part haven't felt much pride in their lives. But I want to tell you about a visit I made to a store near Dallas a couple of years ago: store number 880 in Irving, Texas. The store has a very young and very ethnic work force and customer base. And our manager there was doing a terrible job with his people. I think maybe he just said to himself, "Well, they're young and they're poor whites and blacks and Mexicans, and they're just going to steal, and I can't do anything about it." So he was not, very definitely not, being a servant leader.

This store was as bad off as any Wal-Mart I've ever seen. It had the highest shrinkage of any Wal-Mart ever—around 6 percent, which for us is unheard of. The store was losing more than a half-million dollars a year, and we thought we ought to close it. But we had a real maverick named Ed Nagy, who was then a district manager. Ed's a fella who's always stepping on toes or breaking one rule or another. He's constantly in trouble, and he likes to try new things, and, I have to admit, he reminds me a bit of myself as a youngster. He goes into that store, and he has a talk with the store manager, and he starts training the department heads. And he sets some realistic goals for these folks. And he starts giving them some motivational talks, explaining how we're different from other companies and they're really missing out on something by not participating.

Then he finds out that the associates are just stealing rampant throughout the store, and letting the customers steal too because no one has set any controls. No one was checking on the refunds. No one was checking on the layaways. No one was even checking on the cash registers. If you wanted to steal, you knew you wouldn't get caught. So they started checking on all those things, and they started talking about integrity, and they talked about improving sales. Within a year and a half, this store was turned around completely. The shrink was down to 2 percent. It started turning a profit, and when I went in there to visit I think it was one of the proudest moments I've had in forty years of visiting almost two thousand stores. It was just an unbelievable job of an action-oriented, right-thinking motivator stepping in and saving a horrible situation.

Now, why did it work? Well, for one thing, Nagy—the district manager—took a lot of the department managers out of that store, out of that losing environment, and got them to rubbing shoulders with some of the folks from the successful stores in his district. They had a weekend meeting, and they talked about their departments, and he made these folks participate. Then he had them set their own goals. And maybe while they were having lunch with these winners from the other stores, maybe they started to dream a little and think a little about how they could improve the mess they were in. He and the other managers talked about the numbers with them and began to show them how their jobs and decisions related to those numbers, so they would care about whether their sales were up and not just stand there going through the motions. They began to learn a little about merchandising.

But here's the best part. When they put in their controls to try and stop the stealing, they started checking every empty box that left the back door. Well, one day they found a big box—a baby buggy box—that had $400 worth of tapes in it, and they caught the guy at the door with it. So they had a meeting the next morning, and the manager talked about the woman who discovered the box and caught the thief, and she was a hero. Everybody gave her a big round of applause. The culture was turning around there, in a short period of time. I learned this early on in the variety store business: you've got to give folks responsibility, you've got to trust them, and then you've got to check on them.

It's true that we have more difficulty in the cities with our approach. We have more trouble coming up with educated people who want to work in our industry, or with people of the right moral character and integrity. Folks in small towns in Iowa and Mississippi are more likely to want to work for what we can pay than folks in Houston or Dallas or St. Louis. And, yes, they're probably more likely to buy our philosophy in the country than they are in the city. But let me tell you this: a smart, motivational, good manager can work what some outsiders call Wal-Mart magic with folks anywhere. It may take more time. You may have to sift through more people, and you may have to become more skilled with your hiring practices. But I truly believe that people anywhere will eventually respond to the same sorts of motivational techniques we use—if they are treated right and are given the opportunities to be properly trained. If you're good to people, and fair with them, and demanding of them, they will eventually decide you're on their side.

And I want to tell you something else: Wal-Mart is not a big success merely because we grew up out here in the country, where people are just naturally friendly and therefore make great retail employees. It's true that we have many fine associates from the country, but they have had to enter our culture and learn retailing just like anybody else, and we have spent a good deal of time teaching many of them to overcome their natural shyness and learn to speak up and help our customers. So I think some folks outside our company may be putting a little too much emphasis on the supposed low quality of workers in the city, and not enough emphasis on the failure of some managers to do their jobs in getting those workers going in the right direction. Years ago, if we hadn't done so well, some of these folks might have said you could never build a retailing empire in small-town America because you wouldn't be able to attract a work force that was sophisticated enough.

Another important ingredient that has been in the Wal-Mart partnership from the very beginning has been our very unusual willingness to share most of the numbers of our business with all the associates. It's the only way they can possibly do their jobs to the best of their abilities—to know what's going on in their business. If I was a little slow to pick up on sharing the profits, we were among the first in our industry—and are still way out front of almost everybody—with the idea of empowering our associates by running the business practically as an open book. I've always told people in the stores what was going on with the numbers. But after we decided to act like a partnership, we formalized the sharing of information to a much greater degree.

Sharing information and responsibility is a key to any partnership. It makes people feel responsible and involved, and as we've gotten bigger we've really had to accept sharing a lot of our numbers with the rest of the world as a consequence of sticking by our philosophy. Everything about us gets to the outside. In our individual stores, we show them their store's profits, their store's purchases, their store's sales, and their store's markdowns. We show them all that on a regular basis, and I'm not talking about just the managers and the assistant managers. We share that information with every associate, every hourly, every part-time employee in the stores. Obviously, some of that information flows to the street. But I just believe the value of sharing it with our associates is much greater than any downside there may be to sharing it with folks on the outside. It doesn't seem to have hurt us much so far. And, in fact, I've been reading lately that what we've been doing all along is part of one of the latest big trends in business these days: sharing, rather than hoarding, information.

All I know is that nothing ever makes me feel better than when I visit a store and some department head comes up to me with pride and shows me all her numbers and tells me she's number five in the company but she plans to be number one next year. I love meeting all these merchants we've got on our team out there. When they show me an endcap display they've got loaded up with charcoal or baby oil or lunch boxes and then tell me they chose that item because of its high profit margin, and then go on to brag about all the volume they've done with that item, I get so proud for them I can hardly stand it. I really mean that. It is just the proudest I get. Because if we, as managers, truly dedicate ourselves to instilling that thrill of merchandising—the thrill of buying and selling something at a profit—into every single one of our associate-partners, nothing can ever stop us.

BERNIE MARCUS, CHAIRMAN AND CO-FOUNDER, HOME DEPOT:

"We feel a great affinity for Sam and Wal-Mart because of the way they treat their people. He's such a great motivator. But the financial incentives have made a big difference too. We modeled our employee stock ownership plan after Sam's, and it worked for us as well.

"We look at his operation—with what, almost 400,000 people—and you walk in there, and they're all smiles. He proved that people can be motivated. The mountain is there, but somebody else has already climbed it.

"But if you ask Sam how's business, he's never satisfied.

He says, 'Bernie, things are really lousy. Our lines are too long at the cash registers. Our people aren't being helpful enough. I don't know what we're gonna do to get them motivated.' Then you ask some of these CEO's from other retail organizations who you know are on the verge of going out of business, and they brag and tell you how great everything is. Really putting on airs. Not Sam. He is down to earth and knows who he is.

"Without question, Sam Walton is one of the great all-time merchants. Period."

Keeping so many people motivated to do the best job possible involves a lot of the different programs and approaches we've developed at Wal-Mart over the years, but none of them would work at all without one simple thing that puts it all together: appreciation. All of us like praise. So what we try to practice in our company is to look for things to praise. Look for things that are going right. We want to let our folks know when they are doing something outstanding, and let them know they are important to us.

You can't praise something that's not done well. You can't be insincere. You have to follow up on things that aren't done well. There is no substitute for being honest with someone and letting them know they didn't do a good job. All of us profit from being corrected—if we're corrected in a positive way. But there's no better way to keep someone doing things the right way than by letting him or her know how much you appreciate their performance. If you do that one simple thing, human nature will take it from there.

ANDY SIMS, MANAGER, WAL-MART NO. 1, ROGERS, ARKANSAS:

"When I started working at Wal-Mart in West Texas, we would anticipate a store visit by the chairman with the same sense you get when you're going to meet a great athlete, or a movie star, or a head of state. But once he comes in the store, that feeling of awe is overcome by a sort of kinship. He is a master at erasing that 'larger-than-life' feeling that people have for him. How many heads of state always start the conversation by wanting to know what *you* think? What's on *your* mind?

"After a visit, everyone in the store has no doubt that he genuinely appreciates our contributions, no matter how insignificant. Every associate feels like he or she does make a difference. It's almost like having your oldest friend come just to see if you're okay. He never lets us down."

There is one more aspect to a true partnership that's worth mentioning: executives who hold themselves aloof from their associates, who won't listen to their associates when they have a problem, can never be true partners with them. Often, this is an exhausting and sometimes frustrating part of the management process, but folks who stand on their feet all day stocking shelves or pushing carts of merchandise out of the back room get exhausted and frustrated too, and occasionally they dwell on problems that they just can't let go of until they've shared it with somebody who they feel is in a position to find a solution. So, as big as we are, we have really tried to maintain an open-door policy at Wal-Mart.

DAVID GLASS:

"If you've ever spent any time around Wal-Mart, you may have noticed that it's not unusual for somebody in Philadelphia, Mississippi, to get in his pickup on the spur of the moment and drive to Bentonville, where you can find him sitting in the lobby waiting patiently to see the chairman. Now, really, how many chairmen of $50 billion companies do you know who are totally, 100 percent accessible to their hourly associates? I know lots of people in big companies who have never even seen their chairman, much less visited with him."

That's not to suggest that they always like what I have to say. I don't always solve their problems, and I can't always side with them just because they bring their situation to my attention. But if the associate happens to be right, it's important to overrule their manager, or whoever they're having the problem with because otherwise the open-door policy isn't any good to anybody. The associates would know pretty soon that it was just something we paid lip service to, but didn't really believe. If I'm going to fly around all over the country telling these folks they're my partners, I sure owe it to them to at least hear them out when they're upset about something.

DEAN SANDERS, EXECUTIVE VICE PRESIDENT OPERATIONS, WAL-MART:

"I've always felt that to Sam, the people in the stores—the managers and the associates—are the kings. He loves them. And there's no doubt they feel they have an open door to him. He'll go out on store visits, and when he gets back he'll call me and say, 'Give this boy a store to manage. He's ready.' Then I'll express some concern about the person's experience level or whatever, and he'll say, 'Give him one anyway. Let's see how he does.' The other thing, of course, is that he has absolutely no tolerance for managers mistreating the associates in the stores. When he finds something like that going on, he gets on us about it instantly."

So you see, when we say Wal-Mart is a partnership, we really believe it. Partnership involves money—which is crucial to any business relationship—but it also involves basic human considerations, such as respect. Wal-Mart is a spectacular example of what happens when 400,000 people come together as a group, with a real feeling of partnership, and are able, for the most part, to put the needs of their individual egos behind the needs of their team.

CHAPTER 10

STEPPING BACK

" 'Heaaah, Maggie!' Sam screams from the cab of his truck.
'Cumoon heaah tuhme!' Up top, Sam's friend, Royce Beall, a
department store owner from Jacksonville, Texas, chuckles.
'Listen to Sam a-hollerin',' he says. 'It don't do no good, but
he'll yell all day like that.' "

—*SOUTHPOINT* magazine,
February 1990

By the time 1974 rolled around, I have to admit we were
feeling pretty good about our accomplishments. By anybody's
standards, we had built a heck of a regional discount chain, with
just under 100 Wal-Marts open for business in eight states. We
were doing nearly $170 million in sales, with more than $6 million in profits. The stock had split twice, and we were on the
New York Stock Exchange. By now, everybody was sharing the
profits so the whole company was pumped up. Wall Street was
buying into our strategy, and whatever reservations anyone up
there might have had about me, they seemed to think pretty
highly of Ron Mayer and the rest of the management team we
had in place. At fifty-six, I was free and clear of debt. My net
worth was far greater than I had ever imagined it could be when I
started out in the retail business. Our kids were out of college and
starting up their own lives. I really don't see how I could have
reasonably expected much more out of life.

If I've given the impression so far that Wal-Mart has occupied most of my competitive energy over the years, that's not completely accurate. I've pursued my other passions all along, too, mostly quail hunting and tennis—and I pursued them both very competitively. A lot of businessmen seem to prefer golf, but I always thought it was a little too country club for me and it took up too much time and wasn't really competitive in the same way that tennis is, you know, in a give-and-take, head-to-head way.

HELEN WALTON:

"When we first met, Sam played golf, but he would get terribly frustrated when he made mistakes. Once, when he was in the Army, he was out playing with some of the officers, and I think their colonel was along that day. Sam had hit off into the woods. It made him so mad that he broke his club on a tree. So he came home that day, threw his clubs down, and said, 'I've had it with golf.' After that, it was mostly tennis for him."

I took my racket with me whenever I was flying, and I had friends to play with when I hit their towns. For some reason, I loved to play around noon—when the sun was hottest—and I guess I was pretty aggressive. I played regularly from the time we got to Bentonville until about two years ago, when my legs just couldn't cut it anymore.

GEORGE BILLINGSLEY, TENNIS PARTNER:

"For about ten years, Sam and I played tennis at high noon— usually on the court over at his house. I think he liked to play during lunch hour because he wouldn't dream of taking any of his associates away from their jobs to play. On the court, he was the most competitive player. He studied his opponents' games, and he knew our strengths and weaknesses as well as his own. If you hit a ball to Sam's forehand, that point was his. He would hit it crosscourt, and it was over.

"He loved the game. He never gave you a point, and he never quit. But he is a fair man. To him, the rules of tennis, the rules of business, and the rules of life are all the same, and he follows them. As competitive as he is, he was a wonderful tennis opponent—always gracious in losing and in winning. If he lost, he would say, 'I just didn't have it today, but you played marvelously.' "

LORETTA BOSS PARKER, POPULARLY KNOWN AS THE VICE PRESIDENT FOR TENNIS:
"If Mr. Walton was out on a trip, his idea of making a tennis date would be to radio our aviation department when he was a few minutes out from landing and have them phone me with a time. I would get the call at eleven, find him a partner, and he would be playing by noon."

So tennis became my outlet for organized competitive sport and exercise. But my real passion outside Wal-Mart has always been my bird hunting. I have to say it's probably my one self-indulgent activity. I loved it so much that I just made it part of my way of doing business from early on.

I never did that much quail hunting growing up, not until I met Helen's father, who was dead serious about it. Anytime I was around Claremore I loved to go out there and hunt with Mr. Robson, or Helen's brothers, Frank and Nick. Her dad and I were both much better than average shots, and we got to be pretty competitive over the hunting.

As I mentioned, Bentonville appealed to me because I could hunt quail seasons in four states. So during the season, I usually took off almost every day around three or four in the afternoon and went out to do a couple of hours' hunting. I had an old hunting car I'd haul my dogs in, and I'd go find a farm or ranch I wanted to hunt. I learned early that the best way to get invited back was to go ask permission and offer the owner a box of chocolate cherries from the store, or, if he preferred it, a take of the game I shot. I've hunted all over these hills and valleys around here.

JOHN WALTON:

"Until Dad was in his mid-sixties, I really had to struggle to keep up with him. I thought I was in pretty good shape, but my tendency is to kind of walk along, take it easy, and enjoy the outdoors. I'd look up, and Dad would be out of sight. He hunted like Sherman marched through Georgia."

When I asked permission to hunt, I always introduced myself as Sam Walton of Sam Walton's variety store down on the square in Bentonville, and I found that it really helped my business. When these farm folks would come to town to shop, they'd naturally do business with that fellow who hunted their land and brought them candy. I still meet folks today who tell me their father recalls me coming out to hunt their land in those days. As we began to expand, and I flew around more, I would throw the dogs in the plane with me so I could hunt between store visits.

I had some crazy times with those dogs out on the road. Usually I made them sleep in the trunk of the car, but if it was Ol' Roy, who was really more of a pet than a bird dog, I would let him sleep in my room with me—unbeknownst, I'm afraid, to the Holiday Inn folks. Once he got in a fight with a skunk, and I am ashamed to even think of what the next person to get my rental car must have thought happened in that thing. I held him by his hind legs and half drowned him trying to wash him off in this lake, but we found out you cannot wash skunk off a dog very easily.

Roy was probably the most overrated bird dog in history. He wasn't much of a hunter at all; he would point rabbits, for example. But the associates and the customers got a kick out of visiting with him in the stores, and once we put his name and picture on our private label dog food, it sold tons. Another thing about Roy that was very unusual: he was a great tennis dog. He would go with me to the tennis court and lay there, and whenever the ball went out of the court, over the fence, or whatever, he would go chasing after it and bring it back to me.

What I really love about hunting is the coordination and the training of the dogs. You have to develop a partnership with

them. You have to motivate them, and they have to do their work
reasonably well.

FROM *SOUTHPOINT* MAGAZINE, FEBRUARY 1990:

> " 'George! Cuminheaartuhme! You're about to get your butt
> shot, George,' Sam says. Then, to a companion: 'I think
> George might be a good one. He's hunting. He's got his nose
> into the wind, and he's hunting back and forth. He acts like
> he knows what he's doing. He may not, but he acts like he
> does. He backed the other dogs, and that was just purely
> instinctive. And a dog with me has to have some instincts.' "

I pride myself on being able to train my own dogs, and I've
never had a dog handler, like some of these country gentlemen
friends of mine. I enjoy picking out ordinary setter or pointer
pups and working with them—yanking them around and cor-
recting them and yelling at them and being patient with them.
They've got to learn to find the birds, and then they've got to
learn the discipline to hold them and wait for the hunter. I have
had some dogs I couldn't handle, and Mr. Robson made a specialty out of resurrecting my failures. He liked nothing better than
to take one of my cast-off dogs and fix it up, then give it back to
me.

As Aside from training the dogs, I like being outdoors in all kinds
of weather. When I'm out there, I'm not thinking about Wal-
Mart or Sam's or anything but where the next covey might be.
Also, some of my best friends are people who like to hunt quail.
I'm extremely prejudiced, but I feel like quail hunters are generally good sportsmen who've got a balanced respect for conservation and wildlife: things that I certainly value.

As good as the quail hunting is around home, Bud and I got
really taken with Texas quail hunting a few years back. We each
got leases on ranches way down in south Texas scrub country, not
too far north of the Rio Grande Valley. My place is about as
simple as they come; Bud's is a good bit fancier. His has a swimming pool.

SOUTHPOINT:

"Sam Walton's Campo Chapote is a rustic little cluster of trailer homes out in the vast middle of South Texas nowhere. This isn't the quail hunting of rich Southern gentry, the kind with white-coated servants and engraved Belgian shotguns and matched mules in silver harness hitched to mahogany dog wagons. Sam calls that variety 'South Georgia quail hunting,' and he's tried it, but it isn't really *him*. In case the *ambiente* of Campo Chapote hasn't sunk in yet, it is, to put it simply: 'All Things Not Trump.' This is a camp where your host hands you your towel, points you to a bedroom in the trailer, and explains: 'Don't let the noise in the ceiling worry you, it's just rats.' "

BUD WALTON:

"One time Sam and I got invited to a fancy quail hunt on one of those south Georgia plantations. They told us they'd pick us up at this landing strip. So we flew in there, and there were all these corporate jets lined up. Well, this guy in a Mercedes pulls up to get us. You should've seen the look on his face when Sam opened up the back of that plane, and his five dogs came flyin' out of there. They weren't expecting anybody to bring their own dogs. They had to haul them in that Mercedes."

As you can see, I'm not all work. I like to play as much as the next guy. And I have to admit, back around 1974 I was awfully tempted to take more time for myself, to step back and let Ron Mayer and the other guys run the company, while I went off to enjoy life. Around that same time, Helen and I went on some of our overseas trips, although I'm sure I spent most of my time over there nosing around stores and doing business.

So for the first time since I had begun retailing in 1945, I was beginning to back off from the business. I was getting slightly less involved in the day-to-day decisions and leaning a bit more on Ron Mayer and Ferold Arend—our two executive vice presidents. I was still chairman and CEO. Ferold, at age forty-five, ran merchandising, while Ron Mayer, who was only forty, ran finance and distribution. To handle the explosive growth, we were bringing on new people in the general office. Ron brought in a lot of people to handle data processing and finance and distribution.

What happened then is the one period in Wal-Mart's history that I am still the least comfortable talking about today. But everybody else has had their say on the subject so I'm going to explain the events the way I saw them unfold and be done with it.

As I look back on that period now, I realize I had split the company in half, setting up two factions which began to compete fiercely with one another. There was the old guard, including many of the store managers, remaining loyal to Ferold, and the new guard, many of whom owed their jobs to Ron. Pretty soon, everybody began to take sides, lining up behind either Ron or Ferold, who didn't get along at all. What I did next—which seems totally out of character for me—only compounded the problem tenfold.

Ferold had been valuable in organizing the company as we began to roll out stores, but because of all the technology and sophisticated systems we were needing, I really felt at the time that Ron was absolutely essential to the company's future. In addition to his ability, he had a lot of ambition. He made it pretty well known that his goal, which I respected, was to run a company, preferably Wal-Mart. He told me one day that if he couldn't run our company, he wanted to get out and run another one. So I thought about that for a few days, and I really worried that we were going to lose Ron. Then I said to myself, "Well, I'm getting pretty old, and we could probably work together. I'll let him be chairman and CEO, and I'll just enjoy myself, step back a little, and, of course, continue to visit stores."

So I became chairman of the Executive Committee. Ron became chairman and CEO of the company. Ferold became president. I moved out of my office down at the end of what they jokingly call "executive row," and let Ron have it. I moved into his office. I made up my mind to stay out of his way and let him run the company, telling myself that I would just check to see how he was getting along. Since I had really been letting other people operate the company day to day all along, I thought things would run real well this way.

Well, I was no more ready to retire in 1974 at the age of fifty-six than the Arkansas sun is ready to start rising out of Oklahoma in the morning. But for a while I did step back and take off a little more time. I'm sure to Ron Mayer it must have seemed like I never took off at all. The truth is, I failed at retirement worse than just about anything else I've ever tried. Actually, I knew it was a mistake almost right after I resigned the chairmanship. I tried to stay out of Ron's way. The problem was that I actually just kept doing exactly the same thing I had been doing all the time. I wanted to see my ideas keep flowing around the company, but I wanted Ron to be successful in operating the company and building an organization. Unfortunately, I just couldn't quite stay away from it to that degree. The situation was quite a burden for Ron, and would have been for any forty-year-old guy wanting to run his own company, I think.

Meanwhile, the house was dividing up against itself. A lot of the newer, younger guys were lining up on Ron's side, and the older bunch who ran the stores were backing Ferold. When I began to sense how deep this split really was, I got real agitated about it, and then I became even more involved in second-guessing everybody.

AL MILES, RETIRED EXECUTIVE VICE PRESIDENT, WAL-MART:

"There was this thing between Ron and Ferold. I wasn't too involved personally because I was out in the field then. But even out there it was very apparent that two camps were building up in the company. You know, you almost felt committed to say, Well, I'm on this team, or I'm on that team. We started seeing a looseness in our organization that had never been there, and things none of us liked were starting to happen regularly. The seriousness of running our stores and taking care of our people wasn't happening. And most of us district managers would get together and talk on the phone on Saturday mornings, and, you know, we thought we were going to hell in a handbasket. I'm not exaggerating. I mean we really did. Also, I remember that when Sam started spending more time in the office, he was very, very intense."

I kept hoping things would work out. And I should say this: Wal-Mart showed real good numbers during this whole period. It was never a question of mismanagement. What we had was a semiretired founder who didn't want to go away, on top of an old-line bunch of store managers at war with an ambitious young guy with big ideas of his own.

FEROLD AREND:

"That period right in there was the only negative I ever experienced in my whole time at the company, which is pretty remarkable in itself. Sam always felt the need for his people to compete with one another because he thought it brought out the best in them, and most of the time it did. But this was a situation that just didn't work. When he stepped aside, it created a tough situation for everybody. Ron's people were loyal to him, and mine were loyal to me. Sam was saying, 'I'll decide the things that need tiebreakers.' That turned out to be a lot more things than he had intended. So once he realized how badly things were really going, he did something about it."

I've always taken most of the blame for this mess I created. But it's also true that I didn't think Ron was handling some things as well as he should. I worried about his people skills, and I felt like the whole clique thing was really hurting our management at the store end, our most unusual strength. And I guess I was pretty unhappy too over some issues of what you'd call personal style— none of them really all that unusual in most corporate environments, but different from the way we had always done things around Wal-Mart.

I agonized over all this. I rarely lose sleep over crises at the office, but this time I did. I didn't want to disappoint Ron, didn't want to lose him. But the company was headed in the wrong direction. So finally I called him in one Saturday in June of 1976, thirty months after I had given up the chairman's job, and just said simply, "Well, Ron, I thought I was ready to step out, but I see that really I wasn't. I've been so involved that in a way it has put you under a real handicap." I told him I wanted to come back in as chairman and CEO, and have him assume another job—vice chairman and chief financial officer, I believe.

My proposal wasn't agreeable to Ron, and I can certainly understand why. He wanted to run the company, and when he couldn't he decided to leave us. Nobody believed it at the time, but although I was unhappy with some of the things going on under Ron's chairmanship, *real* unhappy with a few, I tried as hard as I could to convince him to stay and be part of our growth even though he couldn't be chairman and CEO anymore. I said, "Ron, we are going to miss you, we are going to need you, and I think we're going to suffer a lot because you're not here." I offered him everything to stay, but he felt it was time to go.

As disappointed and unhappy as he was, Ron said, "Sam, I know you're going to think that things are falling apart, and a lot of other people are going to think they're falling apart, but you've got such a strong field organization here, and such loyalty from the associates and the managers in those stores out there, and such loyal customers, and the company is so sound in its operating philosophies, that I think you'll just move right down the road." I appreciated his expressing that confidence in us. I know he meant it, and I'll never forget it.

In company lore, that incident became known as the "Saturday night massacre." What followed became known as "the exodus." First, a whole group of senior managers who had been part of Ron's team—our financial officer, our data processing manager, the guy who was running our distribution centers—all walked out behind him. You can imagine how Wall Street felt about that. A lot of folks wrote us off immediately. They thought, as they have through the years, that we just didn't have the management to hold the place together.

They assumed that Ron Mayer and all his folks were the reason we'd done well, and they just ignored all the basics we had in place, all our principles: keeping our costs down, teaching our associates to take care of our customers, and, frankly, just working our tails off.

Throughout all this turmoil, Jack Shewmaker, one of our brighter, brasher young talents, had been making strong contributions to the company, and I thought he might be just what we needed to get us back on track. But when I named him to be executive v.p. of operations, personnel, and merchandise—passing over some folks who were older and had been with us longer—a bunch more of our managers left. It was a real, bona fide exodus, and by the time it was over, I'll bet one third of our senior management was gone. For the first time in a long time, things looked pretty grim. And at that point, I have to admit I wasn't sure myself that we could just keep on going like before.

As I said back when we lost that first lease in Newport, most setbacks can be turned into opportunities. And as things turned out, this setback presented us with one of the great opportunities in our company's history. Ever since David Glass and I had met at that awful Wal-Mart opening in Harrison, Arkansas, I had been trying to somehow persuade him to work for us. He was a big deal at this discount drug chain up in Springfield, and I was convinced he was one of the finest retail talents I had met. For some time, I had been after Ron Mayer to hire David, but he wouldn't do it. So when Ron left, David was the first person I went to see, and I finally talked him into coming to Wal-Mart. I'm not saying that with David and Jack Shewmaker as executive vice presidents—David for finance and distribution, and Jack for operations and merchandise—we didn't still have some turf fighting left to do between the two sides of the company. But, man, we had as much retail talent and firepower together under one roof as any company could handle.

These two guys are completely different in personality, but they are both whip smart. And with us up against it like we were, everybody had to head in the same direction. Once again, Wal-Mart proved everybody wrong, and we just blew the doors off our previous performances. David made us a stronger company almost immediately. Ron Mayer may have been the architect of our original distribution systems, but David Glass, frankly, was much better than Ron at distribution, and that was one of the big areas of expertise I had been afraid of losing. David also was much better at fine-tuning and honing our accounting systems. He, along with Jack, was a powerful advocate for much of the high technology that keeps us operating and growing today. And not only did he turn out to be a great chief financial officer, he also proved to be a fine talent with people. This new team was even more talented, more suited for the job at hand than the previous one.

All along, the history of Wal-Mart has been marked by having the right people in the right job when we needed them most. We had Whitaker, straight out of the get-after-it-and-stay-after-it old school, to help us get started; Ferold Arend, a methodical, hard-working German, to get us organized; Ron Mayer, a whiz at computers, to get our systems going; Jack Shewmaker, a brilliant shoot-from-the-hip executive with a store manager's mentality, to blow us out of ruts and push us into new ideas we needed to be working with; and David Glass, who could step up in a crisis, keep his cool, and eventually get control of a company that became so big it was hard to comprehend.

From day one, we just always found the folks who had the qualities that neither Bud nor I had. And they fit into the niches as the company grew. Then every so often, we needed even better talents than we sometimes had on board. And that's when the David Glasses would come along. But there's a time for all these things. I tried for almost twenty years to hire Don Soderquist away from Ben Franklin. I even offered him the presidency one time, and he didn't come. But when we really needed him later on, he finally joined up and made a great chief operating officer for David's team.

At any company, the time comes when some people need to move along, even if they've made strong contributions. I have occasionally been accused of pitting people against one another, but I don't really see it that way. I have always cross-pollinated folks and let them assume different roles in the company, and that has bruised some egos from time to time. But I think everyone needs as much exposure to as many areas of the company as they can get, and I think the best executives are those who have touched all the bases and have the best overall concept of the corporation. I hate to see rivalry develop within our company when it becomes a personal thing and our folks aren't working together and supporting one another. Philosophically, we have always said, Submerge your own ambitions and help whoever you can in the company. Work together as a team.

CHAPTER 11

CREATING A CULTURE

"Sam's establishment of the Walton culture throughout the company was the key to the whole thing. It's just incomparable. He is the greatest businessman of this century."

—HARRY CUNNINGHAM,
founded Kmart Stores while
CEO of S. S. Kresge Co.

Not many companies out there gather several hundred of their executives, managers, and associates together every Saturday morning at seven-thirty to talk about business. Even fewer would begin such a meeting by having their chairman call the Hogs. That's one of my favorite ways to wake everybody up, by doing the University of Arkansas's Razorback cheer, real early on a Saturday. You probably have to be there to appreciate the full effect, but it goes like this:

Whoooooooooooooooooooooo Pig. Sooey!
Whoooooooooooooooooooooooooooo Pig. Sooey!
Whoooooooooooooooooooooooooooooooooo Pig. Sooey!
RAZORBACKS!!!!!

And if I'm leading the cheer, you'd better believe we do it loud. I have another cheer I lead whenever I visit a store: our own

Wal-Mart cheer. The associates did it for President and Mrs. Bush when they were here in Bentonville not long ago, and you could see by the look on their faces that they weren't used to this kind of enthusiasm. For those of you who don't know, it goes like this:

Give Me a W!
Give Me an A!
Give Me an L!
Give Me a Squiggly!
(Here, everybody sort of does the twist.)
Give Me an M!
Give Me an A!
Give Me an R!
Give Me a T!
What's that spell?
Wal-Mart!
What's that spell?
Wal-Mart!
Who's number one?
THE CUSTOMER!

I know most companies don't have cheers, and most board chairmen probably wouldn't lead them even if they did. But then most companies don't have folks like Mike "Possum" Johnson, who entertained us one Saturday morning back when he was safety director by taking on challengers in a no-holds-barred persimmon-seed-spitting contest, using Robert Rhoads, our company general counsel, as the official target. Most companies also don't have a gospel group called the Singing Truck Drivers, or a management singing group called Jimmy Walker and the Accountants.

My feeling is that just because we work so hard, we don't have to go around with long faces all the time, taking ourselves seriously, pretending we're lost in thought over weighty problems. At Wal-Mart, if you have some important business problem on your mind, you should be bringing it out in the open at a Friday morning session called the merchandising meeting or at the Saturday morning meeting, so we can all try to solve it together. But while we're doing all this work, we like to have a good time. It's sort of a "whistle while you work" philosophy, and we not only have a heck of a good time with it, we work better because of it. We build spirit and excitement. We capture the attention of our folks and keep them interested, simply because they never know what's coming next. We break down barriers, which helps us communicate better with one another. And we make our people feel part of a family in which no one is too important or too puffed up to lead a cheer or be the butt of a joke—or the target in a persimmon-seed-spitting contest.

We don't pretend to have invented the idea of a strong corporate culture, and we've been aware of a lot of the others that have come before us. In the early days of IBM, some of the things Tom Watson did with his slogans and group activities weren't all that different from the things we do. And, as I've said, we've certainly borrowed every good idea we've come across. Helen and I picked up several ideas on a trip we took to Korea and Japan in 1975. A lot of the things they do over there are very easy to apply to doing business over here. Culturally, things seem so different—like sitting on the floor eating eels and snails—but people are people, and what motivates one group generally will motivate another.

HELEN WALTON:

"Sam took me out to see this tennis ball factory, somewhere east of Seoul. The company sold balls to Wal-Mart, I guess, and they treated us very well. It was the dirtiest place I ever saw in my life, but Sam was very impressed. It was the first place he ever saw a group of workers have a company cheer. And he liked the idea of everybody doing calisthenics together at the beginning of the day. He couldn't wait to get home and try those ideas out in the stores and at the Saturday morning meeting."

Back in 1984, people outside the company began to realize just how different we folks at Wal-Mart are. That was the year I lost a bet to David Glass and had to pay up by wearing a grass skirt and doing the hula on Wall Street. I thought I would slip down there and dance, and David would videotape it so he could prove to everyone back at the Saturday morning meeting that I really did it, but when we got there, it turned out David had hired a truckload of real hula dancers and ukulele players—and he had alerted the newspapers and TV networks. We had all kinds of trouble with the police about permits, and the dancers' union wouldn't let them dance without heaters because it was so cold, and we finally had to get permission from the head of Merrill Lynch to dance on his steps. Eventually, though, I slipped on the grass skirt and the Hawaiian shirt and the leis over my suit and did what I think was a pretty fair hula. It was too good a picture to pass up, I guess—this crazy chairman of the board from Arkansas in this silly costume—and it ran everywhere. It was one of the few times one of our company stunts really embarrassed me. But at Wal-Mart, when you make a bet like I did—that we couldn't possibly produce a pretax profit of more than 8 percent—you always pay up. Doing the hula was nothing compared to wrestling a bear, which is what Bob Schneider, once a warehouse manager in Palestine, Texas, had to do after he lost a bet with his crew that they couldn't beat a production record.

Most folks probably thought we just had a wacky chairman who was pulling a pretty primitive publicity stunt. What they didn't realize is that this sort of stuff goes on all the time at Wal-Mart. It's part of our culture, and it runs through everything we do. Whether it's Saturday morning meetings or stockholders' meetings or store openings or just normal days, we always have tried to make life as interesting and as unpredictable as we can, and to make Wal-Mart a fun proposition. We're constantly doing crazy things to capture the attention of our folks and lead them to think up surprises of their own. We like to see them do wild things in the stores that are fun for the customers and fun for the associates. If you're committed to the Wal-Mart partnership and its core values, the culture encourages you to think up all sorts of ideas that break the mold and fight monotony.

We know that our antics—our company cheers or our songs or my hula—can sometimes be pretty corny, or hokey. We couldn't care less. Sure, it's a little strange for a vice president to dress in pink tights and a long blond wig and ride a white horse around the Bentonville town square, as Charlie Self did in 1987, after he lost a Saturday morning meeting bet that December sales wouldn't top $1.3 billion. And it is odd for a former executive like Ron Loveless to come out of retirement at every year-end meeting and present his annual LEIR report, the Loveless Economic Indicator Report, based on the number of edible dead chickens found on the roadside—with charts and graphs and the whole bit. (The harder times are, the fewer edibles you find on the roadside.)

Maybe it is a little hokey to surprise your president with the gift of a live pig, but that's what a Sam's Club crew did to David Glass at one meeting to kick off a sales competition with a football theme. They told him they had planned to give him a pig-skin, then decided, what the heck, why not leave the pig in it. For that matter, how many other $50 billion companies would have their president put on overalls and a straw hat and ride a donkey around a parking lot? That's what we made David do at the Harrison store to make up for having told *Fortune* magazine his story about the donkey and the watermelons at that store's 1964 opening. Who knows what our competitors thought when they got their issue of *Discount Store News* that week and saw our president sitting on a jackass right there on the front page?

Some of this culture grew naturally out of our small-town beginnings. Back then, we tried literally to create a carnival atmosphere in our stores. We were only in small towns then, and often there wasn't a whole lot else to do for entertainment that could beat going to the Wal-Mart. As I told you, we'd have these huge sidewalk sales, and we'd have bands and little circuses in our parking lots to get folks to those sales. We'd have plate drops, where we'd write the names of prizes on paper plates and sail them off the roofs of the stores. We'd have balloon drops. We'd have Moonlight Madness sales, which usually would begin after normal closing hours and maybe last until midnight, with some new bargain or promotion being announced every few minutes.

We'd play shopping-cart bingo—where each shopping cart

has a number, and if your number is called, you get a discount on whatever you have in the cart. At store openings, we'd stand on the service counters and give away boxes of candy to the customers who had traveled the farthest to get there. As long as it was fun, we'd try it. Occasionally it blew up in our face.

One year, on George Washington's birthday, Phil Green (remember the world's largest Tide display?) ran an ad saying his Fayetteville store was selling a television set for twenty-two cents —the birthday being on February 22. The only hitch was that before you could buy that television set you had to find it first. Phil had hidden it somewhere in the store, and the first person to find it, got it. When Phil arrived at the store that morning, there was such a crowd out front that you couldn't even see the doors. I think all of Fayetteville was there, and a lot of them had been there all night. Our folks had to go in through the back. When they finally opened the front doors, there was a stampede like you wouldn't believe: five hundred or six hundred people tearing through that store looking for one twenty-two-cent television set. Phil sold a ton that day, but the place was so totally out of control that even he admitted playing hide-and-seek with merchandise was a terrible idea.

As we've grown, we've gotten away from the circus approach, but we've made it a point to keep encouraging the spirit of fun in the stores. We want the associates and the management to do things together that contribute to the community and make them feel like a team, even if they don't directly relate to selling or promoting our merchandise. Here are a few of the crazy kinds of things I'm talking about:

—Our Fairbury, Nebraska, store has a "precision shopping-cart drill team" that marches in local parades. The members all wear Wal-Mart smocks and push their carts through a routine of whirls, twirls, circles, and crossovers.

—Our Cedartown, Georgia, store holds a kiss-the-pig contest to raise money for charity. They set out jars with each manager's name on them, and the manager whose jar winds up with the most donations has to kiss a pig.

—Our New Iberia, Louisiana, store fields a cheerleading squad called the Shrinkettes. Their cheers deal mostly with, what else? cutting shrinkage: "WHAT DO YOU DO ABOUT SHRINKAGE? CRUSH IT! CRUSH IT!" The Shrinkettes stole the show at one of our annual meetings with cheers like: "CALIFORNIA ORANGES, TEXAS CACTUS, WE THINK KMART COULD USE SOME PRACTICE!"

—Our Fitzgerald, Georgia, store won first place in the Irwin County Sweet Potato Parade with a float featuring seven associates dressed as fruits and vegetables grown in south Georgia. As they passed the judging stand, the homegrown fruits and vegetables did a homegrown Wal-Mart cheer.

—Managers from our Ozark, Missouri, store dressed up in pink tutus, got on the back of a flatbed truck, and cruised the town square on Friday night, the peak time for teenage cruisers, and somehow managed to raise money for charity by doing it.

As you can see, we thrive on a lot of the traditions of small-town America, especially parades with marching bands, cheer-leaders, drill teams, and floats. Most of us grew up with it, and we've found that it can be even more fun when you're an adult who usually spends all your time working. We love all kinds of contests, and we hold them all the time for everything from po-etry to singing to beautiful babies. We like theme days, where everyone in the store dresses up in costume. Our Ardmore, Okla-homa, store piled hay in front of the store one day, mixed $36 in coins in it—and let the kids dive into it. More of our stores than you would believe hold ladies' fashion shows using ugly old men from the stores as models. Some of our people greeters—the asso-ciates who meet our customers as they come in the door—use their high-profile positions to have a little fun. Artie Hopper, the greeter in Huntsville, Arkansas, dresses in a different costume for every holiday—including Hawgfest, a local celebration.

Then there's the World Championship Moon Pie Eating Contest.

I already told you how I pushed Moon Pies as my item one year and sold $6 million worth. But the Moon Pie contest started back in 1985, when John Love, an assistant manager at the time in Oneonta, Alabama, accidentally ordered four or five times more Moon Pies than he intended to and found himself up to his eyeballs in them. Desperate, John came up with the idea of a Moon Pie Eating Contest as a way to move the Moon Pies out before they went bad on him. Who would have thought something like that would catch on? Now it's an annual event, held every fall—on the second Saturday in October—in the parking lot of our Oneonta store. It draws spectators from several states and has been written up in newspapers and covered by television literally all over the world. As of this writing, by the way, the world record for Moon Pie eating is sixteen double deckers in ten minutes. It was set in 1990 by a guy named Mort Hurst, who bills himself as "the Godzilla of Gluttony."

Corny? How could you get any cornier than that? But when folks get together and do this sort of silly stuff it's really impossible to measure just how good it is for their morale. To know that you're supposed to have a good time, that there's no place for stuffed shirts, or at least that they always get their comeuppance, is a very uplifting thing for all of us.

Take our Saturday morning meetings, for example. Without a little entertainment and a sense of the unpredictable, how in the world could we ever have gotten those hundreds of people—most of our managers and some associates from the general offices here in Bentonville—to get up every Saturday morning and actually come in here with smiles on their faces? If they knew all they could expect in that meeting was somebody droning on about comparative numbers, followed by a serious lecture on the problems of our business, could we have kept the meeting alive? No way. No matter how strongly I felt about the necessity of that meeting, the folks would have revolted, and even if we still held it, it wouldn't be any good at all. As it is, the Saturday morning meeting is at the very heart of the Wal-Mart culture.

Don't get me wrong. We don't get up and go down there just to have fun. That Saturday morning meeting is very much about business. Its purpose is to let everyone know what the rest of the company is up to. If we can, we find heroes among our associates in the stores and bring them in to Bentonville, where we praise them in front of the whole meeting. Everybody likes praise, and we look for every chance we can to heap it on somebody. But I don't like to go to the meeting and hear about just the good things that are happening. I like to hear what our weaknesses are, where we aren't doing as well as we should and why. I like to see a problem come up and then hear suggestions as to how it can be corrected. If we decide we're doing something wrong, and the solution is obvious, we can order changes right then and carry them out over the weekend, while most everybody else in the retail business is off.

The Saturday morning meeting is where we discuss and debate much of our philosophy and our management strategy: it is the focal point of all our communications efforts. It's where we share ideas we've picked up from various places. And while it's not the most exciting part of the meeting, sometimes I like to read from management articles that pertain to our business. Two of our executives, Wesley Wright and Colon Washburn, seem to read just about everything there is in the way of management literature, and they're constantly calling useful articles or books to my attention. At the meeting, we'll talk about competitors, specifically, but also in general. For example, we'll spend ten minutes talking about how Wal-Mart can compete successfully with all the good specialty retailers coming onto the scene. It's often the place where we first decide to try things that seem unattainable. And instead of everybody shouting it down right away, we try to figure out how to make it work. That's exactly how I ended up dancing the hula on Wall Street, by making that bet at a Saturday morning meeting. And, as embarrassing as it was to have to dance on Wall Street, believe me, achieving a pretax profit of more than 8 percent, when most everybody else in the retail industry averages about half that, made it well worth the red face.

AL MILES:

"The great thing about the Saturday morning meeting is how totally unpredictable it is. Sometimes you get your soul bared in there. By that I mean somebody may not have been doing their job so well, and they don't get publicly castigated, but they get gently chided in front of everybody. Or it can be a form of counseling. I'll never forget the chairman saying to me one time in front of everybody that I ought to stop and think sometimes before I talked. And I had it coming. I was being really derogatory in my remarks, really sticking it to another division of the company pretty hard, and it wasn't the right place to do it. I was publicly counseled in that meeting and it stuck.

"Another time, the chairman decided I was going to have to stand up there and sing 'Red River Valley' at a meeting three weeks away. He knew I couldn't carry a tune in a bucket but he made a bigger and bigger deal out of it every week until finally I had to put a group together to sing it so nobody would hear only me. I always figured he just wanted to force me into doing something in public that I wasn't so good at, and that way I had to eat a little humble pie. Anyway, I believe those meetings are managed fun, and I think the chairman manages them very discreetly. He knows when he wants it to be serious, and he knows when he wants it to be fun. Sometimes it's very democratic, and sometimes it's very dictatorial. But he uses it for basically three purposes: to share information, to lighten everybody's load, and to rally the troops. Believe it or not, the majority of our folks wouldn't miss a Saturday morning meeting for anything."

For the meeting to work, it has to be something of a show. We don't ever want to let it become predictable. One day, we might do a few calisthenics. Another day we might sing. Or maybe do the Razorback cheer. We don't want to plan it all out. We just want it to unfold. It is so unconventional that I don't think anyone could really duplicate it even if they wanted to. We have lots of guests, and our folks never know who's going to be there. One day we might have an executive from a company we do business with. It might be somebody they never heard of from some small entrepreneurial outfit with a good idea, or it might be somebody like Jack Welch, the CEO of GE. On the other hand, it might be the comedian Jonathan Winters, who started coming to promote Hefty Bags, one of our vendors' products, and has returned several times. He really cracks everybody up. One time we had a mock boxing match between Sugar Ray Leonard and me. We ask a lot of athletes to join us. Sidney Moncrief, an NBA star and former Razorback great, is one of my favorites, and Fran Tarkenton, the former NFL quarterback, who does a lot of motivational talks, has also spoken at the meeting. Just recently, Garth Brooks, the country singer from Oklahoma, dropped by Wal-Mart for a visit with some of our folks.

DON SODERQUIST:

"One of the real values of our meeting is its spontaneity. We never really have an agenda. Of course the chairman always has his yellow legal pad with notes scribbled on it of things he wants to discuss, and some of the rest of us do the same thing. But one of the things Sam will do is just call someone up at the start and say, 'Okay, you conduct the whole meeting today.' And that meeting will take on the personality of whoever's running it. That way, there's always a sense of anticipation. Something unusual may happen, or somebody may pull off something great."

From the time we started the Saturday meeting, with just four or five store managers getting together somewhere to talk merchandising, it has been a very difficult thing to develop, and there's been a lot of opposition to it, including from my own wife, who I've already told you believes it's unfair to take our folks away from their families on Saturday mornings. There have definitely been times when our folks would have voted it out if we had given them the opportunity. But as I've said, I believe Saturday work is part of the commitment that comes with choosing a career in retail. I can't see asking our folks in the stores to make that sacrifice while our managers are off playing golf.

Very few outsiders ever get to see our Saturday meetings. So the event that gives people the most insight into our corporate culture, the place where they really get a chance to see the Wal-Mart chemistry in action, is our annual stockholders' meeting. I told you how it began as an attempt to do something different for the analysts, taking them on float trips and making them camp out. But since then it's grown into what is probably the largest corporate annual meeting in the world. It's gotten so big now—with over 10,000 shareholders and guests—that we hold it down in Fayetteville at Barnhill Arena, the University of Arkansas's basketball coliseum. Soon we'll be holding it in the new Bud Walton Arena they're building down there, and I know my brother will really take a lot of pride in that.

In some ways, our annual meeting is a bigger version of the kind of show we have on Saturday mornings. We have entertainers, like Reba McEntire, the popular country singer, and we have guest speakers. In other ways, it's a lot like the meetings of many companies—only louder. We make presentations to the shareholders, which focus on our accomplishments over the past year and on our goals and plans for the coming one. But what I think really sets our meeting apart is the degree to which we involve our associates, who, after all, are some of our most important shareholders.

We have always included as many store managers and associates as possible in our annual meeting, to let them see the scope of the whole company and grasp the big picture. We started out letting every store and every distribution center elect an associate to represent them at the meeting. Because we've gotten so big now, I'm sorry to say we've had to stagger the thing. The distribution centers and the Sam's Clubs still send someone every year, but Wal-Mart Stores only send a delegate every other year.

Really, the official part of the meeting takes a backseat to everything else we do, and a couple of times we've been having so much fun that we've actually forgotten to convene the real meeting. We gather our associates early on Friday morning, around seven o'clock, for a real rousing warm-up, a premeeting meeting. We do our cheers and our songs, and raise all sorts of cain. We salute retirees. We bring in all the department managers whose departments have the highest percentage of sales relative to their stores' overall sales. And we recognize the department managers who have the highest sales companywide. We call up the truck drivers who've won the safety awards for the best driving records, and we honor them. We applaud associates who have created particularly successful displays, or who have won one of our VPI (Volume Producing Item) contests, and we honor them. The point is that we're not there to honor our shareholders as much as we are to let them meet the folks who are responsible for the amazing returns on their investments year after year.

After the meeting, Helen and I invite all the associates who attend—about 2,500 of them—over to our house for a big picnic lunch catered by our own Wal-Mart cafeteria. It's a lot of pressure on Helen; not many wives would put up with that kind of crowd streaming through the yard and the house, but I think it's one of the best things we do, and in the end both Helen and I really enjoy it a lot. It gives us a chance to visit with many of our associates who we would otherwise never get to see in a social setting like that. They tend to be the leaders in their stores, which is how they get elected to come. And even with that crush of people there, I still have the opportunity to ask them, "How are we doing at Litchfield, Illinois?" Or "How's your manager working out in Branson, Missouri?" And in a very short time, I can get a pretty good idea from their level of enthusiasm just how things are going in a particular store, and if I hear something I don't like, I just might be out there visiting it within the next week or two.

When the whole thing is over, the guest associates are sent a videotape of the meeting, and they're supposed to share that, and their impressions of the meeting, with their associates who didn't get to go. And, of course, we write a detailed account of the meeting in our company newspaper, *Wal-Mart World,* so everybody gets a chance to read exactly what we did. We like to think that this kind of meeting brings us all closer together, and creates the feeling that we are a family committed to one common interest.

We want our associates to know and feel how much we, as managers and major shareholders, appreciate everything they are doing to make Wal-Mart the great company that it is.

A strong corporate culture with its own unique personality, on top of the profit-sharing partnership we've created, gives us a pretty sharp competitive edge. But a culture like ours can create some problems of its own too. The main one that comes to mind is a resistance to change. When folks buy into a way of doing things, and really believe it's the best way, they develop a tendency to think that's exactly the way things should always be done. So I've made it my own personal mission to ensure that constant change is a vital part of the Wal-Mart culture itself. I've forced change—sometimes for change's sake alone—at every turn in our company's development. In fact, I think one of the greatest strengths of Wal-Mart's ingrained culture is its ability to drop everything and turn on a dime.

We're great at that kind of change when it comes to operating challenges, but sometimes not so great on matters that have more to do with the culture of the company. In the early days, for example, all our old variety store managers had a tremendous prejudice against us hiring college boys because they didn't think they would work hard enough. Three of the first ones we hired— Bill Fields, Dean Sanders, and Colon Washburn—are still with us and, in fact, are among our brightest stars. But they had a heck of a time fitting in at first and could probably tell some real horror stories.

BILL FIELDS, EXECUTIVE VICE PRESIDENT—
MERCHANDISING AND SALES, WAL-MART:

"I had been with the company about five days, and we were opening a store in Idabel, Oklahoma. We had thirteen days to open it, which is still a record. They worked me about 125 hours or more the first week. The second week it was getting worse. Then Sam—who knew who I was because I was a local Bentonville boy—comes walking up to me and says, 'Who hired you?' I told him that Ferold Arend had, and he said, 'Well, do you think you'll ever be a merchant?' Just the way he said it made me mad enough to want to quit. Then Don Whitaker came walking up to me and looked at me almost like he smelled something bad, and said, 'Who in the *hell* hired you?' At the time, it didn't seem like going to college was much of an advantage in this company. We really had to prove ourselves to those old guys."

Obviously if we were going to grow, we had to bring in college-educated folks. But at first, the culture tried to reject them. And now that we have even more complicated needs—in technology, finance, marketing, legal, whatever—our demand for a more sophisticated work force is growing all the time. All this requires some basic changes in the way we think about ourselves, about who's a good Wal-Mart hire for tomorrow and about what we can do for the folks already on board. That's one reason Helen and I started the Walton Institute down at the University of Arkansas in Fort Smith. It's a place where our managers can go and get exposure to some of the educational opportunities they may not have had earlier on. Also, we as a company need to do whatever we can to encourage and help our associates earn their college degrees. We need these folks to get the best training they possibly can. It opens up their career opportunities, and it benefits us.

Traditionally, we've had this attitude that if you wanted to be a manager at Wal-Mart, you basically had to be willing to move on a moment's notice. You get a call that says you're going to open a new store 500 miles away, you don't ask questions. You just pack and go, then sometime later you worry about selling your house and moving your family. Maybe that was necessary back in the old days, and maybe it was more rigid than it needed to be. Now, though, it's not really appropriate anymore for several reasons. First, as the company grows bigger, we need to find more ways to stay in touch with the communities where we operate, and one of the best ways to do that is by hiring locally, developing managers locally, and letting them have a career in their home community—if they perform. Second, the old way really put good, smart women at a disadvantage in our company because at that time they weren't as free to pick up and move as many men were. Now I've seen the light on the opportunities we missed out on with women. (I have to admit that Helen and my daughter Alice have helped me come around to this way of thinking.)

In the old days, retailers felt the same way about women that they did about college boys, only more so. In addition to thinking women weren't free to move, they didn't think women could handle anything but the clerk jobs because the managers usually did so much physical labor—unloading trucks and hauling merchandise out of the stockroom on a two-wheeler, mopping the floors and cleaning the windows if necessary. Nowadays, the industry has waked up to the fact that women make great retailers. So we at Wal-Mart, along with everybody else, have to do everything we possibly can to recruit and attract women.

One other aspect of the Wal-Mart culture which has attracted some attention is simply a matter of lifestyle, but it is one that has bothered me ever since we began to be really successful. The fact is, a lot of folks in our company have made an awful lot of money. We've had lots and lots of millionaires in our ranks. And it just drives me crazy when they flaunt it. Maybe it's none of my business, but I've done everything I can to discourage our folks from getting too extravagant with their homes and their automobiles and their lifestyles. As I said earlier, I just don't believe the lifestyle here in Bentonville should be much different than what would be high moderate income in most other places. But from time to time I've had a hard time holding back folks who have never had the opportunity to get their hands on the kind of money they've made with their Wal-Mart stock holdings. Every now and then somebody will do something particularly showy, and I don't hesitate to rant and rave about it at the Saturday morning meeting. And a lot of times, folks who just can't hold back will go ahead and leave the company.

It goes back to what I said about learning to value a dollar as a kid. I don't think that big mansions and flashy cars are what the Wal-Mart culture is supposed to be about. It's great to have the money to fall back on, and I'm glad some of these folks have been able to take off and go fishing at a fairly early age. That's fine with me. But if you get too caught up in that good life, it's probably time to move on, simply because you lose touch with what your mind is supposed to be concentrating on: serving the customer.

CHAPTER 12

MAKING THE CUSTOMER NUMBER ONE

"Sam Walton understands better than anyone else that no business can exist without customers. He lives by his credo, which is to make the customer the centerpiece of all his efforts. And in the process of serving Wal-Mart's customers to perfection (not quite perfection, he would say), he also serves Wal-Mart's associates, its share owners, its communities, and the rest of its stakeholders in an extraordinary fashion—almost without parallel in American business."

—ROBERTO C. GOIZUETA,
chairman and CEO,
the Coca-Cola Company

For my whole career in retail, I have stuck by one guiding principle. It's a simple one, and I have repeated it over and over and over in this book until I'm sure you're sick to death of it. But I'm going to say it again anyway: the secret of successful retailing is to give your customers what they want. And really, if you think about it from your point of view as a customer, you want everything: a wide assortment of good quality merchandise; the lowest possible prices; guaranteed satisfaction with what you buy; friendly, knowledgeable service; convenient hours; free parking; a pleasant shopping experience. You love it when you visit a store that somehow exceeds your expectations, and you hate it when a store inconveniences you, or gives you a hard time, or just pretends you're invisible.

I learned this lesson as a merchant in small towns, which is where I've spent my whole life. For those of you who've been around as long as I have, and who spent your early days in small towns too, it's not hard to remember how different small-town life was in the first half of this century. Newport was a pretty prosperous little town with a fairly competitive retail environment, but it's still a good example of how things worked back then. It was a cotton town, which meant that a lot of the folks who shopped there really lived outside of town on farms. Most of the men worked long hours in the fields, and most of the women worked at home. Very few women held jobs in those days, although a lot of them had worked during the war, and they were beginning to think about going back to work when they got their families pretty well underway.

The town itself had several small department stores, including, as I mentioned earlier, a Penney's and for a while that little Eagle Store I opened up. It also had a couple of good variety stores—mine and John Dunham's Sterling Store. There were drugstores, hardware stores, tire and auto stores—like Firestone and Western Auto—and little family grocery stores. In lots of little towns, you didn't even have many one-stop groceries. You might have one shop that specialized in butchering meat, another that carried good fresh vegetables, and maybe another that would wring a chicken's neck and dress it for you right there behind the counter while you waited.

Folks back then weren't accustomed to all the variety and abundance of goods and services that we have available today. During the Depression, few of us had enough money to shop very often, and during World War II, everything—meat, butter, tires, shoes, gasoline, sugar—was rationed. But by the time I started out, the shortages were pretty much over, and the economy was growing. Compared to the Depression we had been used to, boom times had arrived.

In a farm-to-market town like Newport, the big shopping day was always Saturday. That's when the whole family would drive to town and spend a few hours—maybe the whole day—walking around looking for what they needed in all the stores. Something had to attract them to a particular store, maybe a combination of things: the storekeeper's personality, the freshness of the goods, the prices—an ice cream machine. We thrived in that competitive environment.

When we arrived in the much smaller town of Bentonville in 1950, we found almost no spirit of competition. A few retailers were scattered around the square, but each of them had sort of carved out their niche, and that was that. If a store didn't have something the customer wanted, he or she would just have to drive to Rogers, or Springdale, or very possibly on into Fayetteville. Using some of the things we had learned in Newport, I'd have to say we changed that way of thinking right off and generally sparked up the atmosphere around town.

ALICE WALTON:

"Saturdays around the Bentonville square were really something special. Dad always had something going on out on the sidewalks or even in the streets, and there was always a crowd. That's where Santa Claus would come, and that's where we had all the parades. To me, as a kid, it seemed like we had a circus or a carnival going on almost every weekend. I loved Saturdays. I had my popcorn machine out on the sidewalk, and I was covered up in business. Everybody wanted some of that popcorn, and of course a lot of my customers would go on into the store. It was a great way to grow up."

As you recall, Fayetteville was where we opened our second store after Bentonville. And it was also where we encountered our first discounter competition—Gibson's. We knew from then on that the retail business was going to be changing in major ways for years to come, and we wanted to be part of it. We knew early on that variety stores weren't going to be as big a factor in the future as they had been in the past, and we were heavily invested in them. The important thing to recognize, though, is that none of this was taking place in a vacuum. In the fifties and sixties, everything about America was changing rapidly.

All the kids who had grown up on farms and in small towns had come home from World War II or Korea and moved to the cities where all the jobs were. Except they weren't really moving to the cities; they were moving to the suburbs and commuting into the cities to work. It seemed like every family had at least one car—and many had two—and the country had started building its interstate highway system, all of which changed a lot of the traditional ways Americans were accustomed to doing business.

The downtowns of big cities started to lose population and business to the suburbs, and the big downtown department stores had to follow their customers and build branch stores out in the suburban malls. Traditional diners and cafés suffered because of the new car-oriented chains like McDonald's and Burger King, and the old city variety stores like Woolworth's and McCrory's just got smashed by Kmart and some of the other big discounters. The oil companies stuck service stations on practically every other corner, and pretty soon something called convenience stores—7-Elevens and such—came along and started filling up the other corners. It was when all this began that Bud and I had opened that Ben Franklin in the shopping center at Ruskin Heights, that big new subdivision community outside Kansas City.

For the most part up where we were—in the small towns of northwest Arkansas, Missouri, Oklahoma, and Kansas—you didn't see much of the mall construction and fast food neon that you saw everywhere else. McDonald's didn't go into the small towns, and neither did Kmart. You saw the small-town commercial centers start to sort of shrivel up. A lot of our customer base had moved on, and the ones who remained behind weren't stupid consumers. If they had something big to buy—say a riding lawn-mower—they wouldn't hesitate to drive fifty miles to get it if they thought they could save $100. Not only that, but with the introduction of TV and new postwar car models, being modern had become a big thing. Everybody wanted to feel up-to-date, and if they knew Kroger or somebody had a big new grocery store in Tulsa or somewhere they'd drive in there to shop it. When they saw that the prices were lower and the selection was better, they would go back again and again, until somebody brought a supermarket to their town.

It was this kind of strong customer demand in the small towns

Meeting as many young people as I do, I'm optimistic that we can rely on a sound future generation of leaders—but it's up to all of us to help ensure the right educational opportunities to guarantee it.

The Wal-Mart cheerleaders help whip up enthusiasm with a hearty Wal-Mart cheer. Give me a "W". . . !

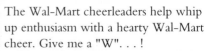

Wal-Mart went on the Big Board in 1972, and I'm proud how well we have served our shareholders. Here we are on the floor of the New York Stock Exchange as we execute the first trade in WMT.

We're thankful for our shareholders' confidence in us, and particularly enjoy how they support us by their participation in our annual shareholders' meeting, the largest in the U.S.A. (June 1987).

I've always enjoyed challenging our people. If you expect great things from folks they'll expect it from themselves. Our people have never let us down.

I always enjoy the new friends I meet at grand openings like this one in Saint Robert, Missouri.

At this Sam's opening I was invited to play the role of John Hancock.

Bud and I share some fond memories with a couple of folks of our generation at the dedication ceremonies for the Wal-Mart Visitors Center (1989).

David Glass is likely to be the best listener and communicator I know. Here he takes in the point of view of some new customers at our Wal-Mart Supercenter in Rolla, Missouri (1992).

Helen and I were treated to an Appreciation Day by our Bentonville friends and neighbors in 1983—and the town really pulled out all the stops.

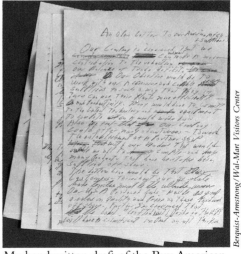

The opening month's financial statement for our first Wal-Mart— which we confidently called Wal-Mart No. 1.

My handwritten draft of the Buy American program we initiated in 1984. I'm real proud of the almost one hundred thousand jobs we have created or preserved for Americans with this plan.

Three generations of Waltons, with Jim getting a little advice from my dad.

Treating one of the grandsons to a canoe trip down the Buffalo River.

Betty Holmes

Elizabeth Dishmon—now in her nineties—worked for our family for over thirty years.

Becky McCoy

Ol' Roy here wasn't much of a hunting dog, but he was a great pet. Thankfully, we don't have to pay him a royalty on what has become the number-two dog food in America—and it's available only in our stores.

Helen with our boys Rob, Jim, and John as she is honored as 1988 Mother of the year by the Florence Crittenton Home.

Alice and her dad.

that made it possible for Wal-Mart to get started in the first place, that enabled our stores to thrive immediately, and that eventually made it possible to spread the idea pretty much all over the country. For many years, we lived entirely off the principle that customers in the country and in small towns are just like their relatives who left the farm and moved to the city: they want a good deal as much as anybody. When we arrived in these little towns offering low prices every day, satisfaction guaranteed, and hours that were realistic for the way people wanted to shop, we passed right by that old variety store competition, with its 45 percent markups, limited selection, and limited hours.

Wal-Mart No. 18 is as good an example as there is of how it worked. That store opened in 1969, and it marked our return to Newport, Arkansas, nineteen years after we had basically been run out of town. By then, I was long over what had happened to us down there, and I didn't have revenge in mind. It was a logical town for us to expand into, and I admit that it did feel mighty good to be back in business down there. I knew it was a town where we would do well. As it happened, we did extraordinarily well with our Newport Wal-Mart, and it wasn't too long before the old Ben Franklin store I had run on Front Street had to close its doors. You can't say we ran that guy—the landlord's son—out of business. His customers were the ones who shut him down. They voted with their feet.

Quite a few smaller stores have gone out of business during the time of Wal-Mart's growth. Some people have tried to turn it into this big controversy, sort of a "Save the Small-Town Merchants" deal, like they were whales or whooping cranes or something that has the right to be protected.

Of all the notions I've heard about Wal-Mart, none has ever baffled me more than this idea that we are somehow the enemy of small-town America. Nothing could be further from the truth: Wal-Mart has actually kept quite a number of small towns from becoming practically extinct by offering low prices and saving literally billions of dollars for the people who live there, as well as by creating hundreds of thousands of jobs in our stores.

I don't have any trouble understanding why some merchant

who's having a hard time competing with us wouldn't be too happy about our being there. What I haven't been able to figure at all is these people who have decided we're somehow responsible for the decline of the small town. My guess is that a lot of these critics are folks who grew up in small towns and then deserted them for the big cities decades ago. Now when they come home for a visit, it makes them sad that the old town square isn't exactly like it was when they left it back in 1954. It's almost like they want their hometown to be stuck in time, an old-fashioned place filled with old-fashioned people doing business the old-fashioned way. Somehow, small-town populations weren't supposed to move out into their own suburbs, and they weren't supposed to go out to the intersections of highways and build malls with lots of free parking. That's just not the way some of these people remember their old towns. But folks who grew up in big cities feel the same way about what's happened to their cities over the last forty or fifty years. A lot of the stores and the movie theaters and the restaurants that they remember loving as kids have boarded up and either gone out of business or moved to the suburbs too.

I think what happened to Wal-Mart in all this is that we got to be a certain size and became so well known as the small-town merchants that we became an easy target. Certain folks figured they could create a niche for themselves, a platform from which to express their views about small-town America, by zeroing in on us. The whole thing taught me a lesson about the way the national media seems to think. When you start out as an unknown quantity with just a dream and a commitment, you couldn't buy a mention of your company in one of these publications. When you become moderately successful, they still ignore you unless something bad happens to you. Then, the more successful you become, the more suspicious they become of you. And if you ever become a large-scale success, it's Katie bar the door. Suddenly, you make a very convenient villain because everybody seems to love shooting at who's on top.

As an old-time small-town merchant, I can tell you that nobody has more love for the heyday of the small-town retailing era than I do. That's one of the reasons we chose to put our little Wal-Mart museum on the square in Bentonville. It's in the old Walton's Five and Dime building, and it tries to capture a little bit of the old dime store feel.

But I can also tell you this: if we had gotten smug about our early success, and said, "Well, we're the best merchant in town," and just kept doing everything exactly the way we were doing it, somebody else would have come along and given our customers what they wanted, and we would be out of business today. I don't know who it would have been. Maybe Gibson's or TG&Y would have pulled it off. But I suspect it would have been a combination of Kmart and Target, which, like McDonald's, would have rolled out into the small towns once they began to saturate their big-city markets.

What happened was absolutely a necessary and inevitable evolution in retailing, as inevitable as the replacement of the buggy by the car and the disappearance of the buggy whip makers. The small stores were just destined to disappear, at least in the numbers they once existed, because the whole thing is driven by the customers, who are free to choose where to shop.

DON SODERQUIST:

"We've never been very sympathetic to this whole small-town argument. What's happened to the small-town merchant isn't any different from what happened when supermarkets first appeared in the fifties. The whole point of retailing is to serve the customer. If you're a merchant with no competition, you can charge high prices, open late, close early, and shut down on Wednesday and Saturday afternoons. You can do exactly what you've always done and probably be just fine. But when competition comes along, don't expect your customers to stick with you for old times' sake. There are plenty of ways to compete successfully with Wal-Mart or any other big retailer. The principle behind all those ways is pretty basic: you have to focus on something the customer wants, and then deliver it."

I don't want to be too critical of small-town merchants, but the truth is that a lot of these folks just weren't doing a very good job of taking care of their customers before we, or somebody else, came in and offered something new. And they didn't do a very good job of reacting to our arrival either. You know, there have been articles, and even one little book, written on how to compete with us. And I've got a few suggestions of my own.

Unless small merchants are already doing a great job, they'll probably have to rethink their merchandising and advertising and promotional programs once a discounter arrives on the scene. They need to avoid coming at us head-on, and do their own thing better than we do ours. It doesn't make any sense to try to underprice Wal-Mart on something like toothpaste. That's not what the customer is looking to a small store for anyway. Most independents are best off, I think, doing what I prided myself on doing for so many years as a storekeeper: getting out on the floor and meeting every one of the customers. Let them know how much you appreciate them, and ring that cash register yourself. That little personal touch is so important for an independent merchant because no matter how hard Wal-Mart tries to duplicate it —and we try awfully hard—we can't really do it.

I think in the case of variety stores, they have to completely reposition themselves, something like the way Don Soderquist did when he was president of Ben Franklin. He saw that there just wasn't any future in competing with Wal-Mart and Kmart so he started converting a lot of their variety stores into craft stores. They offered a much bigger assortment of craft merchandise than any Wal-Mart could, and they held classes in things like pottery and flower arranging, services we could never think about providing. It worked. They stayed in business in the small towns and have been quite successful with many of those stores. The same thing can be done with fabrics: offer higher quality material and throw in some sewing classes. Or ladies' apparel. I don't care how many Wal-Marts come to town, there are always niches that we can't reach—not that we won't try. Just like everybody else, in order to survive, we need to keep changing the things we do.

Now in the case of hardware stores, I don't deny that we've

been hard on some of them too, but if they're in a decent location they shouldn't have that much trouble with Wal-Mart. It's the one kind of store for which I have the least sympathy because, frankly, a good smart hardware store operator can just beat us to death if he thinks about what he's doing and commits to putting up a fight. If he gets his assortment right and makes sure his salespeople have excellent knowledge of the products and how to use them, and goes out of his way to take care of his customers, he can keep plenty of business away from us. We don't have nearly the assortment of a hardware store—plumbing supplies and electrical equipment and specialty tools. And not all of our folks can explain how to fix a leaky faucet or rewire a lamp the way folks in a hardware store should be able to. Our paint customers don't get waited on much either. They have to pick out their own paint and then walk around with it looking for the rest of the things they want. The same is true in sporting goods, where the customer can't expect to get nearly the same kind of service from us as from a specialty store.

DON SODERQUIST:

"I have personally competed with Wal-Mart, so I know it can be done. You develop a uniqueness, a niche, and then you capitalize on it. And let me tell you, not all small merchants in these little towns hate us. Some of them have learned to feed off us rather successfully.

"Shortly after we opened a Wal-Mart in Wheat Ridge, Colorado, I had a lady come up to me and say, 'Oh, I just want to thank you so much for coming here. This is the best thing that could have ever happened.' I thanked her and asked her what she did there in town, and she said, 'Well, I run a paint store right over here, just down in this mall.'

"She went on to say that the day our store opened turned out to be the biggest day she had ever had since her paint store opened. 'You're pulling all these people into our shopping center. And the neatest thing happened to me Saturday. A man came in looking for a particular kind of paint and said he knew we had it. He said he knew because he'd been in the

Wal-Mart looking for it, and the paint department manager told him we had it and sent him on over. I thought that was wonderful.' "

Our guy sent the customer along to the paint store because it was the right thing to do. He was taking care of the customer. What makes me sad these days—and a little angry too—is that some of these stores are starting to shut down before we come to a town. They hear we're coming, and they close up before we ever even get there. We get a bad rap for that, but to my mind somebody who'll close his store just because he hears competition's coming is somebody who must know he's not doing much of a job, somebody who probably shouldn't have been in the retail business to begin with.

For all the press about Wal-Mart being at odds with small towns, I am positive that we are most welcome in almost every community where we do business. That's partly because of our economic contribution. But it's also because we go out of our way to instill a sense of community involvement in our store management and associates so that they'll be even better citizens. We know that some of our store managers do a better job at this than others, and it's a constant effort to make everyone work on community involvement. We already have community scholarship programs and matching charity grant programs, but we're working hard every day to improve the ways in which we give back to the communities we're in. If we ever let our sense of being hometown merchants slip too far, we run the risk of damaging what we think is a unique relationship with our customers.

When we meet opposition to a prospective store site, we try to work with the opponents to see if we can reasonably satisfy them. Occasionally, we will change a proposed location, or make some concessions if they make sense to us. Today, though, we have almost adopted the position that if some community, for whatever reason, doesn't want us in there, we aren't interested in going in and creating a fuss. I encourage us to walk away from this kind of trouble because there are just too many other good towns out there who do want us. For every one that doesn't, I'd say we have another two hundred begging us to come to their town. Wal-Mart wants to go where it's wanted. I've always said that the simplest test of how right we are on this issue would be to go into any town where we've been for a couple of years and let everyone vote on whether they wanted us there or not. My Lord, they'd go crazy if we left. In fact, every now and then we do have to close up a store someplace because we just can't make it profitable, and the outcry is something awful. It's another part of the price you pay for success.

Small-town merchants, by the way, aren't the only groups we've gotten into controversies with by sticking to our philosophy of putting the customer ahead of everything else. On the surface, the idea of serving the customer sounds so simple, so logical, and so obvious. But from the very beginning, the way we have practiced it has been so radical that it has frequently gotten us into trouble with what folks call "the system." In the early days, the department stores put a lot of pressure on vendors to keep them from selling to discounters like us because they hated what we were doing: offering our customers prices much lower than theirs. In some states, the department stores used so-called "fair trade" laws to try and block discounters from doing business at all.

Our vendors resented us for prying the lowest prices out of them. And some manufacturers' representatives—independent sales agents who generally work on commission to represent several different manufacturers—have complained about some of our practices. We don't have any problem with the idea of paying a middleman a commission on a sale, if his services add value to the purchasing process by making it more efficient.

But from the days when I was hauling that little trailer over into Tennessee to buy panties and shirts and avoid paying Butler Brothers' markup, our philosophy on this has always been simple: we are the agents for our customers. And to do the best job possible, we've got to become the most efficient deliverer of merchandise that we can. Sometimes that can best be accomplished by purchasing goods directly from the manufacturer. And other times, direct purchase simply doesn't work. In those cases, we need to use middlemen to deal with smaller manufacturers and make the process more efficient. What we believe in strongly is our right to make that decision—whether to buy directly or from a rep—based on what it takes to best serve our customers.

This controversy is another case, I think, of a group of people believing for some reason that they're just entitled to take a piece of the action, no matter how little they contribute to the transaction or what it means to the customer. The argument is as simple as the small-town merchant controversy. If American business is going to prevail, and be competitive, we're going to have to get accustomed to the idea that business conditions change, and that survivors have to adapt to those changing conditions. Business is a competitive endeavor, and job security lasts only as long as the customer is satisfied. Nobody owes anybody else a living.

To understand Wal-Mart's point of view on middlemen, and our relationship with our vendors, you have to look back to our beginnings in the discount business. In the early days of the industry, most discounters were served entirely by middlemen, jobbers, or distributors who came in and said to those old promoters, "We'll keep your shelves filled for 15 percent of the gross." In other words, the price on every item included a 15 percent commission to the jobber for supplying the merchandise. That's how the fast-buck promoters got into the business without even having to think much like merchants. They took what the jobbers gave them, added on the 15 percent, and still underpriced the department stores by a long shot.

But as I mentioned, we couldn't find anybody who wanted to run their trucks sixty or seventy miles out of the way into these little towns where we were operating. We were totally ignored by the distributors and the jobbers. That's not only how we came to build our own distribution system, it's also how we got used to beating the heck out of everybody on prices. We had a time getting good merchandise for our stores back then, but our cost of acquiring the goods was rock bottom—because we sat out there with absolutely no help from distributors. And because we got used to doing everything on our own, we have always resented paying anyone just for the pleasure of doing business with him.

CLAUDE HARRIS:

"There's a difference between being tough and being obnoxious. But every buyer has to be tough. That's the job. I always told the buyers: 'You're not negotiating for Wal-Mart, you're negotiating for your customer. And your customer deserves the best price you can get. Don't ever feel sorry for a vendor. He knows what he can sell for, and we want his bottom price.'

"And that's what we did, and what Wal-Mart still does. We would tell the vendors, 'Don't leave in any room for a kickback because we don't do that here. And we don't want your advertising program or your delivery program. Our truck will pick it up at your warehouse. Now what is your best price?' And if they told me it's a dollar, I would say, 'Fine, I'll consider it, but I'm going to go to your competitor, and if he says 90 cents, he's going to get the business. So make sure a dollar is your best price.' If that's being hard-nosed, then we ought to be as hard-nosed as we can be. You have to be fair and upfront and honest, but you have to drive your bargain because you're dealing for millions and millions of customers who expect the best price they can get. If you buy that thing for $1.25, you've just bought somebody else's inefficiency.

"We used to get in some terrific fights. You have to be just as tough as they are. You can't let them get by with anything because they are going to take care of themselves, and your job is to take care of the customer. I'd threaten Procter & Gamble with not carrying their merchandise, and they'd say, 'Oh, you can't get by without carrying our merchandise.' And I'd say, 'You watch me put it on a side counter, and I'll put Colgate on the endcap at a penny less, and you just watch me.' They got offended and went to Sam, and he said, 'Whatever Claude says, that's what it's going to be.' Well, now we have a real good relationship with Procter & Gamble. It's a model that everybody talks about. But let me tell you, one reason for that is that they learned to respect us. They learned that they couldn't bulldoze us like everybody

else, and that when we said we were representing the customer, we were dead serious."

In those days, of course, we desperately needed Procter &
Gamble's product, whereas they could have gotten along just fine
without us. Today, we are their largest customer. But it really
wasn't until 1987 that we began to turn a basically adversarial
vendor/retailer relationship into one that we like to think is the
wave of the future: a win–win partnership between two big companies both trying to serve the same customer. Believe it or not,
as big as we had become by then, I don't believe Wal-Mart had
ever been called on by a corporate officer of P&G. We just let our
buyers slug it out with their salesmen and both sides lived with the
results.

Then one day my close friend and longtime tennis buddy here
in Bentonville, George Billingsley, called me up and asked me to
join him on a canoe trip down the Spring River. He said he was
bringing along an old friend named Lou Pritchett, who was a
vice president with P&G at the time, and who wanted to meet
me and talk about some things relating to our two companies. So
I went along, and it turned out to be the most productive float
trip I ever took with George.

LOU PRITCHETT:

"During that time on the river, we both decided that the
entire relationship between vendor and retailer was at issue.
Both focused on the end-user—the customer—but each did it
independently of the other. No sharing of information, no
planning together, no systems coordination. We were simply
two giant entities going our separate ways, oblivious to the
excess costs created by this obsolete system. We were communicating, in effect, by slipping notes under the door.

"As a result, we assembled the top ten officers of both
companies in Bentonville for two days of soul-searching and
thinking, and within three months we had created a P&G/
Wal-Mart team to build a whole new kind of vendor-retailer
relationship. We formed a partnership to conduct our busi-

ness, with one of the most important outcomes being that we started sharing information by computer. P&G could monitor Wal-Mart's sales and inventory data, and then use that information to make its own production and shipping plans with a great deal more efficiency. We broke new ground by using information technology to manage our business together, instead of just to audit it."

Following the P&G/Wal-Mart partnership, many other companies began to view the supplier as an important partner. The partnership was also a model for many of our other vendor relationships. In our situation today, we are obsessed with quality as well as price, and, as big as we are, the only way we can possibly get that combination is to sit down with our vendors and work out the costs and margins and plan everything together. By doing that, we give the manufacturer the advantage of knowing what our needs are going to be a year out, or six months out, or even two years out. Then, as long as they are honest with us and try to lower their costs as much as they can and keep turning out a product that the customers want, we can stay with them. We both win, and most important, the customer wins too. The added efficiency of the whole process enables the manufacturer to reduce its costs, which allows us to lower our prices.

One thing we don't ever want to do, though, is let all these complex strategic issues between us and other big companies—or these controversies like small-town merchants and middlemen—get in the way of our thinking like customers, which may be the most basic way in which we make the customer number one.

DAVID GLASS:

"I was in a store recently where a manager and an assistant manager were taking a department manager through her department. They were saying, 'If you were a customer, how would you buy that item?' She was cramped for space and had put this item out of reach of the average customer. And they kept going. 'If you were a customer, what related items would you want to buy with this? And how would you find them?'

"I loved it. So many times we overcomplicate this business. You can take computer reports, velocity reports, any kind of reports you want to and go lay out your counters by computer. But if you simply think like a customer, you will do a better job of merchandise presentation and selection than any other way. It's not always easy. To think like a customer, you have to think about details. Whoever said 'retail is detail' is absolutely 100 percent right. On the other hand it's simple. If the customers are the bosses, all you have to do is please them."

I couldn't agree with David more. Everything we've done since we started Wal-Mart has been devoted to this idea that the customer is our boss. The controversies it has led us into have surprised me, but they've been easy to live with because we have never doubted our philosophy that the customer comes ahead of everything else.

CHAPTER 13

MEETING THE COMPETITION

"Sam phoned to tell me he was going to start a wholesale club. It was no surprise. He is notorious for looking at what everybody else does, taking the best of it, and then making it better."

—SOL PRICE,
*founder—1955—Fed-Mart,
and founder—1976—Price Club*

I don't know what would have happened to Wal-Mart if we had laid low and never stirred up the competition. My guess is that we would have remained a strictly regional operator. Then, eventually, I think we would have been forced to sell out to some national chain looking for a quick way to expand into the heartland market. Maybe there would have been 100 or 150 Wal-Marts on the street for a while, but today they would all have Kmart or Target signs in front of them, and I would have become a full-time bird hunter.

We'll never know, because we chose the other route. We decided that instead of avoiding our competitors, or waiting for them to come to us, we would meet them head-on. It was one of the smartest strategic decisions we ever made. In fact, if our story doesn't prove anything else about the free market system, it erases any doubt that spirited competition is good for business—not just customers, but the companies which have to compete with one another too. Our competitors have honed and sharpened us to an edge we wouldn't have without them. We wouldn't be nearly as good as we are today without Kmart, and I think they would admit we've made them a better retailer. One reason Sears fell so far off the pace is that they wouldn't admit for the longest time that Wal-Mart and Kmart were their real competition. They ignored both of us, and we both blew right by them.

BUD WALTON:

"Competition is very definitely what made Wal-Mart—from the very beginning. There's not an individual in these whole United States who has been in more retail stores—all types of retail stores too, not just discount stores—than Sam Walton. Make that all over the world. He's been in stores in Australia and South America, Europe and Asia and South Africa. His mind is just so inquisitive when it comes to this business. And there may not be anything he enjoys more than going into a competitor's store trying to learn something from it."

At first, we only butted heads with other regional discounters, like Gibson's and the Magic Mart discount division of Sterling. We didn't compete directly with Kmart. To put things into perspective, compare Kmart and Wal-Mart after they had both been on the street for ten years. Our fifty-plus Wal-Marts and eleven variety stores were doing about $80 million a year in sales compared to Kmart's five hundred stores doing more than $3 billion a year. But Kmart had interested me ever since the first store went up in 1962. I was in their stores constantly because they were the laboratory, and they were better than we were. I spent a heck of a lot of my time wandering through their stores talking to their people and trying to figure out how they did things.

For a long time, I had been itching to try our luck against them, and finally, in 1972, we saw a perfect opportunity in Hot Springs, Arkansas—a much larger city than we were accustomed to moving into but still close to home and full of customers we understood. We saw Kmart sitting there all alone, really having their way with the market. They had no competition, and their prices and margins were so high that they almost weren't even discounting. We sent Phil Green in to open store number 52, which, you may remember, is where he stirred up all the fuss with the world's largest Tide display and all his other outrageous promotions. He cut prices to the bone and stole a bunch of Kmart's customers.

Coincidentally, it was right about that time that Harry Cunningham chose to retire as the CEO of Kmart, which he had founded while he was chairman of S. S. Kresge. This was a big break for us. Harry was really the guy who, in just ten years, had legitimized the discount industry and made Kmart into the model for us all—though my good friend, John Geisse, who helped found the Target and Venture stores, was another pioneer way ahead of his time.

HARRY CUNNINGHAM:

"From the time anybody first noticed Sam, it was obvious he had adopted almost all of the original Kmart ideas. I always had great admiration for the way he implemented—and later enlarged on—those ideas. Much later on, when I was retired but still a Kmart board member, I tried to advise the company's management of just what a serious threat I thought he was. But it wasn't until fairly recently that they took him seriously."

I guess we really were a flea attacking an elephant, and the elephant didn't respond right away. Maybe Harry's right. Maybe they didn't take us seriously until much later. But I always believed it made them mad, our going in on them like that in Hot Springs. Just a few years later, around 1976 and 1977, we definitely got the message that Kmart—with 1,000 stores—thought Wal-Mart—with 150—had gotten too big for its britches. All of a sudden they took a direct shot right into our backyard, by opening up in four of our better towns: Jefferson City and Poplar Bluff, Missouri; and Fayetteville and Rogers, Arkansas. They were expanding like that all over the country at the time, and all the regional discounters were worried. In 1976, we had a session of our discounters' trade group in Phoenix, and a lot of guys were talking about ways to avoid competing with Kmart directly. I got a little mad, and told everybody they ought to stand up and fight them. I made it clear we planned to.

HERB FISHER, FOUNDER, CHAIRMAN, AND CEO, JAMESWAY CORPORATION:

"Kmart was opening so many stores it was regarded as the Genghis Khan of the discounting business. Sam has always been clear about his attitude: 'Meet them head-on. Competition will make us a better company.'

"He is that way with everyone. Personally, he's such a fine, unassuming, quiet gentleman. But he's always picking your brain, and he always has a notebook or that tape recorder. He'll learn everything you know, but he shares his information freely with you in return.

"Now, of course, he's a competitor to Jamesway. But he wouldn't ever apologize for that. He thinks it makes us a better company. And he's right."

Something else happened in late 1976 which really helped us gear up for competition. A research group set up by a bunch of us regional discounters—who at the time didn't compete in each other's territories—had its first meeting here in Bentonville. Guys like Herb Fisher of Jamesway, and Herb Gillman of Ames, and Dale Worman of Fred Meyer all came down here and went through our stores to give us their opinion of how they thought we were doing. And, man, what they had to say really shocked us.

NICK WHITE, EXECUTIVE VICE PRESIDENT, WAL-MART:

"Bill Fields was running the Rogers store, Dean Sanders was running Siloam Springs, and I was running Springdale—all close to Bentonville—so we were all on the tour. These guys —the presidents of all these companies—they just ripped our stores apart, telling us how poorly we did *everything*. 'The signing isn't worth a damn.' 'You've got your prices too high on this.' 'This stuff isn't even priced.' 'You've got too much of this and not enough of that.' I mean, it was really critical.''

That was really a turning point in our business. We listened to everything they had to say, and made huge adjustments based on those critiques. It helped us gear up for any competition, especially Kmart, whose attack on us was probably the best single external event in Wal-Mart's history. We pulled ourselves together and designed a big plan—a promotional program and a people program and a merchandising program—for how we were going to react. Since our run on Kmart in Hot Springs had turned out well, we were confident we could compete.

THOMAS JEFFERSON:

"Kmart really took us on in about 1977, and I remember Little Rock particularly. They took us on there in North Little Rock, where store number 7 had been one of our better stores. They got aggressive, and we fought back. We told our manager there, 'No matter what, don't let them undersell you at all, on anything.' I remember he called me one Saturday night and said, 'You know, we have Crest toothpaste down to six cents a tube now.' And I said, 'Well, just keep it there and see what they do.' They didn't lower it any more than that, and we both just kept it at six cents. Finally, they backed off. I always thought they learned something about us at that store —that we don't bend easy—because they never came at us with that degree of price cutting anywhere else.''

We got so much better so quickly it was hard to believe. We totally stood Kmart off in those small towns of ours. Almost from the beginning, they weren't very successful at taking our customers away in Jeff City and Poplar Bluff. Once Kmart arrived, we worked even harder at pleasing our customers, and they stayed loyal. This gave us a great surge of confidence in ourselves.

But at the time, remember, our sales were about 5 percent of Kmart's. And we had recently suffered that exodus of executives following the Ron Mayer departure. So we were having a heck of a time convincing Wall Street to stick with us. A lot of people didn't think we could stand up to *real* competition. One analyst, Margo Alexander of Mitchell Hutchins Inc., really worried about the exodus in her report on Wal-Mart. She wondered if it wouldn't discourage other executives from coming on board. She said they might see an inevitable conflict with "the entrepreneur who will never be satisfied with another person running 'his' company," in other words, me. She also questioned whether I, having retired once, was as committed to running the business as I had been previously.

Here's some of what she wrote about us in January of 1977:

> One of the key elements in Wal-Mart's success has been the lack of competition in its small, rural markets . . . It is clearly easier to operate in this kind of situation than in a competitive one: pricing need not be so sharp, and the "right" merchandise is less critical, simply because customers have no alternative . . . Although Wal-Mart says its stores compete effectively against Kmart, the company will avoid a Kmart if possible. While we don't expect Kresge to stage any massive invasion of Wal-Mart's existing territory, Kresge could logically act to contain Wal-Mart's geographical expansion . . . Assuming some containment policy on Kresge's part, Wal-Mart could run into serious problems in the next few years.
>
> We would very much like to recommend purchase of the stock . . . Unfortunately, however, the future of the company appears uncertain, and we think that Wal-Mart is one of those threshold companies that runs the risk of stumbling.

Reports like that one didn't help us much, but the truth is that her analysis of the situation wasn't necessarily as wrong as it looks today. All those things could have come true. She missed a few key points, though. Her biggest mistake was the uncertainty she felt about the management team that followed Ron Mayer. As I said earlier, having David Glass and Jack Shewmaker both on board in senior positions gave us about as much talent under one roof as any one retailer could ever hope to have. In recent years, I've taken a lot of pride in the fact that our fastest expansion—the greatest growth period in the history of retail—actually came after everybody thought our goose was cooked and ready to be eaten by the Kmart folks from Detroit.

Another point missed by Margo Alexander and others was that a very fortunate thing happened to us on the competitive front: Kmart was developing its own problems. Toward the end of 1976, they had purchased more than two hundred store locations left over from the defunct Grant's chain, and they had their hands full trying to make that work. Not only that, they seemed to have a management philosophy at the time of avoiding all change, something that never works in this business. I'm sure that worrying about Wal-Mart fell way down on their priority list, and I occasionally think back to how lucky we were not to have had to face Harry Cunningham—or Kmart's current management team —during that period.

Regardless of what was going on at Kmart, the new team we had in place in Bentonville by the late seventies had us well positioned for the next decade of growth. It was around this same time that many of the high-flying promoters in the discounting business began to struggle for their lives. The national economy weakened in the mid-seventies, and the intense competition among the real merchants began to drive the fast-buck types out of the business. The more efficient Kmart, Target, Wal-Mart, and some of the regionals became, and the more we bumped into each other in competitive situations, the more we were able to lower prices.

The percentage of gross margin in this industry—really, the markup on merchandise—has dropped steadily from around 35 percent in the early sixties to only 22 percent today. Almost all of that represents increased value and savings to the customers who shop discount stores. So the guys who weren't running efficient operations, who had taken on lots of debt and were living high and not taking care of their associates, who weren't scrambling around to get the best deals on merchandise and passing those deals on to their customers, these guys got into trouble. When we saw Kmart headed right after us in 1976 and 1977, we decided we could pick up some speed in our expansion efforts by acquiring some struggling discounters.

Because Wal-Mart had always been such a homegrown operation, this whole period sparked a lot of philosophical debate around our offices, and, frankly, I changed sides so often that I drove everybody involved pretty crazy. I didn't have many problems at all with our first real acquisition, which came in 1977. My brother Bud and David Glass negotiated a deal to buy a small chain called Mohr Value discount stores up in Illinois. Their stores had been averaging $3 million to $5 million a year per store, and it seemed like a good way to put a beachhead into some new territory. We closed five stores and converted the remaining sixteen to Wal-Marts, and it wasn't much of a shock to our system.

It sure didn't slow us down any because two years later, in 1979, with about 230 stores on the street, we hit a billion dollars in sales for the first time. Of all the milestones we ever reached, that one probably impressed me the most. I have to admit, I was amazed that Wal-Mart had turned into a billion-dollar company. But I couldn't see any logic to stopping there, and right about then another acquisition opportunity came our way.

This one was a good bit more disruptive, but it helped us make a geographic leap that was very important to our expansion. A lot of people back East who don't know much about Wal-Mart still think of us today as a "Southern" discount operator. Maybe it's because we're in Arkansas, which most people think of as a Southern state, even though where we are is really more Midwestern. Or maybe it's because of our downhome image. But the truth is that until 1981, we had almost no stores east of the Mississippi. We were big in Arkansas, Louisiana, Mississippi, and Texas, but had nothing in Tennessee, Alabama, Georgia, or the Carolinas. We weren't much of a competitor in the South at all.

On the other hand, Kuhn's Big K stores had become a good-sized player in the South. Based in Nashville, Tennessee, Kuhn's had started as a single variety store back sometime before 1920. Jack Kuhn and his brother Gus had converted the company into a discounter, made an acquisition or two, and grown it into a chain of 112 stores, concentrated in Tennessee, but also doing business in Kentucky, Alabama, Georgia, and South Carolina—all states where we thought we could do well. We were a good bit bigger than they were, but the two of us had been watching each other pretty closely. It was sort of like the old variety store days when one chain, like TG&Y, wouldn't go into the territory of another chain, like Hested's. We knew that one way or another we had to head on into the South, and I guess we stirred them up by crossing the Mississippi and opening a store in Jackson, Tennessee. They retaliated by opening stores in West Helena and Blytheville, Arkansas. The truth is, we were closing in on Kuhn's and really doing a better job than they were. In fact, they were beginning to falter. They had taken on some debt and built a fancy headquarters building. And they were showing some losses.

I had a heck of a time making up my mind what to do. I wanted to get into that territory before Kmart or somebody else woke up and stole our thunder there. It seemed like a great competitive move to make. But we'd never bitten off anything close to this size before, and we didn't know what it would be like trying to digest it. We went round and round on it. We were on again, off again for probably two years. Finally, the Executive Committee sat down to vote on it one morning, and it came out split right down the middle, fifty-fifty. It was just as well because it gave me the opportunity to take the ultimate responsibility for the decision. The whole thing had been really cloudy all along, with a lot of arguing. Finally, I voted to do it. We didn't know how to go about folding Kuhn's into Wal-Mart, but we put Paul Carter in charge and he commuted back and forth between Nashville and Bentonville for quite a while.

PAUL CARTER, EXECUTIVE VICE PRESIDENT AND CHIEF FINANCIAL OFFICER, WAL-MART:

"It was one of the few times we ever saw the chairman use his prerogative and say, 'We are going to do this.' It was a new kind of proposition for Wal-Mart. At first we thought we were going to run everything from Nashville, as a separate division. Then we changed our minds and decided to close all their offices down and bring everything over here. It was the furthest out we'd ever been geographically, and, looking back, I guess the decision to run it from here had a big influence on how we've run the company ever since, with all the regional managers based in Bentonville.

"I went over there to Big K weighing 190 pounds and came back at 165. It was a struggle for all of us involved, and a stretch for the whole company. But I'm not sure that's not good for every organization at some point. Jack Shewmaker took the situation as an opportunity to learn and implement a lot about communications in a spread-out situation. Hard as it was, the Big K thing was really good for this company. It was like a caterpillar that turns into a butterfly. As a company, we were really ready to fly after we emerged from that one."

We closed down some of Kuhn's money-losing stores, and for the first time we tried to supply our stores using an outside company, a third-party distributor, which didn't work at all. But once we figured out how to handle it, the acquisition put us in a great position for growth. We exploded from that point on, almost always opening 100 new stores a year, and more than 150 in some years. I think the Kuhn's deal gave us a new confidence that we could conquer anything.

I don't know how the folks around our executive offices see me, and I know they get frustrated with the way I make everybody go back and forth on so many issues that come up. But I see myself as being a little more inclined than most of them are to take chances. On something like the Kuhn's decision, I try to play a "what-if" game with the numbers—but it's generally my gut that makes the final decision. If it feels right, I tend to go for it, and if it doesn't, I back off.

Sometimes, of course, that leads me into mistakes. Back in the early eighties, for example, I traveled all over the world looking at global competition in retailing. I went to Germany, France, Italy, South Africa, Great Britain, Australia, and South America, and saw several concepts which interested me. I was impressed with the giant Carrefours stores in Brazil, which got me started on a campaign to bring home a concept called Hypermart—giant stores with groceries and general merchandise under one roof. I checked them out in Europe and came back pushing the concept hard. I argued that everybody except the U.S. was successful with this concept and we should get in on the ground floor with it. I was certain this was where the next competitive battlefield would be.

Eventually, we opened two Hypermarts in the Dallas-Fort Worth area, one in Topeka, and one in Kansas City. By now we had gotten enough respect in the business so that Kmart jumped right in behind us with their own Hypermart concept called American Fare. Our Hypermarts weren't disasters, but they were disappointments. They were marginally profitable stores, and they taught us what our next step should be in combining grocery and general merchandising—a smaller concept called the Supercenter. But I was mistaken in my vision of the potential the Hypermart held in this country.

We conducted other similar, but less publicized, experiments that didn't work out so well either. Our dot Discount Drug concept grew to twenty-five stores before we decided it wasn't going to be profitable enough. And we tried one home improvement center called Save Mor in the building which had housed the original Wal-Mart in Rogers, which was also not a success. As David Glass says about me, once I decide I'm wrong, I'm ready to move on to something else.

But when one of our experiments works, watch out. Take Sam's Clubs, for example. It was an experiment when we started it up in 1983, and now nine years later it's a $10 billion business with more than 217 stores and terrific growth potential. Sam's are big stores in warehouse-type buildings aimed at small-business owners and other customers who buy merchandise in bulk. A membership fee entitles a customer to shop at Sam's, which charges wholesale prices for name-brand, often high-end merchandise—everything from tires to cameras to watches to office supplies to cocktail sausages and soft drinks. If you've never been in one, they're a lot of fun to shop, and the people who work there are a little crazy. Like the old days at Wal-Mart, they're liable to do anything on a moment's notice to move the merchandise.

Just like discounting, I'm sorry to say we can't take any of the credit for inventing the wholesale club concept. Put yourself in our position for a moment, though, and you can see why we had to steal the idea from those who did roll it out. It was the early eighties, and we'd been in the discount business for around twenty years. Only the efficient operators were still in business, because prices, and margins, had been falling steadily the whole time. Suddenly, we noticed a whole new class of sub-discounter undercutting our prices, wholesalers with very low overhead who were selling at margins way below the 22 percent in the discount business—5 to 7 percent. Since "Low Prices Every Day" had brought us this far, we had to explore the business. Especially since we knew that Sol Price—one of the original discount pioneers—was behind this idea. He had started his Price Club stores in 1976.

So one day in 1983 I went to see Sol in San Diego. I had met him earlier when my son Rob and I called on him. This time, though, Helen and I were out on the West Coast already for a meeting of the mass merchandisers, so we dropped down to have dinner with Sol and his wife Helen at Lubock's. And I admit it. I didn't tell him at the time that I was going to copy his program, but that's what I did.

I came home and went over to Oklahoma City, where we rented an old building for about ninety cents a square foot, or maybe even seventy-five cents. We remodeled it and, to manage it, put together a pickup crew of mavericks who were sort of underappreciated at Wal-Mart. We had two or three buyers. We whipped up a program and a design, and put the whole thing in motion. We opened our first club in 1983. It had that same feel of chaos and excitement as the early days at Wal-Mart. And we went out of our way from the very beginning to separate the Sam's Club culture from the Wal-Mart culture. One of the guys I picked was Rob Voss. He was not really looked on as a top management talent at Wal-Mart because he was always swimming against the current more than he was going with it. He was a little bit of an agitator.

ROB VOSS, FIRST GENERAL MERCHANDISE MANAGER, SAM'S CLUB:

"I told Sam up front that he had a lot of egos around this company, and that they needed to understand we were going to be doing our own merchandising. So he got up at a Saturday morning meeting and told everybody—this is a direct quote—'The Sam's Club operation will be doing their own merchandising. If any of you buyers out here with Wal-Mart take exception to that, and feel that because you're the buyer of a category you should be buying it for the entire company, I suggest you come and visit with me in my office on a one-on-one basis, and then I'll explain it to you in a little more detail.' From that day on, we never had a problem."

We quickly went on to open Sam's in Kansas City and Dallas and then two units in Houston. It was a lot like Wal-Mart. Once we had those five units up and going, I knew we could run with it, and we did. I hate to say it, but I guess it was almost what you'd call a second childhood for me—a second challenge anyway. I had a chance to build a company all over again, and I tried to be as hands-on as I could, although David Glass was heavily involved with Sam's from early on too.

RON LOVELESS, RETIRED SENIOR VICE PRESIDENT, WAL-MART:

"I came over from Wal-Mart to help set up Sam's. Since we were patterned after Price Clubs, sometimes we copied them without exactly knowing what we were doing. We were bringing a West Coast idea to the Midwest, and we didn't know how it would be received. I remember one idea that didn't transfer too well. Price Club had a huge stack of wine in the front of its stores. We bought the same amount for our stores in the Midwest, and we learned the hard way that Mid-westerners aren't exactly wine drinkers."

TOM COUGHLIN, SENIOR VICE PRESIDENT,
SAM'S CLUBS:

> "This business is fun. It really is. It's so *basic*. So straightfor-
> ward. We do no advertising, but our whole business is based
> on selling the concept. We sell small business operators on the
> idea that for $25 a year they can have a just-in-time warehouse
> with all the same price advantages for goods that large compa-
> nies get. And just like Wal-Mart, our customers get to know
> and love our culture. They know there are no frills whatso-
> ever in those warehouses. They know our management peo-
> ple are likely to be the ones to grab the forklift and pull the
> goods down for them, and they come to expect it. And like
> it."

The competition in the club business can get pretty spirited
sometimes. Once I was in the big Price Club on Marino Avenue
in San Diego, and I had my little tape recorder with me—like I
always do—and I was making notes to myself about prices and
merchandising ideas. This guy, a big guy, comes up to me and
says, "I'm sorry but I'll have to take your tape recorder and erase
the material you've got on it. We have a policy against people
using them in the stores." Well, we have the same policy, and I
knew I was caught. So I said, "I respect that. But I've got things
on here from other stores that I don't want to lose, so let me write
a note to Robert Price"—that's Sol's son. So I wrote: "Robert,
your guy is just too good. I was trying to get some information
on this recorder about some of the items you were carrying and
some of my impressions of your store, and he caught me. So
here's the tape. If you want to listen to it, you certainly have that
privilege, but I have some other material on here I would like
very much to have back." So in about four days I got a nice note
back from Robert, with the tape, and none of it had been blurred
or scratched out. He probably treated me better than I deserved.

The Sam's launch reflects another part of my management
style that applies not only to the competition, but to our own
people as well. I like to keep everybody guessing. I don't want our

competitors getting too comfortable with feeling like they can predict what we're going to do. And I don't want our own executives feeling that way either. It's part of my strong feeling for the necessity of constant change, for keeping people a little off balance.

A lot of folks in my position would have been perfectly content with the situation as it stood in 1984. Our 640 Wal-Marts were earning almost $200 million a year on sales of more than $4.5 billion, we were still growing like wildfire, and we were underway with Sam's. But I felt like we had to make a change. So I called in Jack Shewmaker, by now our president and chief operating officer, and asked him if he would mind swapping jobs with David Glass, our chief financial officer. Not your everyday request from the chairman in most companies, I guess. I valued the talents of both of these guys enormously, but I had my own reasons for wanting to see how the switch might work out. Jack is so smart and aggressive and sure of himself that sometimes he could be a little rough on folks, and I wanted to see how somebody with David's smoother manner would handle the job.

Jack said he already knew he didn't want to stay at Wal-Mart until he was an old man, so after some discussion, we agreed on the switch. David took the president's job, and Jack stayed on for three more years as chief financial officer, and he did a great job. Today, he does international consulting work, and he remains a valuable Wal-Mart board member. David, of course, turned into a fantastic president, and about five years ago I relinquished my CEO title to him. At that time, Jack retired.

As well as all that worked out for everyone—and it really did —I won't pretend there wasn't tension surrounding that period in our history. This is a highly competitive business, and an even more competitive company. It naturally attracts a lot of ambitious people, sometimes with egos to match. Ever since my peewee football days, I've believed almost any kind of competition is great. I expect our folks to compete with one another and as I have said, what I hate is to see a rivalry become a personal thing, where the folks don't support one another.

Competition is actually the reason I love retailing so much. The Wal-Mart story is just another chapter in that history of competition—a great chapter, mind you—but it's all part of the evolution of the industry. There's always a challenger coming along. There may be one on the street right now formulating a plan to get to the top. To stay ahead of those challengers, we have to keep changing and looking back over our shoulder and planning ahead. That's one reason we bought the McLane company a few years ago. It's a big distributor to grocery stores, and it should be a great base for us to push on into that market, where we feel customers are ready for our way of doing business.

Right now, I see a lot of new challengers coming from offshore with some very sophisticated programs. Some of the emerging competitors in this country who have come from Holland, Germany, and France bear close watching. And it won't be long before we have a wave of Japanese retail concepts arriving. I don't know if Wal-Mart can truly maintain our leadership position by just staying in this country. I think we're going to have to become a more international company in the not-too-distant future. We've created an international division in the company, and we have a joint venture with a Mexican company called CIFRA for the development of Club Aurrera, a wholesale club concept. We've opened two with plans for more soon. Absorbing people from other cultures quickly and smoothly into the company will present a real challenge to Wal-Mart in the near future—but our folks are up to it.

On the domestic front, competition in the discount business has improved tremendously in the last few years. Our competitors are doing a better job of serving their customers, of getting them through the checkout lines. They're running cleaner stores with better merchandise presentations. They're making our job a lot harder. But so far, none of our competitors has yet been able to operate on the volume that we do as efficiently as we do. They haven't been able to get their expense structure as low as ours, and they haven't been able to get their associates to do all those extra things for their customers that ours do routinely: greeting them, smiling at them, helping them, thanking them. And they haven't been able to move their merchandise as efficiently, or keep it in stock as efficiently, as we do.

If anyone is ever able to top us in any of those areas, we will have real concern. At this point, no one has been able to do it.

CHAPTER 14

EXPANDING THE CIRCLES

"Distribution and transportation have been so successful at Wal-Mart because senior management views this part of the company as a competitive advantage, not as some afterthought or necessary evil. And they support it with capital investment. A lot of companies don't want to spend any money on distribution unless they have to. Ours spends because we continually demonstrate that it lowers our costs. This is a very important strategic point in understanding Wal-Mart."

—JOE HARDIN,
executive vice president,
logistics and personnel

Some of our guys around here find it amusing that I get so much credit for Wal-Mart's reputation as a world leader in retailing and distribution technology. It's not because we're not on the cutting edge. We are. They're amused because, as I told you, ever since I went to that IBM school in 1966, I've put up a pretty good fight every time somebody wants to buy some new system for this, that, or the other. I want them to think hard about how they're going to justify the expense before they even come to me with it.

But there's no question about it: one of the main reasons we've been able to roll this company out nationally was all the pressure put on me by guys like David Glass and, earlier, Jack Shewmaker and Ron Mayer, to invest so heavily in technology. Yes, I argued and resisted, but I eventually signed the checks. And we have been able to move way out front of the industry in both communications and distribution. During that period in the late seventies when Kmart's management had such a strong resistance to any kind of change, that resistance included investment in systems. At the same time, our fellows were just absolutely convinced that computers were essential to managing growth and keeping down our cost structure. Today, of course, they've been proven so right that they look like geniuses. I would go so far as to say, in fact, that the efficiencies and economies of scale we realize from our distribution system give us one of our greatest competitive advantages.

Many people have contributed over the years, but David Glass has to get the lion's share of the credit for where we are today in distribution. David had a vision for automated distribution centers—linked by computer both to our stores and to our suppliers—and he set about building such a system, beginning in 1978 at Searcy, Arkansas.

DAVID GLASS:

"Searcy probably was built about two years later than we needed it, so there was a lot of pressure on us to get it up and running. The big knock on Wal-Mart was that we weren't going to be able to expand much beyond the 350-mile ring around our distribution center in Bentonville. Because of that logistical problem, our disbelievers said we would always be a medium-sized regional retailer confined to this area. I pushed hard for Searcy as the solution. It was a real ambitious plan: our first remote, mechanized distribution center. Unfortunately, we needed it so badly that we had to rush it into service, and the crunch turned it into a disaster—my disaster. It was as bad as Sam's opening at Harrison, only more serious.

"We were shipping freight out of there before we had a roof on the building, and nothing—not even the toilets—worked like it was supposed to. We had guys like Glenn Habern, our data processing manager, and Paul Carter down there driving forklifts—until Habern tore down a rack and spilled Listerine all over the place. Working conditions were terrible, and the next thing you know the union was down there organizing.

"It was such a nightmare that Sam began to question the whole idea of mechanized distribution. He really wasn't sure it worked at all. Fortunately, he hired Don Soderquist from Ben Franklin around that time, and Don came in as a big supporter of what we were trying to do. He believed in mechanized distribution all the way, and he eventually took over distribution from me in 1980. He went on to do a great job expanding it, helping introduce a lot of innovation, including a badly needed new inventory management system.

"Fortunately, we turned Searcy around and made it work because it saved our neck after we took on all those Kuhn's stores. We had to figure out how to supply them, and our arrangement with a third-party distributor turned into a nightmare. So we built an addition at Searcy to service them, and it solved the problem. Searcy—which is one of our best-performing distribution centers today—really was the key to our whole distribution system. After we proved it would work, we were able to duplicate the model anywhere, and that's what we've done."

I think it's fair to say that our distribution system today is the envy certainly of everyone in our industry, and in a lot of others as well. We now have twenty of these centers placed strategically in our trade areas around the country—still mostly within a day's drive, or about 350 miles, of the stores they serve. Combined, they account for more than 18 million square feet of distribution space. We stock over 80,000 items in our stores, and our warehouses directly replenish almost 85 percent of their inventory, compared to only about 50 to 65 percent for our competition. As a result, the gap from the time our in-store merchants place their computer orders until they receive replenishment averages only about two days. That probably compares to five or more days for a lot of our competitors, which don't ship as much merchandise through their own network.

The time savings and flexibility are great, but the cost savings alone would make the investment worthwhile. Our costs run less than 3 percent to ship goods to our stores, while it probably costs our competitors between 4½ to 5 percent to get those same goods to their stores. The math is pretty simple: if we both sell the same goods for the same price at retail, we'll earn 2½ percent more profit than they will right there.

JOE HARDIN:

"When you own and manage your distribution and logistics channel, you have a great competitive advantage over companies that rely on third-party suppliers. It automatically shortens your lead times, but also you can constantly look for ways to improve your operation and try to make it more efficient. You never have to rely on what's going on in somebody else's shop. In our case, we generally know where things are in relationship to when we want them to arrive, so we can schedule and plan to move goods into the stores at the right time. That maximizes our in-stock positions, which is vital. You can't generate sales unless you have the product there when the customer wants it."

Not only do we stock more of our merchandise in our own distribution centers, we also rely on our own private truck fleet to a much greater degree than our competitors do. Our private fleet is one of the nation's largest, maybe *the* largest. Last year, David asked Lee Scott, our vice president who oversees transportation, to try and locate every truck and trailer in the fleet on a single day just to show that we could do it. Of course he did, and at last count, Lee says we have more than two thousand over-the-road tractors and more than eleven thousand trailers. Unlike both Kmart and Target, which contract out with third parties to deliver a lot of freight from their distribution centers, we've always felt that we needed our own fleet.

To have the kind of flexibility we want—that ability to respond above and beyond what we could ask some outsider to do for us—we need drivers who are part of our team, drivers who are as dedicated to serving our customers as the associates in the stores. And, man, do we ever have them. When you're out on the highway and you pass by a Wal-Mart truck, you can bet your bottom dollar that the guy behind the wheel is a true professional. He's not just driving a truck. He's dedicated to servicing those stores, and he knows he's an ambassador of Wal–Mart and everything we stand for out on the road. I'll just say it: we have the best damned truck drivers in America, and their loyalty and their can-do attitude have made a huge difference to this company.

LEE SCOTT:

"Our drivers really are extremely loyal to their mission, which is to serve the stores. They report back to Wal–Mart continually on things like merchandise thrown out behind the store that looked like it was good, attitude and morale problems in the stores. For a long, long time, Sam would show up regularly in the drivers' break room at 4 A.M. with a bunch of doughnuts and just sit there for a couple of hours talking to them.

"He grilled them. 'What are you seeing at the stores?' 'Have you been to that store lately?' 'How do the people act there?' 'Is it getting better?' It makes sense. The drivers see more stores every week than anybody else in this company. And I think what Sam likes about them is that they're not like a lot of managers. They don't care who you are. They'll tell you what they really think."

Of course, the only thing that makes the whole distribution system work so well is the dedication of the people all across it. The technology and hardware are just tools. The people in the system believe, just as firmly as the associates in the stores, that their primary job is to take care of the customer. Except in their case, the customer is the Wal–Mart store or Sam's Club they're supplying.

With that idea at the root of everything, we've developed a unique ability to customize what we do to meet the needs of our stores. Until recently, for example, we bragged that we were making deliveries every day to 97 percent of our stores. Then we discovered that wasn't necessarily the best thing for all of our stores, particularly the smaller ones. So now we've gone into a customized delivery program in which stores can pick one of four different delivery plans. Every six months, each store decides which plan it prefers. And we also have a plan called accelerated delivery, designed for stores located within a certain distance of a distribution center. A store in that plan can order merchandise on Monday night and get it on Tuesday night. Nobody else in the business can deliver like that on any kind of widespread basis.

When all this comes together at one of our distribution centers, it's really a sight to behold. You really have to see one of these places in action to appreciate them, and sometimes I can hardly believe them myself. But I'll try to describe the activity at one. Start with a building of around 1.1 million square feet, which is about as much floor space as twenty-three football fields, sitting out somewhere on some 150 acres. Fill it high to the roof with every kind of merchandise you can imagine, from toothpaste to TV's, toilet paper to toys, bicycles to barbecue grills. Everything in it is bar-coded, and a computer tracks the location and movement of every case of merchandise, while it's stored and when it's shipped out. Some six hundred to eight hundred associates staff the place, which runs around the clock, twenty-four hours a day. On one side of the building is a shipping dock with loading doors for around thirty trucks at a time—usually full. On the other side is the receiving dock, which may have as many as 135 doors for unloading merchandise.

These goods move in and out of the warehouse on some 8½ miles of laser-guided conveyor belts, which means that the lasers read the bar codes on the cases and then direct them to whatever truck is filling the order placed by one of the stores it's servicing that night. On a heavy day, those belts might handle up to 200,000 cases of goods. When the thing is running full speed, it's just a blur of boxes and crates flying down those belts, red lasers flashing everywhere, directing this box to that truck, or that box to this truck. Out in the parking lot, whole packs of Wal-Mart trucks rumble in and out all day. I get tremendously excited going out to these centers, talking with our associates and drinking coffee with them and the truck drivers. It's amazing to me how many ideas they always have for fine-tuning the system. If you get the idea that I'm awfully proud of what we've managed to do in distribution, you're right.

To get the whole picture, though, it's important to realize that the same thing is happening simultaneously at nineteen other almost identical distribution centers every day. Not only that, for us to continue expanding the way we do, we have to constantly plan the construction and staffing of more and more of these giant mechanized warehouses, and that's no small task for Joe Hardin and his folks. We'll probably have thirty in operation in just the next few years. They're already on the drawing boards.

From the time David Glass came on board in 1976, he's been pushing me to invest and invest and invest in that system, and thank goodness he managed to be so persuasive. At the same time, he and Jack Shewmaker were also pushing hard for heavy investment in more and more, better and better computer systems, so that we could track sales and merchandise and inventories across the company—especially in-store transactions. When Jack became our president and chief operating officer in 1978, he worked really hard at getting me to invest in bar coding and SKU item control, which is a computerized stockkeeping unit inventory system. Jack also was heavily involved in the creation of our satellite system, which turned out to be another one of our tremendous competitive advantages.

JACK SHEWMAKER:

"Glenn Habern was our data processing manager, and he and I had this dream of an interactive communications system on which you could communicate back and forth between all the stores and the distribution centers and the general office. Glenn came up with the idea of using the satellite, and I said, 'Let's pursue it without asking anybody.' So we got it to the point where we were ready to make a proposal, and we told Sam. He just listened. He didn't necessarily discourage me. But he didn't encourage me either. Sam never gets excited about systems.

"The technology didn't really exist to do this for a retailer in the early eighties. But we got together with the Macom &

Hughes Corporation, and worked out a contract, and eventually we committed $24 million to build it. We launched it in 1983, and I mean, Sam liked to killed me the first two years. It was not an immediate success. But we got it working, and now, of course, everybody has one."

The satellite turned out to be absolutely necessary because, once we had those scanners in the stores, we had all this data pouring into Bentonville over phone lines. Those lines have a limited capacity, so as we added more and more stores, we had a real logjam of stuff coming in from the field. As you know, I like my numbers as quickly as I can get them. The quicker we get that information, the quicker we can act on it. The system has been a great tool for us, and our technical people have done a terrific job of figuring out how to use it to our best advantage.

Jack is absolutely right about me and systems, though. I rarely get excited about them. A few years ago, we built this huge building right next to our main offices—around 135,000 square feet—just to house the computers, and everyone at the time told me how much room we'd have to grow. I mean it was really empty in there just two or three years ago. Well, already it's completely full of computer equipment. And when I look back, it's no wonder. We've spent almost $700 million building up the current computer and satellite systems we have. I'm told it's the largest civilian data base of its kind in the world—even bigger than AT&T's.

None of that matters to me. What I like about it is the kind of information we can pull out of it on a moment's notice—all those numbers. For one thing, we keep a sixty-five-week rolling history of every single item we stock in Wal-Mart or Sam's. That means I can pick anything, say a little combination TV/VCR like I use here in my office, and tell you exactly how many of them we've bought over the last year and a quarter, and exactly how many of them we've sold. Not only overall, but in any or every region, every district, every store. It makes it tough for a vendor to know more about how his product is doing in our stores than we do. I guess we've always known that information gives you a certain power, but the degree to which we can retrieve it in our computer really does give us the power of competitive advantage.

I can walk in that satellite room, where our technicians sit in front of their computer screens talking on the phone to any stores that might be having a problem with the system, and just looking over their shoulder for a minute or two will tell me a lot about how a particular day is going. Up on the screen I can see the total of the day's bank credit card sales adding up as they occur. I can see how many stolen bank cards we've retrieved that day. I can tell if our seven-second credit card approval system is working as it should be and monitor the number of transactions we've conducted that day. If we have something really important or urgent to communicate to the stores and distribution centers—something important enough to warrant a personal visit—I, or any other Wal-Mart executive, can walk back to our TV studio and get on that satellite transmission and get it right out there. And, as I told you earlier, I can go in every Saturday morning around three, look over those printouts, and know precisely what kind of week we've had.

So you see, technology and distribution *are* every bit as important to Wal-Mart's ability to grow and maintain control as you may have heard or read over the years. But when you see all those satellite dishes outside our building, or hear about all the computers inside it, or look at some videotape of our laser-guided distribution centers, don't let anybody kid you. Without the right managers, and the dedicated associates and truck drivers all across the system, all that stuff is totally worthless.

CHAPTER 15

THINKING SMALL

"Well, now, Sam, how big do you really want this company to be? What is your plan?"

—FEROLD AREND,
*shortly after coming
to work at Wal-Mart*

"Ferold, we're going to take it as it comes, and if we can grow with our own money, we'll maybe add a store or two."

—SAM WALTON

Not long ago somebody showed me an article written for a local magazine in 1960. It was called "Success Story of the Year," and it described how we had built up an empire of nine variety stores. Then it quoted me as saying that we probably wouldn't grow much more because I believed in personally supervising the nine-store group, and I thought any more stores would be "unwieldy" to manage without additional supervisors. So what the heck happened? How did we ever get to be the largest retailer in the world with a philosophy like that?

I really believed what I said then, and I still do. But we figured out a way to grow, and stay profitable, and there was no logical place to stop. The way I approached managing the business, I always tried to maintain a sense of hands-on, personal supervision —usually by flying around to take a look at our stores on a regular basis. But from the very beginning, even on my paper routes in college, I have also been a delegator, trying to hire the best possible people to manage our stores. That's been the case since back in Newport.

An awful lot of water has washed over the dam since 1945, when we bought that little Front Street store in Newport, but almost every single thing we learned, every basic principle we applied in building that store up into a respectable business, still applies to our company today. It's hard to think of another company that sustained the kind of growth we did over thirty years without experiencing any major financial problems or dips in profitability. During that time, our business was growing at annual rates of anywhere from 30 to an incredible 70 percent in some years.

Along the way, we always had lots of people waiting for us to stumble and fall—especially Wall Street types. They said we'd never be able to keep doing things our way after we reached $1 billion in sales. But we did, and kept right on going. Then they said everything would fall apart at $10 billion because you just couldn't manage a company that big with our little down-home management philosophies. We roared past that, and then hit $20 billion and $30 billion, and in the coming year we should hit around $53 billion. Two years ago, we earned $1 billion in profits for the first time. That's a jump from only $41 million just ten years before. Here's a chart that completely amazes me:

	1960	1970	1980	1990
SALES	$1.4 million	$31 million	$1.2 billion	$26 billion
PROFITS	$112,000	$1.2 million	$41 million	$1 billion
STORES	9	32	276	1,528

So now we're the largest retailer in the world, and still growing like a weed. If my chart doesn't paint a clear enough picture for you of how large the company is, here are some other ways to think about Wal-Mart's size. Every week, nearly 40 million people shop in Wal-Mart. Last year, we sold enough mens' and women's underwear and socks to put a pair on every person in America, with some to spare. We sold 135 million men's and boys' briefs, 136 million panties, and 280 million pairs of socks.

We sold one quarter of all the fishing line purchased in the U.S., some 600,000 miles of it, or enough to go around the earth twenty-four times. We sold 55 million sweatsuits and 27 million pairs of jeans, and we sold almost 20 percent of all the telephones bought in the U.S. And here's one I'm really proud of: in one week last year, we sold as much Ol' Roy private label dog food as we did in all of 1980. With sales of $200 million last year, Ol' Roy became the number-two dog food in America, and remember, we only sell it in Wal-Mart. Another one: Procter & Gamble sells more product to Wal-Mart than it does to the whole country of Japan.

I could go on and on, but you get the idea. We're big. Really big. That's not something I like to focus on. I always wanted to be the best retailer in the world, not necessarily the biggest. In fact, as I said in that article thirty something years ago, I've always been a little bit afraid that big might get in the way of doing a good job. Of course, being this big has some real advantages. Until we reached a billion dollars, a lot of suppliers and vendors just ignored us way out here in the Arkansas outback. For years, some suppliers wouldn't even call on us. Now, of course, we're too big to ignore. But being big also poses dangers. It has ruined many a fine company—including some giant retailers—who started out strong and got bloated or out of touch or were slow to react to the needs of their customers.

Here's the point: the bigger Wal-Mart gets, the more essential it is that we think small. Because that's exactly how we have become a huge corporation—by not acting like one. Above all, we are small-town merchants, and I can't tell you how important it is for us to remember—when we puff up our chests and brag about all those huge sales and profits—that they were all made one day at a time, one store at a time, mostly by the hard work, good attitude, and teamwork of all those hourly associates and their store managers, as well as by all those folks in the distribution centers. If we ever get carried away with how important we are because we're a great big $50 billion chain—instead of one store in Blytheville, Arkansas, or McComb, Mississippi, or Oak Ridge, Tennessee—then you probably can close the book on us. If we ever forget that looking a customer in the eye, and greeting him or her, and asking politely if we can be of help is just as important in every Wal-Mart today as it was in that little Ben Franklin in Newport, then we just ought to go into a different business because we'll never survive in this one.

BILL FIELDS:

> "I'm sure that our whole focus on thinking small all relates to Sam running that store in Newport, where he was the entrepreneur, and he was out there involved as a leader of the community. He sees that entrepreneurial element as being so important and something he never wants us to lose. He saw the big change in Ben Franklin and all those other companies that lost it because they got too big and distracted, and he's just determined it won't happen here."

For us, thinking small is a way of life, almost an obsession. And I suspect thinking small is an approach that almost any business could profit from. The bigger you are, the more urgently you probably need it. At our size today, there's all sorts of pressure to regiment and standardize and operate as a centrally driven chain, where everything is decided on high and passed down to the stores. In a system like that, there's absolutely no room for creativity, no place for the maverick merchant that I was in the early days at Ben Franklin, no call for the entrepreneur or the promoter. Man, I'd hate to work at a place like that, and I worry every single day about Wal-Mart becoming that way. I stay on these guys around here all the time about it. Of course, all those vendors and suppliers would love to see us get that way. It would make their jobs a lot simpler for sure. If anybody at Wal-Mart thinks we as a company are immune to Big Disease, I wish they'd just pack up and leave right now because it's always something we'll have to worry about.

For several decades now we've worked hard at building a company that's simple and streamlined and takes its directions from the grass roots. It's a pretty tall order for an outfit that is spreading out all over the country as fast as we are. But along the way we've learned some practical things about thinking small and developed some principles that have had a big effect on our company's success. Before you can fully understand how we got where we are today, it's important to understand these principles. Then you can recognize how we've applied them all along the way in the building of the company. Seeing how we've done some of these things might help other folks out there who face the same challenge of growing their business without losing touch with the customer.

There's nothing at all profound about any of our principles. In fact, they're all common sense, and most of them can be found in any number of books or articles on management theory—many of which I've read and studied over the years. But I think the way we've applied them at Wal-Mart has been just a little different. Here are six of the more important ways we at Wal-Mart try to think small:

Think One Store at a Time

That sounds easy enough, but it's something we've constantly had to stay on top of. Because our sales and earnings keep going up doesn't mean that we're smarter than everyone else, or that we can make it happen because we're so big. What it means is that our customers are supporting us. If they stopped, our earnings would simply disappear, and we'd all be out looking for new jobs. So we know what we have to do: keep lowering our prices, keep improving our service, and keep making things better for the folks who shop in our stores. That is not something we can simply do in some general way. It isn't something we can command from the executive offices because we want it to happen. We have to do it store by store, department by department, customer by customer, associate by associate.

For example, we've got one store in Panama City, Florida, and another only five miles away in Panama City Beach, but actually they're worlds apart when it comes to their merchandise mix and their customer base. They're entirely different kinds of stores. One is built for tourists going to the beach, and the other is more like the normal Wal-Mart, built for folks who live in town. That's why we try our best to put a merchant in charge of each store, and to develop other merchants as the heads of each department in those stores. If the merchandise mix is really going to be right, it has to be managed by the merchandisers there on the scene, the folks who actually deal face to face with the customers, day in and day out, through the seasons.

That makes it management's job to listen to those merchandisers out in the stores. We have these buyers here in Bentonville —218 of them—and we have to remind them all the time that their real job is to support the merchants in the stores. Otherwise, you have a headquarters-driven system that's out of touch with the customers of each particular store, and you end up with a bunch of unsold workboots, overalls, and hunting rifles at the Panama City Beach store, where folks are begging for water guns and fishing rods and pails and shovels; and at the Panama City store in town you've got a bunch of unsold beach gear stacked up gathering dust.

So when we sit down at our Saturday morning meetings to talk about our business, we like to spend time focusing on a single store, and how that store is doing against a single competitor in that particular market. We talk about what that store is doing right, and we look at what it's doing wrong.

DAVID GLASS:

"We believe that we have to talk about and examine this company in minute detail. I don't know any other large retail company—Kmart, Sears, Penney's—that discusses their sales at the end of the week in any smaller breakdown than by region. We talk about individual stores. Which means that if we're talking about the store in Dothan, Alabama, or Harrisburg, Illinois, everybody here is expected to know something about that store—how to measure its performance, whether a 20 percent increase is good or bad, what the payroll is running, who the competitors are, and how we're doing. We keep the company's orientation small by zeroing in on the smallest operating unit we have. No other company does that."

Focusing on a single store can accomplish a number of things. First, of course, it enables us to actually improve that store. But if in the process we also happen to learn a particular way in which that Panama City Beach Wal-Mart is outsmarting the competition on, say, beach towels, then we can quickly get that information out to all our other beach stores around the country and see if their approach works everywhere. Which brings us to the next principle.

Communicate, Communicate, Communicate

If you had to boil down the Wal-Mart system to one single idea, it would probably be communication, because it is one of the real keys to our success. We do it in so many ways, from the Saturday morning meeting to the very simple phone call, to our satellite system. The necessity for good communication in a big company like this is so vital it can't be overstated. What good is figuring out a better way to sell beach towels if you aren't going to tell everybody in your company about it? If the folks in St. Augustine, Florida, don't get the word on what's working over in Panama City until winter, they've missed a big opportunity. And if our buyers back in Bentonville don't know we're expecting to double our sales of beach towels this summer, the stores won't have anything to sell.

Nowadays, I see management articles about information sharing as a new source of power in corporations. We've been doing this from the days when we only had a handful of stores. Back then, we believed in showing a store manager every single number relating to his store, and eventually we began sharing those same numbers with the department heads in our stores. We've kept doing it as we've grown. That's why we've spent hundreds of millions of dollars on computers and satellites—to spread all the little details around the company as fast as possible. But they were worth the cost. It's only because of information technology that our store managers have a really clear sense of how they're doing most of the time. They get all kinds of information transmitted to them over the satellite on an amazingly timely basis: their monthly profit-and-loss statement, up-to-the-minute point-of-sale data that tells them what's selling in their own store, and a lot of other paper they probably wish we wouldn't send them.

I'm not going to pretend we're perfect at this. We do have our share of miscommunication, like that time the Moon Pies were shipped to stores in Wisconsin, where they didn't exactly jump off the shelves. And sometimes a simple attitude is as valuable as all the technology in the world. For example, we've got this one rule I hope we never give up enforcing: our buyers here in Bentonville are required to return calls from the stores first, before they return the calls of vendors or anybody else, and they are required to get back to the stores by sundown of the day they get the call.

Obviously, we're too doggoned big to have every department head in every Wal-Mart spend a lot of time with the vendors who call on us in Bentonville, so we try to think up ways to get at a similar result. Recently, we've started seminars for our department managers. We'll pick a department, like sporting goods or lawn and garden, then we'll pick one department head—these are the hourly associates who actually run those departments in their stores—from each of our store districts. That's 184 folks right now. We'll bring all of them in to Bentonville to talk to the buyers about what's working for them, and what's not. Then they meet with the vendors and explain what kinds of complaints we're getting about their products, or what's working well. Together, all these folks formulate their plan for the coming season, and then the department heads go back to their districts and share what they've learned with their counterparts in neighboring stores.

As much as we travel to our stores, and bring our folks in to Bentonville, though, sometimes I have the feeling that the word is not getting out. And if it's on a subject I feel strongly enough about, I'm not above getting in front of one of our TV cameras here and going out by satellite to all our associates gathered in front of their TV's in the break rooms of our stores. A few years ago, I had an idea around Christmastime that was just burning me up to tell people about, so I went on the camera and visited with everybody about how our sales were doing, and talked a little about my hunting, and let them know that I hoped their holiday season was going well. Then I got to the point: "I don't think any other retail company in the world could do what I'm going to propose to you. It's simple. It won't cost us anything. And I believe it would just work magic, absolute magic on our customers, and our sales would escalate, and I think we'd just shoot past our Kmart friends in a year or two and probably Sears as well. I want you to take a pledge with me. I want you to promise that whenever you come within ten feet of a customer, you will look him in the eye, greet him, and ask him if you can help him. Now I know some of you are just naturally shy, and maybe don't want to bother folks. But if you'll go along with me on this, it would, I'm sure, help you become a leader. It would help your personality develop, you would become more outgoing, and in time you might become manager of that store, you might become a department manager, you might become a district manager, or whatever you choose to be in the company. It will do wonders for you. I guarantee it. Now, I want you to raise your right hand—and remember what we say at Wal-Mart, that a promise we make is a promise we keep—and I want you to repeat after me: From this day forward, I solemnly promise and declare that every time a customer comes within ten feet of me, I will smile, look him in the eye, and greet him. So help me Sam."

Now, I had no way of knowing how much effect a little communication like that would have on our associates, or on our customers. But I felt so strongly about the idea that it was worth calling attention to it by satellite, and I really meant it when I said I didn't think any other retailer in the country could do it. I do know this—a lot of our associates started doing what I suggested, and I'm sure a lot of our customers appreciated it. We used mass communications to transmit the idea, but it was a small idea, aimed at the folks on the front lines, the ones most responsible for keeping our customers happy and coming back to our stores over and over. And I'm not saying one way or another whether my little pep talk had anything to do with it, but we went on from that Christmas to pass both Kmart and Sears in sales at least two years before even the most optimistic Wall Street analysts thought we could do it.

Keep Your Ear to the Ground

As chairman of Wal-Mart, I, of course, was the one who ultimately authorized all those expenditures for technology, which proved absolutely crucial to our success. But truthfully, I never viewed computers as anything more than necessary overhead. A computer is not—and will never be—a substitute for getting out in your stores and learning what's going on. In other words, a computer can tell you down to the dime what you've sold. But it can never tell you how much you could have sold.

That's why we at Wal-Mart are just absolute fanatics about our managers and buyers getting off their chairs here in Benton-ville and getting out into those stores. We have twelve airplanes— only one of them a jet, I'm proud to say—in our hangars out at the Rogers, Arkansas, airport, and that's why they're there. We stay in the air to keep our ear to the ground. Our whole travel system is really an outgrowth of the way I managed those nine stores back in 1960 when I said I didn't want to grow anymore. Back then, as you now know, I would get in my old Tri-Pacer and fly to those stores once a week to find out what was selling and what wasn't, what the competition was up to, what kind of job our managers were doing, what the stores were looking like, what the customers had on their minds. Of course, I have continued to visit stores almost constantly ever since, and it is the part of my job I enjoy the most, the part where I feel I make the greatest contribution, but with almost two thousand stores today, a lot of other folks have to get in on the act with me.

Today, the idea is pretty much the same. Our district managers are doing the job that I did back in 1960—the real hands-on, get-down-in-the-store stuff. But also, we have eighteen regional managers, all of them based here in Bentonville. Every Monday morning, they pile into those airplanes and head across the country to the stores in their regions. It's a condition of their employment. They stay out three to four days, usually coming back in on Thursday. We've drummed into their heads the belief that they should come back with at least one idea that will pay for the trip. Then they gather with the senior management of the company—all of whom should also have been visiting stores earlier in the week if they expect to ask any intelligent questions or know the first thing about what's going on—for our Friday morning merchandising meeting.

In addition to the fieldwork, of course, we have computer printouts at the meetings which tell us what's selling and what's not. But the really valuable intelligence that surfaces in these sessions is what everybody has brought back from the stores. If they're doing their jobs right, they'll know why things are or aren't selling, and what we ought to be thinking about selling next, or dropping from our assortment. If they've been to that Panama City Beach store and seen a suntan cream display that's blowing the stuff out the door, they can share that with the other regionals for their beach stores. Or if they've been to a big store in the Rio Grande Valley and found out that we're getting beat by a competitor on ladies' dresses because their assortment is more suited to the particular tastes of that area, we can start fixing it. When that meeting is over, every one of those regionals should be on the phone to the district managers, who should be passing the word along to the store managers, who'll get the department managers to act on it right away.

DAVID GLASS:

"Our Friday merchandising meeting is unique to retailing as far as I can tell. Here we have all these regional managers who have been out in the field all week long—they are the operations guys who direct the running of the stores. Then you have all your merchandising folks back in Bentonville—the people who buy for the stores. In retailing, there has always been a traditional, head-to-head confrontation between operations and merchandising. You know, the operations guys say, 'Why in the world would anybody buy this? It's a dog, and we'll never sell it.' Then the merchandising folks say, 'There's nothing wrong with that item. If you guys were smart enough to display it well and promote it properly, it would blow out the doors.' That's the way it is everywhere, including Wal-Mart. So we sit all these folks down together every Friday at the same table and just have at it.

"We get into some of the doggonedest, knock-down drag-outs you have ever seen. But we have a rule. We never leave an item hanging. We will make a decision in that meeting even if it's wrong, and sometimes it is. But when the people come out of that room, you would be hard-pressed to tell which ones oppose it and which ones are for it. And once we've made that decision on Friday, we expect it to be acted on in all the stores on Saturday. What we guard against around here is people saying, 'Let's think about it.' We make a decision. Then we act on it."

Once these regional managers have come back on Thursdays, we load up the planes with some buyers and send them out to visit the individual stores. As we've gotten bigger, we've added on all kinds of ways to keep our buyers responsive to the store needs. These days we've got folks called regional buyers, who go around and help the store managers customize the merchandise for their own stores. My favorite buyer program is one called Eat What You Cook. Once a quarter, every buyer has to go out to a different store and act as manager for a couple of days in the department he or she buys merchandise for. I guarantee you that after they've eaten what they cooked enough times, these buyers don't load up too many Moon Pies to send to Wisconsin, or beach towels for Hiawatha, Kansas.

Push Responsibility—and Authority—Down
The bigger we get as a company, the more important it becomes for us to shift responsibility and authority toward the front lines, toward that department manager who's stocking the shelves and talking to the customer. When we were much smaller, I probably

wasn't as quick to catch on to this idea as I should have been. But as an avid student of management theory, back in the mid-seventies I started reading the work of W. Edwards Deming, the famous statistician who taught so much to the Japanese about improving their productivity and competitiveness. Then Helen and I took a trip to Japan and Korea, which got me thinking about a whole bunch of different things we could do to improve our company. That's probably when I first began thinking about some of the very real ways that we could improve our teamwork and put more authority in the hands of our people in the stores.

Our most famous technique for doing this is a textbook example of thinking small. We call it Store Within a Store, and it's the simplest idea in the world. Again, in many big retail companies the department head is just an hourly employee going through the motions, somebody who punches a clock, then rips open boxes and stacks whatever's in them onto shelves. But we give our department heads the opportunity to become real merchants at a very early stage of the game. They can have the pride of proprietorship even if they weren't fortunate enough to go to college or be formally trained in business. They only have to want it bad enough, pay close attention, and work very hard at developing merchandising skills. We've had many cases where the experience has fired people up with ambition, and they've gone on to work their way through college and move on up in the company, and I hope we have many more cases like that.

Again, this only works because we decided a long time ago to share so much information about the company with our associates, rather than keep everything secretive. In Store Within a Store we make our department heads the managers of their own businesses, and in some cases these businesses are actually bigger in annual sales than a lot of our first Wal-Mart stores were. We share everything with them: the costs of their goods, the freight costs, the profit margins. We let them see how their store ranks with every other store in the company on a constant, running basis, and we give them incentives to want to win.

We're always trying for that fine balance between autonomy and control. Like any big retailer, Wal-Mart obviously has certain procedures which we require our stores to follow or items they must stock. But we have taken steps to make sure our stores have some autonomy. The responsibility for ordering merchandise lies with the department head. The responsibility for promoting merchandise is with the store manager. Our buyers have much more responsibility for deciding what's carried in our stores than buyers at most other companies. We run them hard, and we give them a tough time because we don't want them getting a big head and thinking they're all-powerful. But the fact is that our buyers—just like our folks in the stores—are in unique positions of authority for the retail business.

Force Ideas to Bubble Up

This goes hand-in-hand with pushing responsibility down. We're always looking for new ways to encourage our associates out in the stores to push their ideas up through the system. We do a lot of this at Saturday morning meetings. We'll invite associates who have thought up something that's really worked well for their store—a particular item or a particular display—to come share those ideas with us.

The VPI (Volume Producing Item) contest is a perfect example of how we put this into practice. Everybody from the department manager level on up can choose an item of merchandise they want to promote—with big displays or whatever—and then we see whose item produces the highest volume. I've always thought of the VPI contest not just as a way to stimulate sales, but as a method of teaching our associates how to become better merchants, to show them what can be done by picking an item that's available and figuring out a creative way to sell it, or buy it, or both. It gives them the opportunity to act the way we used to in the early days. They can do crazy things, like pick an item and hang it all over a tree filled with stuffed monkeys in the middle of the store. Or drive a pickup truck into action alley and fill it with car-washing sponges.

We're not just looking for merchandising ideas from our associates. Our latest effort is a program called Yes We Can, Sam!—

which, by the way, I did not name. Again, we invite hourly associates who have come up with money-saving ideas to attend our Saturday morning meeting. So far, we figure we've saved about $8 million a year off these ideas. And most of them are just common-sense kinds of things that nobody picks up on when we're all thinking about how big we are. They're the kinds of things that come from thinking small. One of my favorites came from an hourly associate in our traffic department who got to wondering why we were shipping all the fixtures we bought for our warehouses by common carrier when we own the largest private fleet of trucks in America. She figured out a program to backhaul those things on our own trucks and saved us over a half million dollars right there. So we brought her in, recognized her good thinking, and gave her a cash award. When you consider that there are 400,000 of us, it's obvious that there are more than a few good ideas out there waiting to be plucked.

TOM COUGHLIN:

"Let me tell you how Wal-Mart came to have people greeters. Back in 1980, Mr. Walton and I went into a Wal-Mart in Crowley, Louisiana. The first thing we saw as we opened the door was this older gentleman standing there. The man didn't know me, and he didn't see Sam, but he said, 'Hi! How are ya? Glad you're here. If there's anything I can tell you about our store, just let me know.'

"Neither Sam nor I had ever seen such a thing so we started talking to him. Well, once he got over the fact that he was talking to the chairman, he explained that he had a dual purpose: to make people feel good about coming in, and to make sure people weren't walking back out the entrance with merchandise they hadn't paid for.

"The store, it turned out, had had trouble with shoplifting, and its manager was an old-line merchant named Dan McAllister, who knew how to take care of his inventory. He didn't want to intimidate the honest customers by posting a guard at the door, but he wanted to leave a clear message that if you came in and stole, someone was there who would see it.

"Well, Sam thought that was the greatest idea he'd ever heard of. He went right back to Bentonville and told everyone we ought to put greeters at the front of every single store. A lot of people thought he'd lost his mind.

"Our folks felt that putting someone at the door was a waste of money. They just couldn't see what Sam and Dan McAllister were seeing—that the greeter sent a warm, friendly message to the good customer, and a warning to the thief. They fought him all the way on it. Some people tried hard to talk him out of it. They tried to ignore it.

"Sam just kept pushing and pushing and pushing. Every week, every meeting, he'd talk about greeters. He'd throw fits whenever he went into a store and didn't find one. Gradually, he wore everyone down and got his way. I'd say it took about a year and a half because they really resisted it. But Sam was relentless.

"I guess his vindication had to be the day in 1989 when he walked into a Kmart in Illinois and found that they had installed people greeters at their front doors."

If people greeters were the only good idea I'd picked up from the associates in the stores over the years, I'd still say that visiting the stores and listening to our folks was one of the most valuable uses of my time as an executive. But really, our best ideas usually do come from the folks in the stores. Period. I should say, though, that the people greeters were an exception in that I'm not generally disposed to ideas that require adding on people and expenses.

Stay Lean, Fight Bureaucracy

Anytime a company grows as fast as Wal-Mart has, pockets of duplication are going to build up, and there will be areas of the business which we may no longer need. No boss or employee really likes to dwell on such matters: it's only human nature not to want to have your job, or the jobs of the people who work for you, eliminated. But it is absolutely the responsibility of a company's top management to be thinking about this issue all the time —to ensure a sound future for the overall company.

One way I've approached this is by sticking to the same formula I used back when we had about five stores. In those days, I tried to operate on a 2 percent general office expense structure. In other words, 2 percent of sales should have been enough to carry our buying office, our general office expense, my salary, Bud's salary—and after we started adding district managers or any other officers—their salaries too. Believe it or not, we haven't changed that basic formula from five stores to two thousand stores. In fact, we are actually operating at a far lower percentage today in office overhead than we did thirty years ago, and that includes tremendous expenses for computer support and distribution center support—though not the actual cost of running the distribution centers. Really, it includes everything that we supply centrally in the way of support for the stores.

Some folks in the retail business have asked me where I came up with the 2 percent formula, and the truth is I just pulled it out of the air. In the early days, most companies charged 5 percent of their sales to run their offices. But we have always operated lean. We have operated with fewer people. We have had our people do more than in other companies. I think we came to work earlier and stayed later. It has been our heritage—our obsession—that we would be more productive and more efficient than our competition. And we've accomplished that goal.

A lot of first-time visitors are kind of shocked by our executive offices. Most people say my office and those of all the other Wal-Mart executives look like something you'd find in a truck terminal. We're in a one-story office-warehouse building. The offices aren't real big, and the walls are covered with inexpensive paneling. We never had fancy furniture or thick carpet, or suites with bars for our executives. I like them just like they are. We sure as heck won't win any interior decorating awards, but they're all we need, and they must be working fine. Just ask our shareholders.

DAVID GLASS:

"If you don't zero in on your bureaucracy every so often, you will naturally build in layers. You never set out to add bureaucracy. You just get it. Period. Without even knowing it. So you always have to be looking to eliminate it. You know when Tom Watson, Sr., was running IBM, he decided they would never have more than four layers from the chairman of the board to the lowest level in the company. That may have been one of the greatest single reasons why IBM was successful.

"A lot of this goes back to what Deming told the Japanese a long time ago: do it right the first time. The natural tendency when you've got a problem in a company is to come up with a solution to fix it. Too often, that solution is nothing more than adding another layer. What you should be doing is going to the source of the problem to fix it, and sometimes that requires shooting the culprit.

"I'll give you an example that just drove Sam crazy until we started doing something about it. When merchandise came into the back of a store, it was supposed to be marked at the right price or marked correctly on the spot. But because it often wasn't getting done properly, we created positions called test scanners, people who go around the stores with hand-held scanners, making sure everything is priced correctly. There's another layer right there, and Sam didn't ever visit a store without asking if we really needed these folks.

"Well, we still have some, but what we've done is overhaul our back-office procedures to make sure we get it right more often the first time, and, in the process, we eliminated one and a half people out of the office in every Wal-Mart store in the company. That's big bucks.

"Really it's a pretty simple philosophy. What you have to do is just draw a line in the dirt, and force the bureaucracy back behind that line. And then know for sure that a year will go by and it will be back across that line, and you'll have to do the same thing again."

I guess one reason I feel so strongly about not letting egos get out of control around Wal-Mart is that a lot of bureaucracy is really the product of some empire builder's ego. Some folks have a tendency to build up big staffs around them to emphasize their own importance, and we don't need any of that at Wal-Mart. If you're not serving the customer, or supporting the folks who do, we don't need you. When we're thinking small, that's another thing we're always on the lookout for: big egos. You don't have to have a small ego to work here, but you'd better know how to make it look small, or you might wind up in trouble.

So you see what I mean when I say you have to think small to grow big. And really, I don't have any doubt that Wal-Mart will stay the course and reach $100 billion in sales by the year 2000. It's a challenge. Nothing like it has ever been done before, but our folks will do it. And now I'm going to confess to a really radical thought I've been having lately. I probably won't do anything about it, but the folks who come after me are eventually going to have to face up to this question. Even by thinking small, can a $100 billion retailer really function as efficiently and productively as it should? Or would maybe five $20 billion companies work better?

CHAPTER 16

GIVING SOMETHING BACK

"I believe that every right implies a responsibility; every opportunity an obligation; every possession a duty."

—JOHN D. ROCKEFELLER, JR.

By now, I hope I've given you a pretty clear impression of what my business priorities have been over the years. If I've explained myself well, you know that I have concentrated all along on building the finest retailing company that we possibly could. Period. Creating a huge personal fortune was never particularly a goal of mine, and the proof of that lies in the fact that even to this day most of my, and my family's, wealth remains in the form of Wal-Mart stock. I think most people in our position would have hedged their bets a long time ago and diversified into all kinds of investments. As it's happened, though, our very simplistic, very personal investment strategy has turned out far better than anyone could ever have expected. So Wal-Mart stock has made the Waltons a very wealthy family—on paper anyway.

I won't deny for a second that my approach has been single-minded. I've concentrated on keeping our Wal-Mart stores and Sam's Clubs on track, and I have to admit that I never have spent a great deal of my time, or energy, thinking about what some of the broader implications of our family's wealth could be. Maybe it's because we have never had any intention of liquidating our stock. Even so, the annual dividend income from that stock has become large in its own right, and it's that income which represents the actual wealth available to us.

As I told you early on, this kind of wealth seems to naturally attract all kinds of folks who just want us to give them a handout. We have never been inclined to give any undeserving stranger a free ride, and we will never change our minds about that. Nor do we believe that because we have money, we should be called upon to solve every personal problem that comes to our attention, every problem of the community, the state, or, for that matter, the country.

We do, however, believe in worthy causes, and we realize how fortunate we've been as a family. So we are committed to using our personal resources for as much benefit as possible—in the areas we feel need the most help, employing the methods we think hold the most promise. And our family's gifts reflect a wide variety of interests, spread across numerous organizations, with a heavy emphasis on education.

Most of the giving we have done has been either anonymously, or linked to strict requests for no publicity, and I'm not going to go into the financial details of our charitable activities here because I don't think it's anybody's business but our own. I will tell you, though, that we think we do our part.

In addition to a lot of educational institutions, recipients of Walton family gifts include church groups and community projects like zoos and libraries and recreation facilities. We support hospitals and medical research programs. We fund arts groups and theater groups and symphonies. We give to conservation and environmental causes and veterans' groups, as well as to economic development groups and free enterprise groups. We support public schools and private schools. Since charity almost always begins at home, many of the recipients are in the communities or at institutions to which Helen and I, or our children, have personal ties. But we have also supported national organizations and even a few local causes of national importance in such cities as New York and Washington. Helen has been actively, and publicly, supportive of a number of institutions, including the Presbyterian Church, the University of the Ozarks, and the National Museum for Women in the Arts. And I have supported such groups as the Citizens Against Government Waste, Students in Free Enterprise, and the Arkansas Business Council—which folks around here insist on calling "The Good Suit Club."

We also have some pet projects to which Helen and I together are strongly, and personally, committed. In the last ten years we have funded a special scholarship program we started which sends kids from Central America to college here in Arkansas. Right now we've got about 180 of them enrolled at three different Arkansas schools, and we pay about $13,000 a year per student to provide tuition, transportation, books, and room and board. We got the idea while we were traveling around down in that part of the world. And when we learned that the then Soviet Union and Cuba had programs to teach their values to kids from other places, we decided Americans ought to be doing the same sort of thing with our values. We want kids to learn about the tremendous potential of the free enterprise system and to see for themselves what all the advantages are of a stable, democratic government. Besides that, it will help some of these students, who wouldn't have otherwise received any college education, to return to their countries and do something about their serious economic development problems. Who knows, maybe one day some of them will be running Wal-Marts or Sam's Clubs in Honduras or Panama or Guatemala—or even Nicaragua. Closer to home, the Walton family sponsors seventy scholarships of $6,000 each every year for children of Wal-Mart associates.

So we feel pretty good about what we've done up until now. But I do realize there's a bigger issue at stake here, and I've been doing a lot of thinking on it lately. As a family, we've been in the planning stages of how we want to leverage our resources for a while now, but really the serious business of getting it done will begin after I'm gone. Helen and I expect that an amount at least equal to our share of the family assets will go to nonprofit organizations over a number of years.

In all likelihood, education is going to be the issue we focus on the most. It is the single area which causes me the most worry about our country's future. As a nation, we have already learned that we must compete worldwide with everybody else, and our educational process has more to do with our ability to compete successfully than anything else. Unless we get ourselves on the right track pretty quickly, and start rebuilding our system into one that compares favorably with the rest of the world's, we could seriously jeopardize the future of this great country of ours. Frankly, I'd like to see an all-out revolution in education. We've got to target the inner-city schools and the rural poverty pockets like the Mississippi Delta and figure out a way to make a difference. We have to start at the preschool level, and develop ways to change the environment for children so they have a chance to stay in school and learn to value their educations. We have to look at the effects of so many single mothers and fathers leaving their kids at home with no guidance, and find ways to help them encourage their kids.

Incidentally, my share of the proceeds from this book will go to the New American School Corporation, which is a private initiative started by business leaders who have pledged to raise $200 million for the development of "break-the-mold schools." It's a true nonpartisan effort aimed at helping American schools meet the six goals established by a national governors' task force, which was convened by President Bush, and chaired by Arkansas governor Bill Clinton.

As the family focuses more broadly on educational reform, we want to be very careful. We are devout believers in the Wal-Mart way of doing things, and we want some basis by which to measure our investment. We're not satisfied that the traditional methods by which charitable foundations are operated really meet our criteria. Some people have crowed a great deal about all their philanthropy over the years, but too many of these foundations, I suspect, were only begun as tax shelters without much real sense of purpose. Many of them seem to have become very nice places to work for a small group of folks who have built up pretty thick crusts of administration and bureaucracy. Those are two of the things we have fought the hardest to keep out of our company, so naturally we don't want them clogging up our nonprofit efforts.

We are going to insist that whatever program we support incorporates those same values. When it comes to college educations and scholarships, for example, I've always favored programs that require the recipients to work and kick in some of their own money. For that matter, I've always preferred to hire people who had to at least partly work their way through school—no doubt because of my own background. The secret lies in motivating kids who aren't getting educated today to *want* to put themselves through school, and to make them understand the rewards they can expect when they do.

So we are going to approach philanthropy with the same lack of reverence we gave to the traditional methods of the retail business when we started out there. We are going to see if we can't shake up some of the time-honored assumptions about what you can teach people, about what you can do with people whose self-esteem has been beaten down, and about how you can motivate ordinary people to do extraordinary things. As just one example of the kinds of folks we're calling on in putting this effort together, we asked Lamar Alexander, the former governor of Tennessee and now U.S. Secretary of Education, to attend our last family meeting here in Bentonville and talk with us about some of the ideas he's come across for improving our public education system.

We don't come by this passion for improving education out of some fuzzy-headed notion or something we read somewhere. We see the need every day at Wal-Mart. In the old days, just being bright and willing to work hard was enough to give you all the opportunity you needed at our company. But we are such a sophisticated company today, and have moved so rapidly in the areas of technology and communications, that skill and knowledge in these fields have become a vital part of our business. None of this is news to anyone who keeps up with world business trends. This is the direction in which we're all headed. And to succeed, we're just going to have to do a better job of educating and training our work force.

One aspect of this whole philanthropy issue that has annoyed me considerably over the years is the criticism by some of our detractors that Wal-Mart doesn't do its fair share of giving to charities. The criticism seems to come from folks who say we don't meet the standard guidelines for corporations, guidelines which are set, I guess, by the people who run the charity business.

Wal-Mart, like many other corporations, conducts a very aggressive United Way campaign which meets with great success among our associates every year. In fact, we keep our United Way goal sign in the yard right outside my office here so everybody can see how we're doing. We strongly believe in United Way because—in spite of all the publicity it received recently for some problems in the national office—most all the money that's collected in these campaigns is directed locally. We believe in locally directed charities, so we have a matching grant program for associates who want to raise money for charities of their choice. We're also a big contributor to the Children's Miracle Network Telethon—which supports locally directed children's hospitals. Last year, Wal-Mart and its associates were the largest single contributors to this campaign—at $7.5 million.

I think quite a few companies use charitable giving guidelines as a way to say, in effect, "We gave at the office," when it comes to thinking about what overall good the companies should be accomplishing. In my opinion, Wal-Mart is an entirely different sort of enterprise from that and I would argue that our relentless effort to improve our business has always been tied to trying to make things better for the folks who live and work in our communities. We have built a company that is so efficient it has enabled us to save our customers billions of dollars, and whether you buy into the argument or not, we believe it. That in itself is giving something back, and it has been a cornerstone philosophy of our company.

For example, we did $43 billion in sales this year. For the last ten years—1982 to 1992—we have averaged sales of, say, $13 billion a year. So that's about $130 billion in sales. If we only saved our customers 10 percent over what they would be paying if we weren't there—and I think that's very conservative—that would be $13 billion we've saved them. That's $13 billion which is a product of a free market system that allows us to operate efficiently, and it's the reason our customers love us so. The truth is that Wal-Mart has been a powerful force for improving the standard of living in our mostly rural trade areas, and our customers recognize it.

We do a lot of things to take care of our own. Some of them you already know about. Our associates have almost $2 billion in their profit sharing fund, some of which I suppose the company could have given to charity instead. We have a relief fund for associates who are the victims of natural disasters. And each year, every Wal-Mart store sponsors one student in its community to a $1,000 scholarship.

Beyond that, we feel very strongly that Wal-Mart really is *not,* and *should not* be, in the charity business. We don't believe in taking a lot of money out of Wal-Mart's cash registers and giving it to charity for the simple reason that any debit has to be passed along to somebody—either our shareholders or our customers. A few years ago, when Helen convinced me that our associates here in Bentonville needed a first-class exercise facility, she and I paid the million dollars in construction costs ourselves, plus an annual subsidy for a few years to get it started. We paid for it to show our sincere appreciation to the associates, but also because I don't believe in asking the customers or the shareholders to pay for something like that—as worthy a cause as it may be. By not designating a large amount of corporate funds to some charity which the officers of Wal-Mart may happen to like, we feel we give our shareholders more discretion in supporting their own charities. And I have been particularly proud of the really generous community support shown by some of our shareholders who have been with us since way back when—especially the early store managers. Willard Walker and Charlie Baum are two guys who have just done great things for the community with some of what they've accumulated through their Wal-Mart holdings.

In 1987 I proudly accepted the Libertas Award at Enterprise Square, U.S.A. I guess I couldn't resist the opportunity to give a pitch for my VPI choice that year: Chattanooga Bakery's Deluxe Double Decker Moon Pie.

I've shared so much with Helen, my wife of forty-nine years—and my original partner.

Helen frying up a mess of quail with her special recipe.

Grandma helps tie a shoe while in the fields with our son Jim's boy.

Pitching in with Helen to help wash the dishes after a church supper.

Catching my breath with Helen after a tough tennis doubles match.

Standing proudly with my family, Rob, Jim, Helen, Alice, and John, while in New York City to accept *Financial World*'s CEO of the Decade Award (1989).

Our comfortable home was designed by E. Fay Jones. It was built on the site of the earlier home we had raised our family in (also designed by Fay), which burned to the ground in 1972 after being struck by lightning.

My brother Bud and I not only share a passion for retailing, we also love to spend time together quail hunting—especially on our lease camp on the Dick Jones Ranch in south Texas.

The first Walton's Five and Dime on the square in Bentonville; it was rededicated as the Wal-Mart Visitors Center in 1989.

We used these Beat Yesterday ledger books to monitor our performance in the early years of Wal-Mart.

This photo of our second Walton's Five and Dime in Fayetteville, Arkansas, gives a flavor of heartland America in the mid-fifties.

The Grand Opening ad for the first Wal-Mart (Rogers, Arkansas, 1962).

©1991 Clifton Eoff

I have always had a passion for flying and have flown literally millions of miles—most recently in my Cessna Chancellor 414A. It got me out of . . .

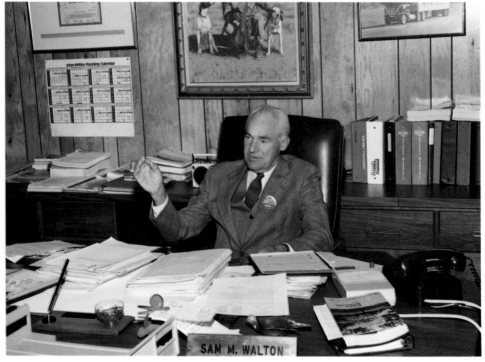

bob's of fayetteville

. . . my office . . .

Wal-Mart World

. . . and into the stores . . .

Mass Market Retailers

. . . to meet with our valued customers and associates.

Our people have *always* made the difference. I loved the enthusiasm of this group celebrating the grand opening of our one hundredth Sam's Club in Joliet, Illinois, 1988.

Wal-Mart's talented Executive Committee members. Left to right: David Glass, Paul Carter, Donald Soderquist, John Tate, Rob Walton, A. L. Johnson. Not shown: J. L. "Bud" Walton (1990).

Wal-Mart's Board of Directors. Top row, left to right: Robert Kahn, Robert Dedman, A. L. Johnson, William Seay, F. Kenneth Iverson, J. L. "Bud" Walton, Donald Soderquist, Paul Carter, and James Jones. Bottom row, left to right: Jack Shewmaker, David Glass, Hillary Rodham Clinton, Rob Walton, John Cooper, Jr., and John Tate (1990).

Our associates who drive the trucks and work at our distribution centers do a fine job keeping the shelves of our stores stocked with merchandise for our customers.

David Glass is all too eager to help me don a grass skirt and lei as I get ready to keep a promise to "do the hula on Wall Street" in 1984 after we turned in an exceptional year.

Welcoming associates, elected to represent each of our stores, to the annual post–shareholders' meeting picnic that Helen and I host in our backyard.

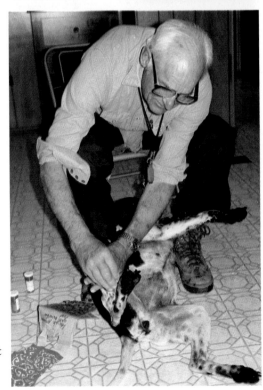

Tending to Queenie's sore foot—I've trained some great dogs over the years and Queenie may be the best.

Kimberly J. Slavan/Wal-Mart World

It was the greatest day of my life when President and Mrs. Bush came to Bentonville to honor me with the Presidential Medal of Freedom.

Berquist-Armstrong/Wal-Mart Visitors Center

The Citation.

It's a Wonderful Life.

Maybe the most important way in which we at Wal-Mart believe in giving something back is through our commitment to using the power of this enormous enterprise as a force for change. One of the better examples of what I'm talking about is our Bring it Home to the U.S.A. program, which we started in 1985 in response to the soaring U.S. trade deficit.

Wal-Mart, like every other American retailer, is a huge importer of merchandise from overseas. In some cases—too many in my opinion—importing is really our only alternative because a lot of American-made goods simply aren't competitive, either in price, or quality, or both. We committed ourselves to seeing if we could do anything to improve the situation. The remedy we envisioned wasn't some blind patriotic idea that preaches buying American at any cost. We, like any other retailer, will only buy American if those goods can be produced efficiently enough to offer good value. We're not interested in charity here; we don't believe in subsidizing substandard work or inefficiency. So our primary goal became to work with American manufacturers, and see if our formidable buying power could help them deliver the goods and, in the process, save some American manufacturing jobs. I sent out an open letter to our suppliers, inviting them to work with us on the program. "Wal-Mart believes American workers can make the difference," I told them, "if management provides the leadership."

We were surprised ourselves at the results. It turned out that if Wal-Mart committed to high volume purchases well in advance of shipping deadlines, a lot of American manufacturers could save enough on the purchase of materials, personnel scheduling, and inventory costs to realize significant efficiency gains. So, in fact, they could turn out a wide variety of merchandise—flannel shirts, candles, men's knit shirts, ladies' sweaters, bicycles, beach towels, film, videotapes, furniture, even toys—at competitive prices. We also took a close look at our overseas buying practices and discovered a number of hidden costs, such as having to own inventory from the time it leaves port on a ship. Using that data, we developed a formula which enabled us to make a true apples-to-apples cost comparison of buying something overseas versus buying it at home. Now, if we can get within 5 percent of the same price and quality, we take a smaller markup and go with the American product.

What we learned was that we had fallen into a pattern of knee-jerk import buying without really examining possible alternatives. In the past, we would just take our best-selling U.S.-made items, send them to the Orient, and say, "See if you can make something like this. We could use 100,000 units of this, or more, if the quality holds up." I'm sure a lot of other retailers do the same thing. Today, we instruct our buyers to make trips to places like Greenville, South Carolina; Dothan, Alabama; Aurora, Missouri; and hundreds of other out-of-the-way places in Pennsylvania, New York, Ohio, or New Hampshire, before just routinely dashing off a letter of credit to the Far East. If we could all take a little extra trouble to work some of these deals out—and the manufacturers will continue to come up with their own creative programs—I think there's still a tremendous amount of untapped potential left in this idea.

As usual, some of our critics—mostly unions in this case—took a shot at me for this idea. They said I was wrapping myself in the flag and pulling a typical Sam Walton promotion to hide the fact that we sell a lot of import goods. These folks, I'm afraid, are really living in the past. They don't believe in a free market. They're not interested in new solutions. And they only care about jobs if they are *union* jobs, many of which, frankly, have priced themselves out of the market either with unrealistic wages or total inflexibility. With this approach, we estimate we have saved or created almost 100,000 American manufacturing jobs. So before anybody dismisses Bring it Home as a publicity stunt, they should listen to the people whose jobs were saved, or created, by the program.

FARRIS BURROUGHS, PRESIDENT, FARRIS FASHIONS —BRINKLEY, ARKANSAS:

"It's the best thing that ever happened to Brinkley, and certainly the best thing that ever happened to me. Before, we had a contract with Van Heusen for Penney's and Sears, but in

1984 they told us they were moving everything to China. We were struggling from season to season with ninety jobs, when I got this call from a guy claiming to be Sam Walton. It turns out he actually was Sam Walton, and he wanted to know if we thought we could make 50,000 dozen flannel shirts for him. I'll tell you what, though. He's the only guy I ever worked for who looked me right in the eye and said, 'Son, if you can't make money off this project, don't do it.' Most retailers couldn't care less whether the manufacturer makes money or not.

"Anyway, today we're making about two and a half million Wal-Mart shirts, and we've gone from 90 employees the week Mr. Sam called to 320 today. And we know where it comes from. Every Christmas, we give our employees Wal-Mart gift certificates."

There's no charity at all involved in this program, and, in fact, I'm proud to say that it benefits us at Wal-Mart in a very direct way. Every job we save creates another potential Wal-Mart customer who's not worrying about where his or her next dollar's coming from. They have a job, and we have a customer. So we all come out ahead. Farris was one of our early success stories, and since then we've worked out all kinds of Buy American deals with small and large manufacturers, including Fieldcrest Cannon, 3M, Sunbeam, Mirro Foley, U.S. Electronics, Kentogs, Capital-Mercury, Mr. Coffee, Lasko, and Huffy.

From the time the program began in 1985, until the end of last year—1991—we estimate that we bought American-made goods with a retail value of more than $5 billion that would previously have been purchased overseas. And just to keep everybody thinking along these lines, we always post our latest tally and our latest Bring it Home success story right by the door where all our vendors have to enter our building to make sales calls.

In the same spirit, we're in the early stages of an environmental initiative, encouraging suppliers and manufacturers to eliminate any wasteful practices—such as unnecessary packaging—that we can. Also, we have a fairly new program in which we donate

2 percent from purchases of Sam's American Choice products—a selection of our own private label products—toward scholarships for students studying mathematics, hard sciences, and computer sciences.

We aren't the least bit naive about how big a stick Wal-Mart swings in the world of retailing these days. We know we can be very influential—powerful if you prefer. So today I think it's important for our people to remember that things aren't the same as the old days, when we were the scrappy underdog having to fight for every single break. We still want to drive a hard bargain, but now we need to guard against abusing our power. We want to find more ways, like Bring it Home, in which we can use our influence to give something back.

CHAPTER 17

RUNNING A SUCCESSFUL COMPANY: TEN RULES THAT WORKED FOR ME

"One thing you'll notice if you spend very much time talking with Sam about Wal-Mart's success. He's always saying things like 'This was the key to the whole thing,' or 'That was our real secret.' He knows as well as anyone that there wasn't any magic formula. A lot of different things made it work, and in one day's time he may cite all of them as the 'key' or the 'secret.' What's amazing is that for almost fifty years he's managed to focus on all of them at once—all the time. That's his real secret."

—DAVID GLASS

I think we've covered the story of how all my partners and associates and I over the years built Wal-Mart into what it is today. And in the telling, I think we've covered all the principles which resulted in the company's amazing success. A whole lot has changed about the retailing business in the forty-seven years we've been in it—including some of my theories. We've changed our minds about some significant things along the way and adopted some new principles—particularly about the concept of partnership in a corporation. But most of the values and the rules and the techniques we've relied on have stayed the same the whole way. Some of them are such simple commonsense old favorites that they hardly seem worth mentioning.

This isn't the first time that I've been asked to come up with a list of rules for success, but it *is* the first time I've actually sat down and done it. I'm glad I did because it's been a revealing exercise for me. The truth is, David Glass is right. I do seem to have a couple of dozen things that I've singled out at one time or another as the "key" to the whole thing. One I don't even have on my list is "work hard." If you don't know that already, or you're not willing to do it, you probably won't be going far enough to need my list anyway. And another I didn't include on the list is the idea of building a team. If you want to build an enterprise of any size at all, it almost goes without saying that you absolutely must create a team of people who work together and give real meaning to that overused word "teamwork." To me, that's more the goal of the whole thing, rather than some way to get there.

I believe in always having goals, and always setting them high. I can certainly tell you that the folks at Wal-Mart have always had goals in front of them. In fact, we have sometimes built real scoreboards on the stage at Saturday morning meetings.

One more thing. If you're really looking for my advice here, trying to get something serious out of this exercise I put myself through, remember: these rules are not in any way intended to be the Ten Commandments of Business. They are some rules that worked for me. But I always prided myself on breaking everybody else's rules, and I always favored the mavericks who challenged my rules. I may have fought them all the way, but I respected them, and, in the end, I listened to them a lot more closely than I did the pack who always agreed with everything I said. So pay special attention to Rule 10, and if you interpret it in the right spirit—as it applies to you—it could mean simply: Break All the Rules.

For what they're worth, here they are. Sam's Rules for Building a Business:

RULE 1: COMMIT to your business. Believe in it more than anybody else. I think I overcame every single one of my personal shortcomings by the sheer passion I brought to my work. I don't know if you're born with this kind of passion, or if you can learn it. But I do know you need it. If you love your work, you'll be out there every day trying to do it the best you possibly can, and pretty soon everybody around will catch the passion from you—like a fever.

RULE 2: SHARE your profits with all your associates, and treat them as partners. In turn, they will treat you as a partner, and together you will all perform beyond your wildest expectations. Remain a corporation and retain control if you like, but behave as a servant leader in a partnership. Encourage your associates to hold a stake in the company. Offer discounted stock, and grant them stock for their retirement. It's the single best thing we ever did.

RULE 3: MOTIVATE your partners. Money and ownership alone aren't enough. Constantly, day by day, think of new and more interesting ways to motivate and challenge your partners. Set high goals, encourage competition, and then keep score. Make bets with outrageous payoffs. If things get stale, cross-pollinate; have managers switch jobs with one another to stay challenged. Keep everybody guessing as to what your next trick is going to be. Don't become too predictable.

RULE 4: COMMUNICATE everything you possibly can to your partners. The more they know, the more they'll understand. The more they understand, the more they'll care. Once they care, there's no stopping them. If you don't trust your associates to know what's going on, they'll know you don't really consider them partners. Information is power, and the gain you get from empowering your associates more than offsets the risk of informing your competitors.

RULE 5: APPRECIATE everything your associates do for the business. A paycheck and a stock option will buy one kind of loyalty. But all of us like to be told how much somebody appreciates what we do for them. We like to hear it often, and especially when we have done something we're really proud of. Nothing else can quite substitute for a few well-chosen, well-timed, sincere words of praise. They're absolutely free— and worth a fortune.

RULE 6: CELEBRATE your successes. Find some humor in your failures. Don't take yourself so seriously. Loosen up, and everybody around you will loosen up. Have fun. Show enthusiasm—always. When all else fails, put on a costume and sing a silly song. Then make everybody else sing with you. Don't do a hula on Wall Street. It's been done. Think up your own stunt. All of this is more important, and more fun, than you think, and it really fools the competition. "Why should we take those cornballs at Wal-Mart seriously?"

RULE 7: LISTEN to everyone in your company. And figure out ways to get them talking. The folks on the front lines— the ones who actually talk to the customer—are the only ones who really know what's going on out there. You'd better find out what they know. This really is what total quality is all about. To push responsibility down in your organization, and to force good ideas to bubble up within it, you *must* listen to what your associates are trying to tell you.

RULE 8: EXCEED your customers' expectations. If you do, they'll come back over and over. Give them what they want— and a little more. Let them know you appreciate them. Make good on all your mistakes, and don't make excuses—apologize. Stand behind everything you do. The two most important words I ever wrote were on that first Wal-Mart sign: "Satisfaction Guaranteed." They're still up there, and they have made all the difference.

RULE 9: CONTROL your expenses better than your competition. This is where you can always find the competitive advantage. For twenty-five years running—long before Wal-Mart was known as the nation's largest retailer—we ranked number one in our industry for the lowest ratio of expenses to sales. You can make a lot of different mistakes and still recover if you run an efficient operation. Or you can be brilliant and still go out of business if you're too inefficient.

RULE 10: SWIM upstream. Go the other way. Ignore the conventional wisdom. If everybody else is doing it one way, there's a good chance you can find your niche by going in exactly the opposite direction. But be prepared for a lot of folks to wave you down and tell you you're headed the wrong way. I guess in all my years, what I heard more often than anything was: a town of less than 50,000 population cannot support a discount store for very long.

Those are some pretty ordinary rules, some would say even simplistic. The hard part, the real challenge, is to constantly figure out ways to execute them. You can't just keep doing what works one time, because everything around you is always changing. To succeed, you have to stay out in front of that change.

CHAPTER 18

WANTING TO LEAVE
A LEGACY

"With the possible exception of Henry Ford, Sam Walton is the entrepreneur of the century."

—TOM PETERS,
co-author of In Search of Excellence

By now, it's probably clear to you that I've devoted most of my life to Wal-Mart—starting it, growing it, and always refining the concept of this whole phenomenon. My life has been full and fun and challenging and rewarding beyond even my wildest expectations. I've pretty much gotten my own way for the whole run. While a lot of people were working away at jobs they might not have particularly enjoyed, I was having the time of my life. If I wasn't in the stores trying to pump up our associates to do an even better job, or in the office looking over numbers to see where the next trouble spot was going to pop up, or leading cheers at a Saturday morning meeting, I was probably at the stick of my airplane, looking out over some part of this beautiful country of ours—and checking out the number of cars in those Kmart parking lots. Or maybe I was taking a few hours off to get in some tennis or to hunt with my dogs.

All that has wound down for me now. I'm really sick these

days, and I guess when you get older, and illness catches up with you, you naturally turn just a little bit philosophical—especially late at night when you can't sleep and your mind is turning everything over and over trying to take stock of where you've been and what you've done. The truth is that if I hadn't gotten sick, I doubt I would have written this book, or taken the time to try to sort my life out. As you now know, temperamentally, I'm much too biased toward action to undertake such a sedentary project. But since I have, I'm going to go all the way and try to share with you how I feel about some things that seem important to me.

This will sound strange to people who know me well, but lately I've wondered if I should feel bad about having been so wholly committed to Wal-Mart. Was it really worth all the time I spent away from my family? Should I have driven my partners so hard all these years? Am I really leaving behind something on this earth that I can be proud of having accomplished, or does it somehow lack meaning to me now that I'm facing the ultimate challenge?

We could've gone a lot of different ways at several points. Many folks started out in retailing just like I did and built their companies up to a point, and then said, "I've had enough!" and sold out and bought an island. I could have kicked back and played with the grandchildren, or I could have devoted the latter years of my life to good works, I guess. I don't know that anybody else has ever done it quite like me: started out as a pure neophyte, learned his trade, swept the floor, kept the books, trimmed the windows, weighed the candy, rung the cash register, installed the fixtures, remodeled the stores, built an organization of this size and quality, and kept on doing it right up to the end because they enjoyed it so much. No one that I know of has done it that way.

Here's how I look at it: my life has been a trade-off. If I wanted to reach the goals I set for myself, I had to get at it and stay at it every day. I had to think about it all the time. And I guess what David Glass said about me is true: I had to get up every day with my mind set on improving something. Charlie Baum was right too when he said I was driven by a desire to always be on the top of the heap. But in the larger sense—the life and death sense—did I make the right choices?

Having now thought about this a lot, I can honestly say that if I had the choices to make all over again, I would make just about the same ones. Preachers are put here to minister to our souls; doctors to heal our diseases; teachers to open up our minds; and so on. Everybody has their role to play. The thing is, I am absolutely convinced that the only way we can improve one another's quality of life, which is something very real to those of us who grew up in the Depression, is through what we call free enterprise —practiced correctly and morally. And I really believe there haven't been many companies that have done the things we've done at Wal-Mart. We've improved the standard of living of our customers, whom we've saved billions of dollars, and of our associates, who have been able to share profits. Many of both groups also have invested in our stock and profited all through the years.

When we started out, the whole idea was nothing but a pure profit motive: our business strategy was to bring the customers into the tent by selling the highest quality goods we could at the lowest possible prices. It worked, and those few of us who believed in it from early on and invested in the idea got rich off it.

Obviously, everybody who went to work in a Wal-Mart didn't get rich. But there've been many stories over the years of associates who've made enough at least to buy their first car, or own their first home, and we've had several associates who've retired with over a million dollars in profit sharing. We've been able to help our associates to a greater degree than most companies because of what you'd have to call enlightened self-interest; we were selfish enough to see in the beginning the value to the company of letting them share the profits.

Also, I think those associates in our company who believe in our ideals and our goals and get with the program have felt some spiritual satisfaction—in the psychological rather than the religious sense—out of the whole experience. They learn to stand up tall and look people in the eye and speak to them, and they feel better about themselves, and once they start gaining confidence there's no reason they can't keep on improving themselves. Many of them decide they want to go to college, or to manage a store, or take what they've learned and start their own business, or do a good job and take pride in that. Wal-Mart has helped their pocketbooks and their self-esteem. There are certainly some union folks and some middlemen out there who wouldn't agree with me, but I believe that millions of people are better off today than they would have been if Wal-Mart had never existed. So I am just awfully proud of the whole deal, and I feel good about how I chose to expend my energies in this life.

I know one thing for sure. We certainly changed the way retail works in this country. And when I say we, I don't mean just Wal-Mart. Some of the fellows I told you about early in the book, like Sol Price and Harry Cunningham and John Geisse, deserve a lot of the credit too. The whole philosophy has changed in the retail business because of the quality discounters, of whom I believe we are the very best. Almost from the beginning, our objective has been to charge just as little as possible for our merchandise, and to try and use what muscle we've had to work out deals with our suppliers so we can offer the very best quality we can. Many people in this business are still trying to charge whatever the traffic will bear, and they're simply on the wrong track. I'll tell you this: those companies out there who aren't thinking about the customer and focusing on the customers' interests are just going to get lost in the shuffle—if they haven't already. Those who get greedy are going to be left in the dust.

There are lessons in what's happened at Wal-Mart that go beyond retail and apply to many other businesses. You start with a given: free enterprise is the engine of our society; communism is pretty much down the drain and proven so; and there doesn't appear to be anything else that can compare to a free society based on a market economy. Nothing can touch that system—not unless leadership and management get selfish or lazy. In the future, free enterprise is going to have to be done well—which means it benefits the workers, the stockholders, the communities, and, of course, management, which must adopt a philosophy of servant leadership.

Recently, I don't think there's any doubt that a lot of American management has bent over too far toward taking care of itself first, and worrying about everybody else later. The Japanese are right on this point: you can't create a team spirit when the situation is so one-sided, when management gets so much and workers get so little of the pie. Some of these salaries I see out there are completely out of line, and everybody knows it. It's obvious that most companies would be much better served by basing managers' pay on the performance of the company or return on investment to the shareholders or some yardstick which clearly takes into account how well they're doing their job. And the formula has to make sure that profits are divided fairly among workers, management, and stockholders, according to their contributions and risks. At Wal-Mart, we've always paid our executives less than industry standards, sometimes maybe too much less. But we've always rewarded them with stock bonuses and other incentives related directly to the performance of the company. It's no coincidence that the company has done really well, and so have they.

I believe our way of looking at things is going to come into its own in this decade, and the next century. The way business is conducted worldwide is going to be different, and a lot of that difference is going to reflect what we egotistically think of as the Wal-Mart Way. In the global economy, successful business is going to do just what Wal-Mart is always trying to do: give more and more responsibility for making decisions to the people who are actually on the firing line, those who deal with the customers every day. Good management is going to start listening to the ideas of these line soldiers, pooling these ideas and disseminating them around their organizations so people can act on them. That's the way the successful companies out there already are doing it: the 3M's, the Hewlett-Packards, the G.E.'s, the Wal-Marts. Great ideas come from everywhere if you just listen and look for them. You never know who's going to have a great idea.

We can turn the whole world around just the way we've done it in retail. We can do it better than the Japanese because we're more innovative, we're more creative. We can compete with labor in Bangladesh or wherever because we have better technology, which can give us more efficient equipment. We can get beyond a

lot of our old adversarial relationships and establish win–win partnerships with our suppliers and our workers, which will leave us
with more energy and talent to focus on the important thing,
meeting the needs of our customers. But all this requires over-
coming one of the most powerful forces in human nature: the
resistance to change. To succeed in this world, you have to change
all the time.

When you look at what's happened to the American auto
industry, it's tempting to want to treat the Japanese unfairly—the
way they treat us with their protectionist laws. Our auto industry
doesn't play on level ground. But I don't think we should counter
with protectionism because it doesn't address the real problem:
the quality of our product doesn't compete with that of the Japanese, whether we want to admit it or not. The challenge is a great
one for management. What they have to do is build a partnership
with their people.

I understand that this industry has all kinds of problems we
haven't seen in ours. I know that U.S. auto workers make $22 an
hour versus $16 in Japan, and that Mexican auto workers earn
much less. I'm not saying I could solve all these problems, but I'd
love to have the fun of trying to take a unionized company today
and sell its people on the idea of having to be competitive globally
—whether it was in autos, or steel, or electronics. I'd love a
chance at that, the pleasure of seeing if they could be motivated
into a team that would share in all the company's success—and
still have a union. It would take a powerful lot of persuading to
pull this off, but I guarantee it could be accomplished by somebody obsessed and persistent enough. But if American management is going to say to their workers that we're all in this together, they're going to have to stop this foolishness of paying
themselves $3 million and $4 million bonuses every year and riding around everywhere in limos and corporate jets like they're so
much better than everybody else.

I'm not saying every company should necessarily be as chintzy
as Wal-Mart. Everybody's not in the discount business, consumed
by trying to save every possible dollar for their customers. But I
wonder if a lot of these companies wouldn't do just as well if their

executives lived a little more like real folks. A lot of people think it's crazy of me to fly coach whenever I go on a commercial flight, and maybe I do overdo it a little bit. But I feel like it's up to me as a leader to set an example. It's not fair for me to ride one way and ask everybody else to ride another way. The minute you do that, you start building resentment and your whole team idea begins to strain at the seams.

But now it's time for me to forget about all that's past and think about what I really want the legacy of Wal-Mart to be in the future. I'd like to believe that as Wal-Mart continues to thrive and grow, it can come to live up to what someone once called us: the Lighthouse of the Ozarks. Only I hope we can spread the concept further than our home region here in the foothills because we're really a national company now. For Wal-Mart to maintain its position in the hearts of our customers, we have to study more ways we can give something back to our communities. I'm tremendously proud of the things we've done that I've already mentioned. And we're already studying ways we can go further to stay involved, to be more socially conscious all around. As I've said, our country desperately needs a revolution in education, and I hope Wal-Mart can contribute at some level, if for no other reason than selfish ones. Without a strong educational system, the very free enterprise system that allows a Wal-Mart or an IBM or a Procter & Gamble to appear on the scene and strengthen our nation's economy simply won't work. You may have trouble believing it, but every time we've tested the old saying, it has paid off for us in spades: the more you give, the more you get.

Finally, a lot of folks ask me two related questions all the time. The first one is could a Wal-Mart–type story still occur in this day and age? My answer is of course it could happen again. Somewhere out there right now there's someone—probably hundreds of thousands of someones—with good enough ideas to go all the way. It will be done again, over and over, providing that someone wants it badly enough to do what it takes to get there. It's all a matter of attitude and the capacity to constantly study and question the management of the business.

The second question is if I were a young man or woman starting out today with the same sorts of talents and energies and aspirations that I had fifty years ago, what would I do? The answer to that is a little harder to figure out. I don't know exactly what I would do today, but I feel pretty sure I would be selling something, and I expect it would be at the retail level, where I could relate directly to customers off the street. I think I'd study the retail field today and go into the business that offered the most promise for the least amount of money. Probably some kind of specialty retail, something to do with computers maybe, or something like the Gap—even the Body Shop.

Anyway, the next time some overeager, slightly eccentric shopkeeper opens up a business in your neck of the woods, before you write him off too quickly, remember those two old codgers who gave me maybe sixty days to last in my dime store down in Fayetteville. Go check the new store out. See what they've got to offer, see how they treat you, and decide for yourself if you ever want to go back. Because this is what it's really all about. In this free country of ours, that shopkeeper's success is entirely up to you: the customer.

A POSTSCRIPT

For the last two years of Dad's life, he fought a difficult battle against a form of bone cancer, multiple myeloma, which, from the time of diagnosis, he understood would almost certainly prove fatal. Like every other challenge he encountered in his life, he met this one head-on, full of optimism and ready to try new ways of conquering the problem. So, with the encouragement of the whole family—and the meticulous hands-on medical care management of my brother John—Dad embarked on a variety of experimental treatment programs with a group of excellent doctors.

He took his medicine, but he never dwelled on either the illness that had befallen him or its potential cures. Rather, he seized the day. At the time of the diagnosis, in early 1990, he had been working, somewhat ambivalently, on an autobiography. He canceled that project, choosing instead to spend most of his time and energy doing what he enjoyed most: flying his plane from town to town, going from Wal-Mart to Wal-Mart, visiting with his beloved associates. Toward the end of 1991, when he began to realize that his illness was catching up with him and would soon limit his mobility, Dad—at the urging of our family and others—again turned his attention to the idea of putting his story down on paper while he still could. Once he decided to write it, he threw himself into this book project with the same focus and energy he applied to everything he did in life. He was very particular about what he wanted his book to be, and he worked at it daily, making revisions, adding anecdotes, refining style points, urging others to contribute their memories.

By early March, his spirits remained high as he continued work on the book, but his physical condition was worsening. Then he received one of the great surprises of his life. The White House wanted to present him with the Presidential Medal of Freedom, our nation's highest civilian award. President Bush and the First Lady would be traveling to Bentonville to present the medal to Dad, and he was thrilled by the honor. At such an occasion, of course, Dad could have invited anyone he wanted to attend the ceremony, but we hardly had to ask whom he wanted to be there with him: his Wal-Mart associates.

The award was presented on the morning of Tuesday, March 17, in the auditorium of the Wal-Mart general offices, where Dad had held forth on so many Saturday mornings. The room was filled with several hundred of his associates, and their affection for Dad on this special day was particularly moving. They really outdid themselves, and I think they may even have startled President and Mrs. Bush—not to mention the White House press corps—by giving one of the most enthusiastic Wal-Mart cheers we've heard around here in some time. Dad's pleasure was evident, and he called it "the highlight of our entire career." Of course, he shared all the credit with his associates. But it was a poignant day. He had to be rolled onto the stage in a wheelchair, and I think most of the associates sensed that it would be their last get-together with him. The room was full of pride that day—but also lots of memories, and many tears.

Here is what the presidential citation said of Dad:

An American original, Sam Walton embodies the entrepreneurial spirit and epitomizes the American dream. Concern for his employees, a commitment to his community, and a desire to make a difference have been the hallmarks of his career. By sponsoring scholarships for Latin America, he has also worked to bring peoples closer together and to share with others the American ideals he so well represents. A devoted family man, business leader, and statesman for democracy, Sam Walton demonstrates the virtues of faith, hope and hard work. America honors this captain of commerce, as successful in life as in business.

A few days later, Dad entered the University of Arkansas hospital in Little Rock. Even in the final weeks of his life, he took great pleasure in doing what he had always done. One of the last people he spoke with outside the family was a local Wal-Mart manager who, at our request, dropped by to chat with Dad about his store's sales figures for the week. Then, less than three weeks after receiving the Medal of Freedom, and just days after his seventy-fourth birthday, Dad's struggle with cancer finally ended. On Sunday morning, April 5, he died peacefully—as inspirational in facing death as he had been in facing life.

We will all miss him.

—ROB WALTON
Chairman, Wal-Mart Stores
Bentonville, Arkansas
May 1992

CO-AUTHOR'S NOTE

Sam Walton had a long history of avoiding those who wanted to write about him, and this book never would have come to be without several people whose persistent pursuit of its subject spanned a number of years.

Much of the credit for my own involvement belongs to Marshall Loeb, managing editor of *Fortune*—and my boss—who first dispatched me to the Ozarks in December of 1988, with a clear understanding that taking no for an answer simply wasn't an option. Kris Dahl, my agent at ICM, first encouraged me to write a book, and listened patiently to the ups and downs of this particular one for years.

More than anyone else, Doubleday vice president Bill Barry—the fast-talking, letter-writing New York book "merchant"—deserves credit for somehow first convincing Sam to write a book at all. His ongoing efforts have transcended all normal roles of a publisher. Not the least of his contributions was selecting editor

Deb Futter, who rushed in where any sane person would have feared to tread. She turned in a remarkable performance despite unbelievable deadline pressure, as have so many people in other essential roles at Doubleday.

Inside Wal-Mart, there were co-conspirators as well. Without the patient, shrewd encouragement of Sam's personal secretary, Becky Elliott, he would have found some excuse to permanently postpone the book. From the outset, Wal-Mart CEO David Glass lent it his official seal of approval, which meant all the difference. And the entire Walton family supported the book. Helen Walton's grace and hospitality under difficult circumstances were most appreciated, as were her Razorback basketball tickets. Rob Walton's professional shepherding of the project made it easier on everyone.

Finally, personal thanks to Kate Ellis and Jake Huey for enduring my absence and peripatetic schedule without complaint. My only regret is that I am unable to thank Sam Walton for giving me the opportunity to help him chronicle his extraordinary life. Collaborating with Sam on anything was usually the experience of a lifetime, and this book proved no exception.

—JOHN HUEY
Atlanta, Georgia
May 1992

INDEX